Polished Ru Programming

Build better software with more intuitive, maintainable, scalable, and high-performance Ruby code

Jeremy Evans

BIRMINGHAM—MUMBAI

Polished Ruby Programming

Copyright © 2021 Packt Publishing

Group Product Manager: Aaron Lazar
Publishing Product Manager: Alok Dhuri
Senior Editor: Rohit Singh
Content Development Editor: Tiksha Lad
Technical Editor: Pradeep Sahu
Copy Editor: Safis Editing
Project Coordinator: Deeksha Thakkar
Proofreader: Safis Editing
Indexer: Pratik Shirodkar
Production Designer: Shankar Kalbhor

First published: June 2021

Production reference: 2100821

Published by Packt Publishing Ltd.
Livery Place
35 Livery Street
Birmingham
B3 2PB, UK.

ISBN 978-1-80107-272-4

www.packt.com

To Allyson, Jaden, Ruby, Jennifer, and Veronica, who most shaped my life.

- Jeremy Evans

Contributors

About the author

Jeremy Evans is a Ruby committer who focuses on fixing bugs in Ruby, as well as improving the implementation of Ruby. He is the maintainer of many popular Ruby libraries, including the fastest web framework (Roda) and fastest database library (Sequel). His libraries are known not just for their performance, but also for their code quality, understandability, documentation, and how quickly any bugs found are fixed. For his contributions to Ruby and the Ruby community, he has received multiple awards, such as receiving the prestigious RubyPrize in 2020 and being chosen as a Ruby Hero in 2015. He has given presentations at over 20 Ruby conferences. In addition to working on Ruby, he is also a committer for the OpenBSD operating system.

I would like to thank the editors, technical reviewers, and other Packt staff for their help in creating this book. I would especially like to thank Janko Marohnić for his reviews and recommendations, which resulted in so many improvements to this book.

About the reviewers

Jagdish Narayandasani has more than 14 years of experience in software development and almost a decade of experience in working on Ruby on Rails. He is currently working as a Technology Specialist with a New York-based Fintech firm. He often contributes as a echnical reviewer for technical books. He has worked on a variety of technologies, such as Java, Ruby, Elixir, and the AWS cloud for different companies. He has worked in various industries, such as finance, retail, healthcare, and wealth management. At the moment, he is trying his hand at blockchain technology. In his free time, he loves to spend time with his family, explore new places, and try new food.

Janko Marohnić is a seasoned Ruby developer with big love for open source. He has authored many Ruby libraries, spoken at conferences, and writes on his blog about his discoveries in the Ruby ecosystem (most of them are libraries created or maintained by the author of this book). He values well-tested code, separation of responsibilities, and doing more with less. Outside of programming, Janko enjoys dancing, acrobatic activities, and playing the piano.

Table of Contents

3
Proper Variable Usage

4
Methods and Their Arguments

5
Handling Errors

6
Formatting Code for Easy Reading

Section 2:
Ruby Library Programming Principles

10
Designing Useful Domain-Specific Languages

11
Testing to Ensure Your Code Works

12
Handling Change

13
Using Common Design Patterns

14
Optimizing Your Library

Section 3:
Ruby Web Programming Principles

15
The Database Is Key

16

Web Application Design Principles

17

Robust Web Application Security

Assessments

Other Books You May Enjoy

Index

Preface

The purpose of this book is to teach useful principles for intermediate to advanced Ruby programmers to follow. The focus is not generally on how to implement solutions, but on different implementation approaches, the trade-offs between them, and why some approaches are better in certain situations. While the main focus of the book is teaching principles, in some cases this book also teaches advanced Ruby programming techniques.

This book starts by teaching some fundamental principles, such as how best to use the core classes, when and how best to use each variable type, and how best to use the different types of method arguments. After building on the fundamental principles, the book teaches principles for better library design, such as how best to design extensible plugin systems, trade-offs when using metaprogramming and DSLs, and how best to approach testing, refactoring, and optimization. This book concludes with a few small chapters that are focused on principles specific to web programming in Ruby, with a separate chapter each on database design, application design, and web application security.

Who this book is for

The target audience for the book is intermediate to advanced Ruby programmers who are interested in learning principles to improve their Ruby programming.

What this book covers

Chapter 1, *Getting the Most out of Core Classes*, focuses on the optimal usage of the built-in classes.

Chapter 2, *Designing Useful Custom Classes*, focuses on when it makes sense to implement a custom class, applying SOLID design to custom classes, and the trade-offs between having large classes and having a large number of classes.

Chapter 3, *Proper Variable Usage*, focuses on how best to use each of Ruby's variable types.

Chapter 4, *Methods and Their Arguments*, focuses on method naming principles, the best usage of each of the method argument types, and choosing proper method visibility.

Chapter 5, Handling Errors, focuses on the trade-offs between using exceptions and return values for handling errors, handling transient errors, and designing exception class hierarchies.

Chapter 6, Formatting Code for Easy Reading, focuses on different viewpoints on the importance of syntactic complexity and the downsides of arbitrary limits.

Chapter 7, Designing Your Library, focuses on designing your library around the user experience and complexity trade-offs when designing methods for your library.

Chapter 8, Designing for Extensibility, focuses on designing useful plugin systems to allow for extensibility in libraries.

Chapter 9, Metaprogramming and When to Use It, focuses on the pros and cons of abstraction, avoiding redundancy, and trade-offs between the two approaches Ruby has for metaprogramming.

Chapter 10, Designing Useful Domain-Specific Languages, focuses on when and how best to design DSLs.

Chapter 11, Testing to Ensure Your Code Works, focuses on why testing is so important, how to approach testing and manage complexity during testing, and the importance of code coverage.

Chapter 12, Handling Change, focuses on when and how best to implement refactoring in libraries, and deprecation strategies.

Chapter 13, Using Common Design Patterns, focuses on principles for the best usage of five common design patterns.

Chapter 14, Optimizing Your Library, focuses on determining when optimization is needed and how to approach optimization if it is needed.

Chapter 15, The Database Is Key, focuses on why database design is so important in web programming, how best to use database features, and how best to handle database errors.

Chapter 16, Web Application Design Principles, focuses on trade-offs for different types of application design, different frameworks, and different URL designs.

Chapter 17, Robust Web Application Security, focuses on important web security techniques and how to approach designing web applications for high-security environments.

To get the most out of this book

This book assumes intermediate to advanced knowledge of the Ruby programming language. There are sections of the book that are accessible to those with only basic knowledge of Ruby, but most of the book assumes you already understand how Ruby works and tries to teach principles for more productive usage of Ruby.

While most of the ideas and principles discussed in the book, and most of the code examples used in the book, apply to any version of Ruby, some of the examples and principles are specific to Ruby 3.0, the latest release at the time of publication.

Software/hardware covered in the book	OS requirements
Ruby 3.0 (many examples will work with earlier versions)	Any OS that runs Ruby

If you are using the digital version of this book, we advise you to type the code yourself or access the code via the GitHub repository (link available in the next section). Doing so will help you avoid any potential errors related to the copying and pasting of code.

Download the example code files

You can download the example code files for this book from GitHub at `https://github.com/PacktPublishing/Polished-Ruby-Programming`. In case there's an update to the code, it will be updated on the existing GitHub repository.

We also have other code bundles from our rich catalog of books and videos available at `https://github.com/PacktPublishing/`. Check them out!

Conventions used

There are a number of text conventions used throughout this book.

`Code in text`: Indicates code words in text, database table names, folder names, filenames, file extensions, pathnames, dummy URLs, user input, and Twitter handles. Here is an example: "As an example of this, consider a SQL database library that needs to execute `INSERT`, `UPDATE`, and `DELETE` SQL queries to modify data."

A block of code is set as follows:

```
class Foo
  def self.bar
    :baz
  end
end
```

Any command-line input or output is written as follows:

```
# Warming up ------------------------------------
#     MultiplyProf     28.531k i/100ms
# Calculating ------------------------------------
#     MultiplyProf     284.095k (± 0.3%) i/s
```

Get in touch

Feedback from our readers is always welcome.

General feedback: If you have questions about any aspect of this book, mention the book title in the subject of your message and email us at customercare@packtpub.com.

Errata: Although we have taken every care to ensure the accuracy of our content, mistakes do happen. If you have found a mistake in this book, we would be grateful if you would report this to us. Please visit www.packtpub.com/support/errata, selecting your book, clicking on the Errata Submission Form link, and entering the details.

Piracy: If you come across any illegal copies of our works in any form on the Internet, we would be grateful if you would provide us with the location address or website name. Please contact us at copyright@packt.com with a link to the material.

If you are interested in becoming an author: If there is a topic that you have expertise in and you are interested in either writing or contributing to a book, please visit authors.packtpub.com.

Reviews

Please leave a review. Once you have read and used this book, why not leave a review on the site that you purchased it from? Potential readers can then see and use your unbiased opinion to make purchase decisions, we at Packt can understand what you think about our products, and our authors can see your feedback on their book. Thank you!

For more information about Packt, please visit `packt.com`.

Section 1: Fundamental Ruby Programming Principles

The objective of this section is for you to understand the fundamental principles and trade-offs involved in Ruby programming, at the level of individual classes and methods.

This section comprises the following chapters:

- *Chapter 1, Getting the Most out of Core Classes*
- *Chapter 2, Designing Useful Custom Classes*
- *Chapter 3, Proper Variable Usage*
- *Chapter 4, Methods and Their Arguments*
- *Chapter 5, Handling Errors*
- *Chapter 6, Formatting Code for Easy Reading*

1
Getting the Most out of Core Classes

Ruby is shipped with a rich library of core classes. Almost all Ruby programmers are familiar with the most common core classes, and one of the easiest ways to make your code intuitive to most Ruby programmers is to use these classes.

In the rest of this chapter, you'll learn more about commonly encountered core classes, as well as principles for how to best use each class. We will cover the following topics:

- Learning when to use core classes
- Best uses for `true`, `false`, and `nil` objects
- Different numeric types for different needs
- Understanding how symbols differ from strings
- Learning how best to use arrays, hashes, and sets
- Working with `Struct` – one of the underappreciated core classes

By the end of this chapter, you'll have a better understanding of many of Ruby's core classes, and how best to use each of them.

BigDecimal is similar to rationals in that it is an exact type in most cases, but it is not exact when dealing with divisions that result in a repeating decimal:

```
v = BigDecimal(1)/3
v * 3
# => 0.999999999999999999e0
```

However, other than divisions involving repeating decimals and exponentiation, BigDecimal values are exact. Let's take the first example, but make both arguments BigDecimal instances:

```
f = BigDecimal(1.1, 2)
v = BigDecimal(0)
1000.times do
  v += f
end
v
# => 0.11e4
v.to_s('F')
# => "1100.0"
```

So, as you can see, no error is introduced when using repeated addition on BigDecimal, similar to rationals. You can also see that inspecting the output is less helpful since BigDecimal uses a scientific notation. BigDecimal does have the advantage that it can produce human-friendly decimal string output directly without converting the object to a float first.

If we try the same approach with the second example, we can see that it also produces exact results:

```
f = BigDecimal(1.109375, 7)
v = BigDecimal(0)
1000.times do
  v += f
end
v
# => 0.1109375e4
v.to_s('F')
# => "1109.375"
```

As both examples show, one issue with using a BigDecimal that is created from floats or rationals is that you need to manually specify the initial precision. It is more common to initialize BigDecimal values from integers or strings, to avoid the need to manually specify the precision.

BigDecimal is significantly slower than floats and rationals for calculations. Due to the trade-offs inherent in BigDecimal, a good general principle is to use BigDecimal only when dealing with other systems that support similar types, such as fixed precision numeric types in many databases, or when dealing with other fixed precision areas such as monetary calculations. For most other cases, it's generally better to use a rational or float.

Of the numeric types, most integer and float values are immediate objects, which is one of the reasons why they are faster than other types. However, large integer and float values are too large to be immediate objects (which must fit in 8 bytes if using a 64-bit CPU). Rationals and BigDecimal are never immediate objects, which is one reason why they are slower.

In this section, you learned about Ruby's many numeric types and how best to use each. In the next section, you'll learn how symbols are very different from strings, and when to use each.

Understanding how symbols differ from strings

One of the most useful but misunderstood aspects of Ruby is the difference between symbols and strings. One reason for this is there are certain methods of Ruby that deal with symbols, but will still accept strings, or perform string-like operations on a symbol. Another reason is due to the popularity of Rails and its pervasive use of `ActiveSupport::HashWithIndifferentAccess`, which allows you to use either a string or a symbol for accessing the same data. However, symbols and strings are very different internally, and serve completely different purposes. However, Ruby is focused on programmer happiness and productivity, so it will often automatically convert a string to a symbol if it needs a symbol, or a symbol to a string if it needs a string.

A string in Ruby is a series of characters or bytes, useful for storing text or binary data. Unless the string is frozen, you append to it, modify existing characters in it, or replace it with a different string.

A symbol in Ruby is a number with an attached identifier that is a series of characters or bytes. Symbols in Ruby are an object wrapper for an internal type that Ruby calls `ID`, which is an integer type. When you use a symbol in Ruby code, Ruby looks up the number associated with that identifier. The reason for having an `ID` type internally is that it is much faster for computers to deal with integers instead of a series of characters or bytes. Ruby uses `ID` values to reference local variables, instance variables, class variables, constants, and method names.

Say you run Ruby code as follows:

```
foo.add(bar)
```

Ruby will parse this code, and for `foo`, `add`, and `bar`, it will look up whether it already has an ID associated with the identifier. If it already has an ID, it will use it; otherwise, it will create a new `ID` value and associate it with the identifier. This happens during parsing and the `ID` values are hardcoded into the VM instructions.

Say you run Ruby code as follows:

```
method = :add
foo.send(method, bar)
```

Ruby will parse this code, and for `method`, `add`, `foo`, `send`, and `bar`, Ruby will also look up whether it already has an ID associated with the identifier, or create a new `ID` value to associate with the identifier if it does not exist. This approach is slightly slower as Ruby will create a local variable and there is additional indirection as `send` has to look up the method to call dynamically. However, there are no calls at runtime to look up an `ID` value.

Say you run Ruby code as follows:

```
method = "add"
foo.send(method, bar)
```

Ruby will parse this code, and for `method`, `foo`, `send`, and `bar`, Ruby will also look up whether it already has an ID associated with the identifier, also creating the ID if it doesn't exist. However, during parsing, Ruby does not create an ID value for `add` because it is a string and not a symbol. However, when `send` is called at runtime, `method` is a string value, and `send` needs a symbol. So, Ruby will dynamically look up and see whether there is an ID associated with the `add` identifier, raising a `NoMethodError` if it does not exist. This `ID` lookup will happen every time the send method is called, making this code even slower.

So, while it looks like symbols and strings are as interchangable as the `method` argument to `send`, this is only because Ruby tries to be friendly to the programmer and accept either. The `send` method needs to work with an ID, and it is better for performance to use a symbol, which is Ruby's representation of an ID, as opposed to a string, which Ruby must perform substantial work on to convert to an ID.

This not only affects `Kernel#send` but also affects most similar methods where identifiers are passed dynamically, such as `Module#define_method`, `Kernel#instance_variable_get`, and `Module#const_get`. The general principle when using these methods in Ruby code is always to pass symbols to them, since it results in better performance.

The previous examples show that when Ruby needs a symbol, it will often accept a string and convert it for the programmer's convenience. This allows strings to be treated as symbols in certain cases. There are opposite cases, where Ruby allows symbols to be treated as strings for the programmer's convenience.

For example, while symbols represent integers attached to a series of characters or bytes, Ruby allows you to perform operations on symbols such as `<`, `>`, and `<=>`, as if they were strings, where the result does not depend on the symbol's integer value, but on the string value of the name attached to the symbol. Again, this is Ruby doing so for the programmer's convenience. For example, consider the following line of code:

```
object.methods.sort
```

This results in a list sorted by the name of the method, since that is the most useful for the programmer. In this case, Ruby needs to operate on the string value of the symbol, which has similar performance issues as when Ruby needs to convert a string to a symbol internally.

There are many other methods on Symbol that operate on the internal string associated with the symbol. Some methods, such as `downcase`, `upcase`, and `capitalize`, return a symbol by internally operating on the string associated with the symbol, and then converting the resulting value back to a symbol. For example, `symbol.downcase` basically does `symbol.to_s.downcase.to_sym`. Other methods, such as `[]`, `size`, and `match`, operate on the string associated with the symbol, such as `symbol.size` being shorthand for `symbol.to_s.size`.

In all of these cases, it is possible to determine what Ruby natively wants. If Ruby needs an internal identifier, it will natively want a symbol, and only accept a string by converting it. If Ruby needs to operate on text, it will natively want a string, and only accept a symbol by converting it.

So, how does the difference between a symbol and string affect your code? The general principle is to be like Ruby, and use symbols when you need an identifier in your code, and strings when you need text or data. For example, if you need to accept a configuration value that can only be one of three options, it's probably best to use a symbol:

```ruby
def switch(value)
  case value
  when :foo
    # foo
  when :bar
    # bar
  when :baz
    # baz
  end
end
```

However, if you are dealing with text or data, you should accept a string and not a symbol:

```ruby
def append2(value)
  value.gsub(/foo/, "bar")
end
```

You should consider whether you want to be as flexible as many Ruby core methods, and automatically convert a string to a symbol or vice versa. If you are internally treating symbols and strings differently, you should definitely not perform automatic conversion. However, if you are only dealing with one of the types, then you have to decide how to handle it. Automatically converting the type is worse for performance, and results in less flexible internals, since you need to keep supporting both types for backward compatibility. Not automatically converting the type is better for performance, and results in more flexible internals, since you are not obligated to support both types. However, it means that users of your code will probably get errors if they pass in a type that is not expected. Therefore, it is important to understand the trade-off inherent in the decision of whether to convert both types. If you aren't sure which trade-off is better, start by not automatically converting, since you can always add automatic conversion later if needed.

In this section, you learned the important difference between symbols and strings, and when it is best to use each. In the next section, you'll learn how best to use Ruby's core collection classes.

Learning how best to use arrays, hashes, and sets

Ruby's collection classes are one of the reasons why it is such a joy to program in Ruby. In most cases, the choice of collection class to use is fairly straightforward. If you need a simple list of values that you are iterating over, or using the collection as a queue or a stack, you generally use an array. If you need a mapping of one or more objects to one or more objects, then you generally use a hash. If you have a large list of objects and want to see whether a given object is contained in it, you generally use a set.

In some cases, it's fine to use either an array or a hash. Often, when iterating over a small list, you could use the array approach:

```ruby
[[:foo, 1], [:bar, 3], [:baz, 7]].each do |sym, i|
  # ...
end
```

Or, you could use the hash approach:

```ruby
{foo: 1, bar: 3, baz: 7}.each do |sym, i|
  # ...
end
```

Since you are not indexing into the collection, the simpler approach from a design perspective is to use an array. However, because the hash approach is syntactically simpler, the idiomatic way to handle this in Ruby is to use a hash.

For more complex mapping cases, you often want to use a hash, but you may need to decide how to structure the hash. This is especially true when you are using complex keys. Let's take a deeper look at the differences between arrays, hashes, and sets by working through an example that implements an in-memory database.

Implementing an in-memory database

While many programmers often use a SQL database for data storage, there are many cases when you need to build a small, in-memory database using arrays, hashes, and sets. Often, even when you have the main data stored in a SQL database, it is faster to query the SQL database to retrieve the information, and use that to build an in-memory database for the specific class or method you are designing. This allows you to query the in-memory database with similar speed as a hash or array lookup, orders of magnitude faster than a SQL database query.

Let's say you have a list of album names, track numbers, and artist names, where you can have multiple artists for the same album and track. You want to design a simple lookup system so that given an album name, you can find all artists who worked on any track of the album, and given an album name and track number, you can find the artists who worked on that particular track.

In the following examples, you should assume that `album_infos` is an arbitrary object that has each method that yields the album name, track number, and artist. However, if you would like to have some sample data to work with:

```ruby
album_infos = 100.times.flat_map do |i|
  10.times.map do |j|
    ["Album #{i}", j, "Artist #{j}"]
  end
end
```

One approach for handling this is to populate two hashes, one keyed by album name, and one keyed by an array of the album name and track number. Populating these two hashes is straightforward, by setting the value for the key to an empty array if the key doesn't exist, and then appending the artist name. Then you need to make sure the artist values are unique for the hash keyed just by album name:

```ruby
album_artists = {}
album_track_artists = {}
album_infos.each do |album, track, artist|
  (album_artists[album] ||= []) << artist
  (album_track_artists[[album, track]] ||= []) << artist
end
album_artists.each_value(&:uniq!)
```

With this approach, looking up values is fairly straightforward, and just involves looking in the appropriate hash with the appropriate key:

```ruby
lookup = ->(album, track=nil) do
  if track
    album_track_artists[[album, track]]
  else
    album_artists[album]
  end
end
```

An alternative approach would be to use a nested hash approach, with each album having a hash of tracks:

```
albums = {}
album_infos.each do |album, track, artist|
   ((albums[album] ||= {})[track] ||= []) << artist
end
```

With this approach, looking up values is more complex, especially in the case where a track number is not provided, and you have to dynamically create the list:

```
lookup = ->(album, track=nil) do
  if track
     albums.dig(album, track)
  else
     a = albums[album].each_value.to_a
     a.flatten!
     a.uniq!
     a
  end
end
```

In general, the first approach using multiple hashes is going to take significantly more memory than the second approach if there is a large number of albums, but it will have a much better lookup performance for albums. The first approach will also take much more time to populate the data structure. The second approach is much lighter on memory and has better lookup performance for albums with tracks as it avoids an array allocation, but will exhibit a far more inferior performance for albums.

Each of these approaches does not depend on the types of objects that album_infos. each yields. You probably made the reasonable assumption that album and artist would be strings, and track would be a number. Let's say you knew in advance that the track number was an integer between 1 and 99. You could use that information to design a different approach. You could still have a single of hash keyed by album name, with a value being an array containing arrays of artist names for each track. Since tracks only go from 1 to 99, you could use the 0 index in the array to store all artist names for the album. Populating this combination of hash and array of arrays isn't too difficult:

```
albums = {}
album_infos.each do |album, track, artist|
   album_array = albums[album] ||= [[]]
```

```
    album_array[0] << artist
     (album_array[track] ||= []) << artist
end
albums.each_value do |array|
   array[0].uniq!
end
```

This approach is more memory-efficient than either of the previous approaches, and looking up values is very simple and never allocates an object:

```
lookup = ->(album, track=0) do
   albums.dig(album, track)
end
```

Compared to the previous two approaches, this approach uses about the same amount of memory as the nested hash approach. It takes slightly more time to populate compared to the nested hash approach. It is almost as fast as the two hash approach in terms of lookup performance for albums, and is the fastest approach for lookup performance by albums with tracks.

Maybe the needs of your application change, and now you need a feature that allows users to enter a list of artist names, and will return an array with only the artist names that the application knows are on one of the albums. One way to handle this is to store the artists in an array:

```
album_artists = album_infos.flat_map(&:last)
album_artists.uniq!
```

The lookup can use an array intersection to determine the values:

```
lookup = ->(artists) do
   album_artists & artists
end
```

The problem with this approach is that `Array#&` uses a linear search of the array, so this approach is very slow for a large number of artists.

A better performing approach would use a hash, keyed by the artist name:

```
album_artists = {}
album_infos.each do |_, _, artist|
  album_artists[artist] ||= true
end
```

The lookup can use the hash to filter the values in the submitted array:

```
lookup = ->(artists) do
  artists.select do |artist|
    album_artists[artist]
  end
end
```

This approach performs much better. The code isn't as simple, though it isn't too bad. However, it would be nicer to have simpler code that performed as well. Thankfully, the Ruby Set class can meet this need. Like BigDecimal, Set is not currently a core Ruby class. Set is in the standard library, and you can load it via require 'set'. However, Set may be moved from the standard library to a core class in a future version of Ruby. Using a set is pretty much as simple as using an array in terms of populating the data structure:

```
album_artists = Set.new(album_infos.flat_map(&:last))
```

You don't need to manually make the array unique, because the set automatically ignores duplicate values. The lookup code can stay exactly the same as the array case:

```
lookup = ->(artists) do
  album_artists & artists
end
```

Of the three approaches, the hash approach is the fastest to populate and the fastest to look up. The Set approach is much faster to look up than the array approach, but still significantly slower than hash. Set is actually implemented using a hash internally, so in general, it will perform worse than using a hash directly. As a general rule, you should only use a set for code that isn't performance-sensitive and you would like to use a nicer API. For any performance-sensitive code, you should prefer using a hash directly.

In this section, you learned about Ruby's core collection of classes, arrays, hashes, and sets. In the next section, you'll learn about Struct, one of Ruby's underappreciated core classes.

Working with Struct – one of the underappreciated core classes

The Struct class is one of the underappreciated Ruby core classes. It allows you to create classes with one or more fields, with accessors automatically created for each field. So, say you have the following:

```
class Artist
  attr_accessor :name, :albums

  def initialize(name, albums)
    @name = name
    @albums = albums
  end
end
```

Instead of that, you can write a small amount of Ruby code, and have the initializer and accessor automatically created:

```
Artist = Struct.new(:name, :albums)
```

In general, a Struct class is a little lighter on memory than a regular class, but has slower accessor methods. Struct used to be faster in terms of both initialization and reader methods in older versions of Ruby, but regular classes and attr_accessor methods have gotten faster at a greater rate than Struct has. Therefore, for maximum performance, you may want to consider using regular classes and attr_accessor methods instead of Struct classes.

One of the more interesting aspects of Struct is how it works internally. For example, unlike the new method for most other classes, Struct.new does not return a Struct instance; it returns a Struct subclass:

```
Struct.new(:a, :b).class
# => Class
```

However, the new method on the subclass creates instances of the subclass; it doesn't create future subclasses. Additionally, if you provide a string and not a symbol as the first argument, Struct will automatically create the class using that name nested under its own namespace:

```
Struct.new('A', :a, :b).new(1, 2).class
# => Struct::A
```

A simplified version of the default Struct.new method is similar to the following. This example is a bit larger, so we'll break it into sections. If a string is given as the first argument, it is used to set the class in the namespace of the receiver; otherwise, it is added to the list of fields:

```
def Struct.new(name, *fields)
  unless name.is_a?(String)
    fields.unshift(name)
    name = nil
  end
```

Next, a subclass is created. If a class name was given, it is set as a constant in the current namespace:

```
  subclass = Class.new(self)

  if name
    const_set(name, subclass)
  end
```

Then, some internal code is run to set up the storage for the members of the subclass. Then, the new, allocate, [], members, and inspect singleton methods are defined on the subclass. Finally, some internal code is run to set up accessor instance methods for each member of the subclass:

```
  # Internal magic to setup fields/storage for subclass

  def subclass.new(*values)
    obj = allocate
    obj.initialize(*values)
    obj
  end
```

```
    # Similar for allocate, [], members, inspect


    # Internal magic to setup accessor instance methods


    subclass
end
```

Interestingly, you can still create Struct subclasses the normal way:

```
class SubStruct < Struct
end
```

Struct subclasses created via the normal way operate like Struct itself, not like Struct subclasses created via Struct.new. You can then call new on the Struct subclass to create a subclass of that subclass, but the setup is similar to a Struct subclass created via Struct.new:

```
SubStruct.new('A', :a, :b).new(1, 2).class
# => SubStruct::A
```

In general, Struct is good for creating simple classes that are designed for storing data. One issue with Struct is that the design encourages the use of mutable data and discourages a functional approach, by defaulting to creating setter methods for every member. However, it is possible to easily force the use of immutable structs by freezing the object in initialize:

```
A = Struct.new(:a, :b) do
  def initialize(...)
    super
    freeze
  end
end
```

There have been feature requests submitted on the Ruby issue tracker to create immutable Struct subclasses using a keyword argument to Struct.new or via the addition of a separate Struct::Value class. However, as of Ruby 3, neither feature request has been accepted. It is possible that a future version of Ruby will include them, but in the meantime, freezing the receiver in initialize is the best approach.

Summary

In this chapter, you've learned about the core classes. You've learned about issues with `true`, `false`, and `nil`, and how best to use Ruby's numeric types. You've learned why the difference between symbols and strings is important. You've learned how best to use arrays, hashes, and sets, and when it makes sense to use your own custom structs.

In the next chapter, you'll build on this knowledge of the core classes and learn about constructing your own custom classes.

Questions

1. How are `nil` and `false` different from all other objects?

2. Are all standard arithmetic operations using two BigDecimal objects exact?

3. Would it make sense for Ruby to combine symbols and strings?

4. Which uses less memory for the same data-hash, or `Set`?

5. What are the only two core methods that return a new instance of `Class`?

Further reading

These books will also be applicable to all other chapters in this book, but are only listed in this chapter to reduce duplication:

*   *Comprehensive Ruby Programming*: `https://www.packtpub.com/product/comprehensive-ruby-programming/9781787280649`

*   *The Ruby Workshop*: `https://www.packtpub.com/product/the-ruby-workshop/9781838642365`

2
Designing Useful Custom Classes

In the previous chapter, you learned about how to get the most out of Ruby's core classes. However, outside of small scripts, you'll probably want to create your own classes to organize your code. How you design and structure your classes has a huge effect on how intuitive and maintainable your code is. This chapter will help you learn when a new class is a good idea, how to apply some important object-oriented design principles, how to determine class size, and whether it is worthwhile to introduce a custom data structure.

In this chapter, you'll learn the following principles for designing custom classes:

- Learning when to create a custom class
- Handling trade-offs in SOLID design
- Deciding on larger classes or more classes
- Learning when to use custom data structures

By the end of this chapter, you'll have a better understanding of the principles of Ruby class design and the trade-offs between different design approaches.

Technical requirements

In this chapter and all the chapters of this book, code given in code blocks is designed to execute on Ruby 3.0. Many of the code examples will work on earlier versions of Ruby, but not all. You will find the code files on GitHub at `https://github.com/PacktPublishing/Polished-Ruby-Programming/tree/main/Chapter02`.

Learning when to create a custom class

One of the first questions you need to answer before creating a custom class should probably be, "Do I really need to create a custom class?" Object-oriented design often involves creating classes for each separate type of object. Functional design does away with classes completely, instead having functions that operate on immutable data structures. Procedural design is similar to functional design, but generally involves functions that operate on mutable data structures. No one design approach is best in all cases, and all design approaches have trade-offs. Ruby supports both object-oriented design, functional design, and procedural design, and often maintainable code has a mix of all three.

Choosing to create a custom class is always a trade-off. There is always a cost in creating a custom class versus using a core class, and that is that all classes result in some amount of conceptual overhead. That's true of both core classes and custom classes. It's just that all Ruby programmers have already used most core classes, so they have internalized the conceptual overhead already. Creating a custom class means that everyone who deals with the code needs to learn about the class and how it works so that they are able to use it correctly and be productive while using it.

There are two main benefits of creating a custom class. One is that it encapsulates state, so that the state of the object can only be manipulated in ways that make sense for the object. The second benefit is that classes provide a simple way for calling functions related to the instances of a class (in Ruby, these are called methods). Whether these benefits outweigh the cost of the conceptual overhead is going to be highly dependent on the code you write.

As a simple example, let's say in your application that you need to store a stack of objects (last-in, first-out). With core classes, you can implement this using a standard `Array` class:

```
stack = []

# add to top of stack
stack.push(1)
```

```
# get top value from stack
stack.pop
```

That approach is intuitive and maintainable. However, because a standard array is used, if external code can get a reference to the object, objects can violate the stack design and do this:

```
# add to bottom to stack!
stack.unshift(2)
```

If you want to prevent this, you can encapsulate your logic into a custom class:

```
class Stack
  def initialize
    @stack = []
  end

  def push(value)
    @stack.push(value)
  end

  def pop
    @stack.pop
  end
end
```

If you are sharing this stack object so that users operate on stacks directly and pass the stacks to other objects, this encapsulation makes sense. However, if your stack is just an implementation detail used in another class that has its own encapsulation, then creating a custom Stack class is probably unnecessary complexity. In addition to being less intuitive, it results in slower runtime performance due to additional indirection and slower garbage collection, and greater memory use due to additional allocated objects.

In the previous examples, the only benefit to creating a custom class is information hiding, since push and pop methods both exist on the array. What if you want to require that the values in the stack are symbols, and you want to return the time the symbol spent in the stack when popping the stack? With a custom class, you could implement the behavior by initializing a SymbolStack class with an empty array:

```
class SymbolStack
  def initialize
```

```
    @stack = []
  end
```

Then you could define a `SymbolStack#push` method to check that the object passed is a symbol:

```
def push(sym)
  raise TypeError, "can only push symbols onto stack" unless
      sym.is_a?(Symbol)
  @stack.push([sym, clock_time])
end
```

You can define the `SymbolStack#pop` method to return the symbol and the amount of time the symbol spent in the stack:

```
def pop
  sym, pushed_at = @stack.pop
  [sym, clock_time - pushed_at]
end
```

Finally, in order to calculate times correctly, you can define a private `SymbolStack#clock_time` method. This is more reliable than using `Time.now`, as using `Time.now` to calculate time duration can be affected by changes to the system time:

```
  private def clock_time
    Process.clock_gettime(Process::CLOCK_MONOTONIC)
  end
end
```

In this scenario, where you need both information hiding and custom behavior, defining a custom class usually makes sense.

One final thing to consider before creating a custom class is how many places you will be using it. In the previous example with `SymbolStack`, if you are using `SymbolStack` in three separate classes that have similar needs, that's a strong indication that a separate class is appropriate. However, if you are using `SymbolStack` in only a single class, and it doesn't need to be accessed directly by users, you should consider not creating a custom class for it yet.

In this section, you learned about principles to help you decide whether using a custom class is appropriate. In the next section, you'll learn about SOLID design and the trade-offs involved.

Handling trade-offs in SOLID design

You may have heard about designing classes around SOLID principles. SOLID is an acronym for five separate object-oriented design principles:

- The single-responsibility principle
- The open-closed principle
- The Liskov substitution principle
- The interface segregation principle
- The dependency inversion principle

Using these principles can result in well-structured classes. However, the principles should not be applied dogmatically. You should always consider whether each principle represents a good trade-off for the application or library you are building. In this section, you'll learn about each of these principles and the trade-offs related to each, to help you decide to what extent you would benefit from using them.

The single-responsibility principle

The basic idea of the single-responsibility principle is that a class should basically serve one purpose. On the face of it, this is a good general rule, as classes built to serve a single purpose are fine and easy to use. You've probably designed classes that serve a single purpose, and haven't had problems using them or working with them.

However, the single-responsibility principle is not generally used for justifying designing a class to serve a single purpose. It's almost always used to justify splitting a single class that serves multiple purposes into multiple classes that each serve a single purpose, or at least a smaller number of purposes. This application of the principle can often result in increased complexity, especially if you consider the purpose to be small in scope.

Take Ruby's `String` class as an example. Ruby's `String` class can serve multiple purposes. It can represent text and it can also represent binary data. It can be used as a builder of text or data, or as their modifier. One of the great aspects of Ruby is how flexible the `String` class is, the fact that it can handle many different purposes, and how you don't need to conceptually deal with `Text`, `Data`, `TextBuilder`, `DataBuilder`, `TextModifier`, and `DataModifier` classes. Your use of the single-responsibility principle may be the equivalent of starting with the following code:

```
str = String.new
str << "test" << "ing...1...2"
```

```
name = ARGV[1].
  to_s.
  gsub('cool', 'amazing').
  capitalize

str << ". Found: " << name
puts str
```

And turning it into the following code:

```
builder = TextBuilder.new
builder.append("test")
builder.append("ing...1...2")

modifier = TextModifier.new
name = modifier.gsub(ARGV[1].to_s, 'cool', 'amazing')
name = modifier.capitalize(name)

builder.append(". Found: ")
builder.append(name)

puts builder.as_string
```

In such a case, you should probably reconsider whether the additional complexity you are adding is worth it. In many cases, you can get a design that is more maintainable and easier to use by having a single class with multiple related purposes, compared to splitting the class up and having multiple separate classes, each with its own single purpose.

A good question to ask yourself when deciding whether to use the single-responsibility principle to split up a class is, "Would I be able to use any of the newly split classes in additional places in my application or library?" If the answer is yes, that is an indication that it may be a good idea to separate the classes, since separate parts of the current class are reusable in additional areas. However, if the answer is no, that is an indication that it may not be a good idea.

Another good question to ask yourself is, "Do I want to be able to easily replace certain parts of this class with alternative parts?" Let's say you have a program that prints reports. It starts out with the ability to convert a single type of report to a single format. One design approach is to have a single `Report` class that holds all of the data for the report and has all the methods used for formatting the report:

```
report = Report.new(data)
puts report.format
```

Alternatively, you could have a `ReportContent` class and `ReportFormatter` class, since the storage of data and the formatting of it into a report are separate purposes:

```
report_content = ReportContent.new(data)
report_formatter = ReportFormatter.new
puts report_formatter.format(report_content)
```

Which of these approaches is better depends on whether future changes will be needed. If, in the future, you may have three different types of reports (say, `docx`, `pdf`, and `csv`), using separate classes can allow you to easily replace only part of the class:

```
report_content = ReportContent.new(data)
report_formatter = ReportFormatter.
  for_type(report_type).new
puts report_formatter.format(report_content)
```

If you know in advance that you will need multiple report formats, separating the design into `ReportContent` and `ReportFormatter` classes upfront is probably a good idea. However, if you start out with only a single report format, the single `Report` class design is probably a better approach. You may never need to deal with multiple report formats, and burdening your code with excess complexity will make it harder to use. As a general principle, you should delay increasing complexity in your class designs until you actually need the complexity. It is far easier to add complexity later if needed than to remove complexity later if not needed, at least if you care about backward compatibility.

The open-closed principle

The open-closed principle stipulates that a class should be open for extension, but closed for modification. An extension in Ruby's case would be adding instance variables and methods, and modification would be modifying or removing existing instance variables or methods. The open-closed principle was written mostly to address issues with compiled software written in programming languages that are less expressive than Ruby. In Ruby, pretty much all classes are open for both extension and modification.

Ruby itself completely ignores the open-closed principle, and actively works to make sure classes aren't closed for modification. One of the most significant changes to Ruby's object model happened in Ruby 2.0, with the addition of origin classes. Origin classes are internal classes used to allow the implementation of Module#prepend. Origin classes added a huge amount of complexity to Ruby's object model, for the sole purpose of making modification even easier by programmers to override singleton methods and call super to get the default behavior.

Let's say you actually wanted to try enforcing the open-closed principle in Ruby. How would you go about it? Closing a class for extension and modification is as easy as calling ClassName.freeze, but closing for modification while leaving it open for extension is harder.

There are three general ways in which to add methods to classes. One is to add them by including a module that defines them in the class, and another is prepending a module that defines them to the class. Therefore, if you wanted to prevent modification, you could override include and prepend and have them raise an exception if any of the modules passed have instance methods that overlap with the class's instance methods. You'll want to consider public, protected, and private methods when doing so. You can first create the OpenClosed class and add a singleton meths method to it, returning all instance methods in the given class.

Note that instance_methods returns both public and protected methods, so you need to add the private methods to it:

```ruby
class OpenClosed
  def self.meths(m)
    m.instance_methods + m.private_instance_methods
  end
```

Then you can override the include singleton method:

```ruby
  def self.include(*mods)
    mods.each do |mod|
```

```
    unless (meths(mod) & meths(self)).empty?
      raise "class closed for modification"
    end
  end
  super
end
```

You can alias `include` as `prepend`. When using aliases, super method lookup uses the aliased name, so this doesn't break anything:

```
singleton_class.alias_method :prepend, :include
```

You would probably want to do the same thing for the `extend` method that you did for `prepend` and `include`, as this will handle changes to the class's singleton methods instead of the class's instance methods:

```
def self.extend(*mods)
  mods.each do |mod|
    unless (meths(mod) & meths(singleton_class)).empty?
      raise "class closed for modification"
    end
  end
  super
end
```

The third way to add methods to a class is to define them directly on the class. There isn't a hook called before adding a method, so unlike overriding `include` and `prepend`, you can't prevent the method from being added.

However, you can use the `method_added` hook, which is called after the method has been added, at which point the class or module has already been modified. Since the `method_added` hook is called directly after every method, you can undo the addition of the method and raise an exception as long as you have an alias to the method by overriding the method just defined with the alias. First, you need to make aliases for all methods by appending a double underscore for the method:

```
meths(self).each do |method|
  alias_name = :"__#{method}"
  alias_method alias_name, method
end
```

Then you can define a `method_added` hook. You only want this hook to run when someone else adds a method to the class, and not when you are undoing the addition of the method, so this uses a trick you'll learn more about in *Chapter 3, Proper Variable Usage*, by having a local variable defining outside the method that is modified inside the method:

```
check_method = true
define_singleton_method(:method_added) do |method|
  return unless check_method
```

If the method starts with the double underscore and is not already defined, someone is trying to override the aliased methods, so you can overwrite the aliased method by aliasing the original method again:

```
  if method.start_with?('__')
    unaliased_name = method[2..-1]
    if private_method_defined?(unaliased_name) ||
         method_defined?(unaliased_name)
      check_method = false
      alias_method method, unaliased_name
      check_method = true
      raise "class closed for modification"
    end
```

If the method doesn't start with the double underscore and is already defined, you can fix the issue by aliasing the aliased method back to the original method:

```
  else
    alias_name = :"__#{method}"
    if private_method_defined?(alias_name) ||
         method_defined?(alias_name)
      check_method = false
      alias_method method, alias_name
      check_method = true
      raise "class closed for modification"
    end
  end
end
end
```

This approach handles most cases well, but there are still many ways around it. You could exploit a race condition in the implementation by trying to override methods in different threads in a loop, either exploiting the time slices where `check_method` is set to `false`, or have one thread override the regular method and another thread override the double underscore method at the same time. Alternatively, you could remove the whole check altogether:

```
OpenClosed.singleton_class.remove_method(:method_added)
```

Because a user can always find a way to override the methods you are overriding to attempt to prevent them from modifying the class, it is pointless to try to get Ruby classes to be open for extension and closed for modification. Your choices are either frozen and closed for both modification and extension, or unfrozen and open for both modification and extension.

The Liskov substitution principle

The Liskov substitution principle states that any place in the code where you can use an object of type T, you can also use an object of a subtype of T. In terms of Ruby, this means that any place in your code where you are using an instance of a class, you can also use an instance of a subclass without anything breaking.

In general, this is a good principle to follow. When you subclass an existing class, if you override a method of the class, you should attempt to ensure that it accepts the same argument types and returns the same argument type.

For example, say you have a class named `Max` that stores a maximum value and has an `over?` method for whether a given value is greater than the maximum value:

```
class Max
  def initialize(max)
    @max = max
  end

  def over?(n)
    @max > n
  end
end
```

Then, overriding `over?` to require a separate argument in a subclass for an amount that the value would have to exceed the maximum value by would violate the Liskov substitution principle:

```
class MaxBy < Max
  def over?(n, by)
    @max > n + by
  end
end
```

This is because code that accepts an instance of `Max` and calls `over?` on it with a single argument will break if passed an instance of `MaxBy`. To be compliant with the Liskov substitution principle, you could make the argument optional or a keyword:

```
class MaxBy < Max
  def over?(n, by: 0)
    @max > n + by
  end
end
```

With this approach, passing an instance of `MaxBy` will work because the single argument to `MaxBy#over?` results in the same behavior as `Max#over?`, at least assuming that you initialized the `MaxBy` instance with a numeric value.

While the Liskov substitution principle is useful to follow in general, you should not be dogmatic about applying it. In a strict sense, all subtypes that have different behavior than their supertypes or produce different results could be said to violate Liskov substitutability, even if they expose the same API. And what would be the point of having a subtype with exactly the same behavior?

Fundamentally, attempting to adhere to the Liskov substitution principle means limiting what changes you are willing to allow in a subclass. That may not make sense in all cases. You may want a subclass with different behavior than a superclass in some cases. Does that mean that passing an instance of that subclass to code that expects an instance of a superclass may break? Yes, but that is not necessarily a problem. Just don't pass subclass instances in that case, and you can still happily use instances of subclasses in other cases. If you think the `MaxBy#over?` method, which requires two arguments, is more generally useful since a second argument should almost always be provided, you are probably better off using that approach, and just don't pass `MaxBy` instances to code expecting `Max` instances, at least if the `over?` method will be called on them.

Ruby, in general, respects that the programmer will know to do the right thing. It doesn't prevent behavior simply because there are ways to misuse it. Ruby also uses duck typing and doesn't generally care about what specific classes of objects you are using anyway, so Liskov substitutability doesn't really matter all that much.

There is one method in Ruby that will almost always break Liskov substitutability, and that you should generally avoid, and that is `instance_of?`. Say you have code that does the following:

```ruby
if obj.instance_of?(Max)
  # do something
else
  # do something else
end
```

Then, all subclasses of `Max` will break Liskov substitutability, since instead of taking the `if` branch, they will take the `else` branch. The same is true for comparing the values of using the result of the class method:

```ruby
if obj.class == Max
  # do something
else
  # do something else
end
```

These approaches should almost always use `kind_of?` instead, so that subclasses are allowed:

```ruby
if obj.kind_of?(Max)
  # do something
else
  # do something else
end
```

We have learned that the Liskov substitution principle is useful, but should not be applied in all cases. Next, we'll learn whether the interface segregation principle makes sense in Ruby.

The interface segregation principle

The interface segregation principle states that clients should not be forced to depend on methods they do not use. While this doesn't strictly apply to Ruby directly, since Ruby will only call methods that are used, a looser interpretation is that this applies to how large classes should be in terms of methods.

Classes with a large number of methods, where the programmer is only using a few of the methods, can be more difficult to understand. If 80% of your users use the same 20% of methods of a class, it may make sense to move many of the methods to a separate module (assuming that backward compatibility is not an issue). The 20% of users who need the methods can include the module in the class, while the other 80% can benefit from the smaller class.

In the real world, it's less likely that you'll have 80% of users using the same 20% of the methods. More likely, you'll have 80% of users using 20% of the methods, but which 20% are used varies widely from one user to the next. In that case, there is not an easy way to separate the code.

Ruby in general does not follow this principle, at least if you consider the core classes. Classes such as string, array, and hash have large numbers of methods. Some Rubyists would probably argue that they all have too many methods, but there would probably be differences in which methods they would vote to remove.

As a general principle, splitting up a module that is large simply because it is large is not necessarily beneficial. Having three modules with 10 methods each is not necessarily better than one module with 30 methods. Having multiple modules, where each programmer only uses which ones they need, does reduce the runtime overhead, but the trade-off it makes is that it can increase the cognitive overhead for the programmer.

If you are going to split a large interface into smaller interfaces, do not do so just because the interface is large. Do so if you can clearly separate useful methods in the interface into separate categories, where some categories will be needed in some applications but not in other applications. In *Chapter 8*, *Designing for Extensibility,* you'll learn more about using this kind of interface segregation via plugin systems.

The dependency inversion principle

The dependency inversion principle states that high-level modules should not depend on low-level modules, and both high-level and low-level modules should depend on abstractions. It also states that abstractions should not depend on concrete implementations, but that concrete implementations should depend on abstractions.

In general, more complex code is harder to understand. Whether an abstraction makes code more complex by adding unneeded flexibility, or simpler by unifying separate cases, depends on the abstraction itself. Abstractions are not intrinsically useful; they are only useful to the extent that they can make other code simpler.

One concrete implementation of the dependency inversion principle is dependency injection, or the idea that everything an object depends on should be passed into the object, to allow maximum flexibility. Ruby doesn't require dependency injection as much as other programming languages due to its flexibility of allowing singleton methods on almost all objects. However, dependency injection can still be used in Ruby, and there are Ruby libraries dedicated to it.

Let's say you have a `CurrentDay` class to represent the current day, and you want to have a `work_hours` method that returns the work hours for the current day and a `workday?` method that returns whether the current day is a workday or a non-workday. In your application, you already have a `MonthlySchedule` class that knows the work schedule for a given month, which you initialize with the year and month. Here's one simple approach for implementing this class:

```ruby
class CurrentDay
  def initialize
    @date = Date.today
    @schedule = MonthlySchedule.new(@date.year,
                                    @date.month)
  end

  def work_hours
    @schedule.work_hours_for(@date)
  end

  def workday?
    !@schedule.holidays.include?(@date)
  end
end
```

One issue with this approach is that testing the `CurrentDay` class becomes difficult. How can you test the `workday?` method. If you are testing during a workday, it will always be `true`, and if you are testing outside of a workday, it will always be `false`.

One approach to handling this in the tests without changing the code itself is to override `Date.today`:

```ruby
before do
  Date.singleton_class.class_eval do
    alias_method :_today, :today
    define_method(:today) {Date.new(2020, 12, 16)}
  end
end

after do
  Date.singleton_class.class_eval do
    alias_method :today, :_today
    remove_method :_today
  end
end
```

The problem with this approach is that it prevents you from using multithreaded tests to speed up your testing. There are various ways to get around this, but in general, the approach required to allow multithreaded tests is significantly more complex.

In some cases, you could just use `instance_variable_set` to manually override the instance variables in the object when testing. Unfortunately, that doesn't work in this case because the `@date` instance variable is used to set the `@schedule` instance variable inside `initialize`.

For this type of situation, it makes sense to be able to pass in the date to use as an optional variable. It's probably best to use a keyword argument for this, as it provides flexibility later in case you want to add another positional argument:

```ruby
class CurrentDay
  def initialize(date: Date.today)
    @date = date
    @schedule = MonthlySchedule.new(date.year, date.month)
  end
end
```

This begs the question as to whether you should also allow the `@schedule` instance variable to be overriden, like this:

```
class CurrentDay
  def initialize(date: Date.today,
                 schedule: MonthlySchedule.new(date.year,
                                               date.month))
    @date = date
    @schedule = schedule
  end
end
```

In general, you should probably not do this unless you really need it for some other reason. For one, this can easily result in a caller passing `schedule` for a different month than the month of `date`. One alternative that fixes that is to pass `schedule_class` instead:

```
class CurrentDay
  def initialize(date: Date.today,
                 schedule_class: MonthlySchedule)
    @date = date
    @schedule = schedule_class.new(date.year, date.month)
  end
end
```

However, even this you should not do unless you need it. Dependency injection makes code more complex, so you should only do it if you need it for another reason, such as the ability to mock the `work_hours_for` or `holidays` methods in the schedule.

In this section, you learned how the SOLID design principles can be applied to Ruby programming. In the next section, you'll learn the trade-offs between designing larger classes or a larger number of smaller classes.

Deciding on larger classes or more classes

One of the decisions you will need to make when designing classes is how many classes you should have. The advantage of having fewer classes is that, in general, the code becomes conceptually simpler. The advantage of having more classes is that the code becomes more modular, and it easier to change parts of it. There is a balancing act here. Too few classes can result in large **God** objects that are difficult to change and refactor. Too many classes can result in conceptual overload, and make it difficult for the programmer using the classes to figure out which classes they need to use.

Let's say you are building a library to handle the construction of HTML tables. This library will take an enumerable (rows) of enumerable objects (cells), and construct an HTML table with `table/tbody/tr/td` elements, with all the content in the `td` elements being HTML escaped. One approach is a single class. You can require a standard library to handle the HTML escaping, and define an `HTMLTable` class, which is initialized with the rows of the table:

```
require 'cgi/escape'

class HTMLTable
  def initialize(rows)
    @rows = rows
  end
```

The simplest way to handle this class is to define a `to_s` method, which will convert the rows to a string containing HTML:

```
  def to_s
    html = String.new
    html << "<table><tbody>"
    @rows.each do |row|
      html << "<tr>"
      row.each do |cell|
        html << "<td>" << CGI.escapeHTML(cell.to_s) << "</td>"
      end
      html << "</tr>"
    end
    html << "</tbody></table>"
  end
end
```

This single-class approach contains all the logic in a single method, and will probably perform the best. It does look a little ugly, with the manual concatenation of strings. Perhaps that could be fixed by using separate classes per element type? Ruby makes it fairly easy to metaprogram such element types, using a base class with a to_s method that formats the type, and a subclass for each element type. Then, the HTMLTable#to_s method can just create elements of each of the type subclasses, and the actual HTML generation is confined to a single line in the Element#to_s method. You decide to try that approach. You add an HTMLTable::Element class. This class supports setting the type of the class, which defines the type method, which is used when the element is converted to a string via to_s:

```ruby
class HTMLTable
  class Element
    def self.set_type(type)
      define_method(:type){type}
    end

    def initialize(data)
      @data = data
    end

    def to_s
      "<#{type}>#{@data}</#{type}>"
    end
  end
```

You can then metaprogram the creation of the four element subclasses, one for each type:

```ruby
%i"table tbody tr td".each do |type|
  klass = Class.new(Element)
  klass.set_type(type)
  const_set(type.capitalize, klass)
end
```

Then you can define the `HTMLTable#to_s` method to create instances of each of the element subclasses, nested appropriately:

```
def to_s
  Table.new(
    Tbody.new(
      @rows.map do |row|
        Tr.new(
          row.map do |cell|
            Td.new(CGI.escapeHTML(cell.to_s))
          end.join
        )
      end.join
    )
  ).to_s
end
end
```

This approach uses six classes: the `HTMLTable` class, an `Element` base class, and `Table`, `Tbody`, `Tr`, and `Td` classes, which are created via metaprogramming. Each of these classes is responsible for a single thing, so arguably this does a better job adhering to the single-responsibility principle. However, each of the `Element` subclasses is doing basically the same thing, and you could avoid the use of separate `Element` subclasses by passing the type in as a parameter to a method of the `Element` class.

Definitely, the best part of this design is the fact that all HTML generation happens in a single place. In addition to being overly complex, probably the worst part of this design is that it is probably slow, not just for the additional object creation, but also due to all of the temporary strings. If one of the data cells is large, the memory used will be at least eight times larger than the size of the large data cell, since the following strings will contain the large data:

- The string containing the large data
- The string created by `CGI.escapeHTML`
- The string created in `HTMLTable::Td#to_s`
- The string created in `HTMLTable#to_s` when joining the array of `Td` instances
- The string created in `HTMLTable::Tr#to_s`
- The string created in `HTMLTable#to_s` when joining the array of `Tr` instances

- The string created in `HTMLTable::Tbody#to_s`
- The string created in `HTMLTable::Table#to_s`

Could you get the benefit of all HTML generation in a single place using a single-class design, while keeping the performance of the append-only design? It turns out that this isn't too difficult. You can add a `wrap` method that takes the HTML string being built and the element type and uses an append-only design for building the HTML, yielding between the opening tags and the closing tags:

```
class HTMLTable
  def wrap(html, type)
    html << "<" << type << ">"
    yield
    html << "</" << type << ">"
  end
```

Then, the `to_s` method needs to use nested calls to the `wrap` method:

```
  def to_s
    html = String.new
    wrap(html, 'table') do
      wrap(html, 'tbody') do
        @rows.each do |row|
          wrap(html, 'tr') do
            row.each do |cell|
              wrap(html, 'td') do
                html << CGI.escapeHTML(cell.to_s)
              end
            end
          end
        end
      end
    end
  end
end
```

This approach is slightly more complex than the initial approach, but it performs almost as well and will make it easier to expand later, for example, to add support for HTML attributes on the `table`, `tbody`, `tr`, or `td` tags.

There are still some cases where the separate class approach may make sense; for example, if you wanted to allow users to use individual tags, such as `tr` or `td`, without building the entire table. It's possible that that may be desired if the `table` and `tbody` tags have already been used in a template.

In this case, the trade-off between the approaches comes down to the many classes approach offering additional flexibility, with the single-class approach offering greater simplicity and higher performance. If you need the flexibility, the many classes approach is beneficial, but if you don't need the flexibility, then the benefits of the many classes approach are wasted and the single-class approach makes more sense.

In this section, you learned about a couple of aspects to consider when deciding when to use a more complex class or a greater number of simpler classes. Next, let's learn when it makes sense to use custom data structures in Ruby.

Learning when to use custom data structures

Ruby only offers two main core data structures for collections, arrays, and hashes. However, Ruby arrays and hashes are not simple arrays or hash tables; they are complex internally. Ruby takes care of most of the performance issues when dealing with arrays and hashes. For example, when adding an element to an array when the array does not have any room internally, Ruby expands the array not by a single element, but in relation to how large the array currently is, so that if you keep adding elements to the array, it doesn't need to resize the array each time. Likewise, for small hash tables, Ruby may store the hash table as a simple list if it thinks it will be faster to scan the list than use a real hash table. If the hash table grows, Ruby will internally convert the list into a real hash table, at the point at which it roughly determines that it will be faster to use a separate hash lookup.

In a lower-level language such as C, the choice of data structure for a particular application may be even more important than the choice of algorithm. However, Ruby operates at a high level, and in most cases, trying to recreate a faster data structure than an array or hash in pure Ruby code is likely to be difficult. Most standard libraries that implement data structures use arrays and hashes for the underlying storage, such as Matrix (arrays of arrays) and Set (hash). Exceptions in the standard library would be database libraries such as `dbm` and `gdbm`, which wrap C libraries and are generally used for storing large amounts of data on disk instead of in memory.

In general, you do not need to worry about using custom data structures in Ruby until you have very large datasets that represent a performance bottleneck in your application. To get a substantial performance benefit from a custom data structure in a Ruby program, the custom data structure will probably need to be implemented as a native C extension instead of as a pure Ruby library, as otherwise, the overhead of the Ruby virtual machine is likely to outweigh the benefits of a data structure that better fits the needs of the application.

As an example of the benefits of a custom data structure, you can look at the subset_sum gem. This is a library that implements a solver for the subset sum problem. The subset sum problem is as follows: given a set of values and a target amount, is there a subset of values that sum to the target amount? This is an NP-complete problem, and it quickly becomes impractical to solve for even a moderate number of elements (25-100 depending on the algorithm used). The subset_sum gem implements one of the simpler algorithms for solving this, with two implementations. One implementation is written in Ruby and uses a plain Ruby hash. The second approach is written in C and uses a custom AVL tree. The approach written in C with a custom data structure is only around two times faster than the pure Ruby version that uses a plain Ruby hash.

Another example of performance differences between a plain Ruby hash and a custom data structure comes from GitHub. The GitHub programming language classifier (Linguist) was originally written in pure Ruby, and to achieve better performance and lower memory use, they tested it using an approach written in C with a Judy array for storage. Their approach written in C with a custom data structure was also about twice as fast compared to the Ruby version. One advantage in GitHub's case was the fact that their implementation with a Judy array also used much less memory, about 40% of the memory of the Ruby implementation.

While only you can determine whether a custom data structure is right for your application, if you aren't sure whether a custom data structure will help, chances are that it won't make a huge difference. Unless your code has already been tightly optimized, there are probably better ways to optimize your application than attempting to use a custom data structure instead of a Ruby array or hash. You'll learn about other ways to optimize your application in *Chapter 14, Optimizing Your Library*.

Summary

In this chapter, you've learned when it is a good idea to create a custom class. You've learned about the five principles of SOLID design, and the trade-offs involved in applying them to Ruby classes. You've learned about the important trade-off when deciding how many classes should make up your application. You've also learned when it is appropriate to use custom data structures instead of the core data structures. Now you have a better understanding of the principles of a Ruby class design and the trade-offs between different design approaches.

In the next chapter, you'll learn all about Ruby's different types of variables, and how best to use each of them.

Questions

1. Does creating a custom class make sense if you need both information hiding and custom behavior?

2. Which SOLID principle is almost impossible to implement in Ruby?

3. Is it useful to create classes that the user will not use directly?

4. How often does it make sense to use custom data structures in Ruby?

3
Proper Variable Usage

Anytime you need to store information in a Ruby program and access it later, you will be using some sort of variable. Which types of variables you use has a significant effect on your program's performance and maintainability. In this chapter, you'll learn about Ruby's different variable types and the advantages of using and naming them properly.

We will cover the following topics:

- Using Ruby's favorite variable type – the local variable
- Learning how best to use instance variables
- Understanding how constants are just a type of variable
- Replacing class variables
- Avoiding global variables, most of the time

By the end of this chapter, you'll have a better understanding of the different types of variables and how best to use them.

Technical requirements

In this chapter and all chapters of this book, code given in code blocks is designed to execute on Ruby 3.0. Many of the code examples will work on earlier versions of Ruby, but not all. The code for this chapter is available online at `https://github.com/PacktPublishing/Polished-Ruby-Programming/tree/main/Chapter03`.

Using Ruby's favorite variable type – the local variable

Ruby's favorite variable type is the local variable. Local variables are the only variable type that Ruby doesn't require you to use a sigil (for example, @ or $) or use capitalization. This is not by accident, this is by design, to nudge you toward using local variables as much as possible.

In this section, you'll learn how to improve performance by adding local variables, when it's safe to do so, issues involving scope gates, and the importance of local variable naming.

Increasing performance by adding local variables

You may be wondering, *Why are local variables better than other types of variables?* In Ruby, all other variable types require more indirection. Local variables require the least indirection. When you access a local variable in Ruby, the virtual machine knows the location of the local variable, and can more easily access the memory. Additionally, in most cases, the local variables are stored on the virtual machine stack, which is more likely to be in the CPU cache.

Let's say you want to have a `TimeFilter` class, such that you can pass an instance of it as a block when filtering:

```ruby
time_filter = TimeFilter.new(Time.local(2020, 10),
                             Time.local(2020, 11))
array_of_times.filter!(&time_filter)
```

The purpose of the `TimeFilter` class is to filter enumerable objects such that only times between the first argument and the second argument are allowed through the filter. You also want to be able to leave out either of the ends, to only filter the times in one direction. One other desired usage of the `TimeFilter` class is to separate the times that are in the filter from times that are out of the filter, using `Enumerable#partition`:

```ruby
after_now = TimeFilter.new(Time.now, nil)
in_future, in_past = array_of_times.partition(&after_now)
```

You could implement this as a method on `Enumerable`, but if you are writing a general-purpose library, you should not modify core classes unless that is the purpose of the library. Additionally, by writing a class that can be used as a block, you allow the class to be used by multiple methods since you could pass the block to `filter!` and `partition` as shown previously, but also to methods such as `reject` to remove times that are in the filter.

Here's one way you could implement this class. You need to have a `to_proc` method that returns `proc`, and inside the `proc` you check whether the value is after the start time and before the finish time. If there is a start time and it is before the start time, the proc returns `false`. As this is a proc and not a lambda, you use `next` to quickly return a value for the current block iteration. Likewise, if there is a finish time and it is after the finish time, it also returns `false`. Otherwise, it returns `true`:

```ruby
class TimeFilter
  attr_reader :start, :finish

  def initialize(start, finish)
    @start = start
    @finish = finish
  end

  def to_proc
    proc do |value|
      next false if start && value < start
      next false if finish && value > finish
      true
    end
  end
end
```

One issue with this approach is that it is less efficient than it otherwise could be. The issue is with the implementation of `to_proc`. Every time the proc is called, it calls an `attr_reader` method to get the start time, and if there is a start time, it calls the `attr_reader` method again to get the start time to see whether the value is less than it. Likewise, every time the proc is called, it calls an `attr_reader` method to get the finish time, and if there is a finish time, it calls the `attr_reader` method again to get the finish time to see whether the value is greater than it.

That's four method calls during every block iteration, just to get the start and finish times. At least two of these calls are redundant. You can remove the redundancy by caching the result of the method call in a local variable:

```
def to_proc
  proc do |value|
    start = self.start
    finish = self.finish

    next false if start && value < start
    next false if finish && value > finish
    true
  end
end
```

By calling the `start` method on `self` and setting it to a local variable, and calling the `finish` method on `self` and setting it to a local variable, you've cut the number of `attr_reader` method calls in half. That doesn't quite double the performance of the proc, since there is definitely time spent in the greater than and less than method calls on `value`, and time spent evaluating the `if` conditionals, but this change could improve performance by 50% or so.

However, you could definitely improve performance further. One thing to notice here is that `TimeFilter` doesn't offer a way to modify the start or finish times. There isn't a reason to get the start and finish times in every call of the block, since the result will be the same every time. You can hoist the setting of the local variables before the proc. Code inside the proc can still access the local variables, since the proc operates as a closure, capturing local variables in the surrounding environment. With that change, your `TimeFilter#to_proc` method now looks like this:

```
def to_proc
  start = self.start
  finish = self.finish

  proc do |value|
    next false if start && value < start
    next false if finish && value > finish
    true
  end
end
```

You've now completely removed the `attr_reader` calls from the created proc, providing another large speedup. Now, the only method calls inside the proc are the greater than and less than method calls on `value`.

There is no reason to stop there, as you can improve the performance even more. Because you are retrieving the `start` and `finish` variables before creating the proc, you can use them to make the returned proc more efficient. There are actually four separate cases a `TimeFilter` instance could represent:

- Both `start` and `finish` are used (the common case).
- Only `start` is used, `finish` is `nil`.
- Only `finish` is used, `start` is `nil`.
- Both `start` and `finish` are `nil` (unlikely but possible).

You can produce optimal procs for each case. These procs can be even simpler than the previous case since you don't have to check whether `start` and `finish` are valid inside the proc. If both `start` and `finish` are used, the proc checks that `value` is greater than or equal to `start`, and less than or equal to `finish`. If just `start` is used, only the `start` value is checked. If just `finish` is used, only the `finish` value is checked. If neither is used, there is no filter, and the proc can always return `true`:

```ruby
def to_proc
  start = self.start
  finish = self.finish

  if start && finish
    proc{|value| value >= start && value <= finish}
  elsif start
    proc{|value| value >= start}
  elsif finish
    proc{|value| value <= finish}
  else
    proc{|value| true}
  end
end
```

Using local variables in this way is one of the general principles of writing fast Ruby code. Anytime you have code that can be called multiple times, using a local variable at the highest possible level to cache the results of methods will speed the code up.

In the previous example, you used local variables to store the result of `attr_reader` method calls. However, local variables can be used to replace not just method calls, but also constants. For very performance-sensitive code that accesses constants, you can optimize it by storing constant references in local variables. For example, say you have a large array where you want to count the number of `Array` elements in it:

```
num_arrays = 0
large_array.each do |value|
  if value.is_a?(Array)
    num_arrays += 1
  end
end
```

Assuming that `large_array` is large and this code is very performance-sensitive, you can get a small speed boost by using a local variable for the `Array` reference:

```
num_arrays = 0
array_class = Array
large_array.each do |value|
  if value.is_a?(array_class)
    num_arrays += 1
  end
end
```

As a general rule, you should only use a local variable instead of a constant reference for code that is very performance-sensitive, as the minimal speed improvement is not worth the conceptual overhead in other cases.

Another consideration when using local variables to improve performance is to see whether you can further reduce the need for computation. For example, maybe you are writing a command-line program that will take a large array of floats, and remove values that are at least twice as large as the first argument given on the command line:

```
large_array.reject! do |value|
  value / 2.0 >= ARGV[0].to_f
end
```

Applying the principles that you've learned in this section, and realizing the command-line argument is unlikely to change after program execution, you change this to the following:

```
max = ARGV[0].to_f
large_array.reject! do |value|
  value / 2.0 >= max
end
```

This is certainly a large improvement, but you can further improve this by using the mathematical equivalent of multiplying 2 on both sides:

```
max = ARGV[0].to_f
large_array.reject! do |value|
  value >= max * 2
end
```

Then you can further improve performance by moving that calculation into the local variable:

```
max = ARGV[0].to_f * 2
large_array.reject! do |value|
  value >= max
end
```

In this section, you learned how to add local variables to improve the performance of your code. While this is a great idea most of the time, as you'll see in the next section, it is not always safe to do so.

Avoiding unsafe optimizations

One thing you need to remember when using local variables to optimize code is that you can only use this approach if the expression you are storing in the local variable is idempotent, meaning that it does not have side effects.

For example, consider the following code, where you are processing a large array in order to set values in a hash:

```
hash = some_value.to_hash
large_array.each do |value|
```

```
  hash[value] = true unless hash[:a]
end
```

In this case, it looks like you could use a local variable to improve performance:

```
hash = some_value.to_hash
a_value = hash[:a]
large_array.each do |value|
  hash[value] = true unless a_value
end
```

It may even be tempting to skip the array call entirely by checking whether hash[:a] has already been set:

```
hash = some_value.to_hash
unless a_value = hash[:a]
  large_array.each do |value|
    hash[value] = true
  end
end
```

Unfortunately, such an optimization is not safe in the general case. One issue is that large_array could contain :a as an element, and the purpose of the original code is to stop when :a is found. A less likely but still possible case that could have a problem is that the hash could have a default proc that sets or removes the :a entry from the hash. Before using this optimization safely, you would have to be sure that large_array cannot contain a :a element, and that the hash doesn't have a default proc that deals with the :a entry.

You should also avoid this approach when dealing with values that change over time, at least when you cannot ensure how long the values will last. For example, say you are removing times greater than the current time:

```
enumerable_of_times.reject! do |time|
  time > Time.now
end
```

Maybe it appears that you could use a local variable for the Time.now call:

```
now = Time.now
enumerable_of_times.reject! do |time|
```

```
    time > now
  end
```

However, if `enumerable_of_times` only yields one `time` value per minute, it's probably a bad idea, since `now` will quickly deviate from `Time.now`.

You should be especially careful when using this approach if you are returning a `proc` containing a local variable reference from outside the scope of the `proc`. In any long-running program, it's almost always a bad idea to switch from the following:

```
greater_than_now = proc do |time|
  time > Time.now
end
```

To this:

```
now = Time.now
greater_than_now = proc do |time|
  time > now
end
```

It may not be a bad idea in a small command-line program that runs quickly, but if the program runs quickly, you probably don't need to optimize it.

Handling scope gate issues

Local variables in Ruby are in scope from the first time Ruby comes across them while parsing until the end of the scope they are defined in unless they hit a scope gate. In that case, they are not in scope inside the scope gate. In other words, the scope gate creates a new local variable scope. While you may not be familiar with the term scope gate, you already have a lot of experience with scope gates in Ruby, as the `def`, `class`, and `module` keywords all define scope gates.

The following scope gates show that at the start of each scope gate, there are no local variables:

```
defined?(a) # nil
a = 1
defined?(a) # 'local-variable'
module M
  defined?(a) # nil
  a = 2
```

```
defined?(a) # 'local-variable'
class C
  defined?(a) # nil
  a = 3
  defined?(a) # 'local-variable'
  def m
    defined?(a) # nil
    a = 4
    defined?(a) # 'local-variable'
  end
```

After the scope gate exits, the previous scope is restored and the value of the local variable, a, remains the same as before the scope gate was entered:

```
    a # 3
  end
  a # 2
end
a # 1
```

Additionally, calling a method defined with def in the same scope does not change the current local variables:

```
M::C.new.m
a # 1
```

All scope gates in Ruby have alternatives that do not add scope gates. The def keyword can be replaced with define_method, class with Class.new, and module with Module.new. All replacements accept a block, and blocks in Ruby are not scope gates, they are closures, which share the existing local variables of their surrounding scopes. Any local variables newly defined in a block are local to the block and blocks contained inside of it but are not available to the code outside of the block.

Replacing the scope gates in the previous example with their gateless equivalents, you end up with the following code:

```
defined?(a) # nil
a = 1
defined?(a) # 'local-variable'
M = Module.new do
```

```
  defined?(a)  #  'local-variable'
  a = 2
  self::C = Class.new do
    defined?(a)  #  'local-variable'
    a = 3
    define_method(:m) do
      defined?(a)  #  'local-variable'
      a = 4
    end
```

Unlike the code that uses scope gates, after these blocks return, the value of a remains the same as before the blocks return since each block uses the same local variable. This code shows the danger of not using scope gates and reusing local variables. You can see that the class and module definitions override the local variables in the outer scope:

```
    a # 3
  end
  a # 3
end
a # 3
```

Even worse than that, calling the m method on the M::C instance overrides the local variable of the surrounding scope:

```
M::C.new.m
a # 4
```

This can result in hard-to-debug issues, especially in the case where define_method is used to define methods and where such methods are not called deterministically, such as when they are called based on user input.

The trade-off of using the gateless equivalents is that they can significantly improve performance. If a method is called often and performs a computation that can be cached, it can make sense to precompute the result and use define_method instead of using def. Let's say you are defining a method named multiplier that is based on a constant value and a command-line argument:

```
def multiplier
  Math::PI * ARGV[0].to_f
end
```

This always results in the same value, but Ruby will have to compute it separately every time the method is called. Using a gateless equivalent allows you to precompute the value:

```
multiplier = Math::PI * ARGV[0].to_f
define_method(:multiplier) do
  multiplier
end
```

Note that `define_method` has additional overhead compared to methods defined with `def`, so you should only use it in cases where you can avoid at least one method call inside the defined method.

Another use case for combining local variables with `define_method` is for information hiding. Let's say you want to define a method that is thread-safe, so it uses a mutex:

```
class T
  MUTEX = Mutex.new
  def safe
    MUTEX.synchronize do
      # non-thread-safe code
    end
  end
end
```

The problem with this code is users can easily poke around and use the constant directly:

```
T::MUTEX.synchronize{T.new.safe}
```

This results in thread deadlock. One way to discourage this behavior is to use a private constant:

```
class T
  MUTEX = Mutex.new
  private_constant :MUTEX
  def safe
    MUTEX.synchronize do
      # non-thread-safe code
    end
  end
end
```

This does make something slightly more difficult for the user, as accessing `T::MUTEX` directly will raise `NameError`. However, just as you can work around private methods with `Kernel#send`, you can work around private constants with `Module#const_get`:

```
T.const_get(:MUTEX).synchronize{T.new.safe}
```

In general, users that are accessing private constants deserve what they get, but if you want to make it even more difficult, you can use a local variable and `define_method`:

```
class T
  mutex = Mutex.new
  define_method(:safe) do
    mutex.synchronize do
      # non-thread-safe code
    end
  end
end
```

It is much more difficult for a user to get access to the local `mutex` variable that was defined in the `T` class than it is for them to access a private constant of the class.

Naming considerations with local variables

How you name your variables has a significant effect on how readable your code is. While Ruby allows a lot of flexibility when naming local variables, in general, you should stick to `lower_snake_case` all-ASCII names. Emoji local variable names are cute but lead to code that is difficult to maintain. For teams that are working in a single, non-English language, non-ASCII `lower_snake_case` names in the local language can be acceptable, but it will make it difficult for other Ruby programmers, so strong consideration should be given to whether non-native speakers of the language will ever be working on the code.

In terms of variable length, if you name all your local variables with a single character, it becomes almost impossible to keep track of what each variable actually represents. Likewise, if each of your local variables `is_a_long_phrase_like_this`, simply reading your code becomes exhausting. The central trade-off in variable naming is balancing understandability with ease of reading. Appropriately naming your variables can make it so your code isn't exhausting to read, but it is still easy to comprehend.

How do you decide what length of variable name is appropriate? The general principle in local variable naming is that the length of the variable name should be roughly proportional to the inverse of the size of the scope of the variable, with the maximum length being the length of the name that most accurately describes the variable.

For example, if you are calling a method that accepts a block, and the block is only a single line or a few lines, and the receiver of the method or the method name makes it obvious what block will be yielded, then it may make sense to use a single-letter variable:

```
@albums.each do |a|
  puts a.name
end
```

You could also use a numbered parameter in this case:

```
@albums.each do
  puts _1.name
end
```

Because album is a fairly small name, it would also be reasonable to use album as a local variable name:

```
@albums.each do |album|
  puts album.name
end
```

However, if the context doesn't make it obvious what is being yielded, then using a single variable name is a bad idea:

```
array.each do |a|
  puts a.name
end
```

Additionally, if the fully descriptive variable name is very long, it's a bad idea to use it for single-line blocks:

```
TransactionProcessingSystemReport.each do
  |transaction_processing_system_report|
    puts transaction_processing_system_report.name
  end
```

Using the full name in this case makes this code harder to read, and the clarity of the longer name adds no value. In cases like this, you may not want to use a single variable name, but you should probably at least abbreviate the name:

```
TransactionProcessingSystemReport.each do |tps_report|
  puts tps_report.name
end
```

Or even to this:

```
TransactionProcessingSystemReport.each do |report|
  puts report.name
end
```

If you have a 10-line method, it's probably not a good idea to use a single-letter variable throughout the method. Choose a more descriptive variable name. It doesn't have to be very long, and can certainly use abbreviations, but it should be descriptive enough that a programmer that is familiar with the code base can look at the method and not have any question about what the variable represents.

There are some common block variables for certain methods. `Integer#times` usually uses `i`, following the convention of `for` loops in C:

```
3.times do |i|
  type = AlbumType[i]
  puts type.name
  type.albums.each do |album|
    puts album.name
  end
  puts
end
```

While you could use a more descriptive name such as `type_id`, there is no significant advantage in doing so.

Likewise, when iterating over a hash, it is common to use `k` to represent the current key and `v` for the current value:

```
options.each do |k, v|
  puts "#{k}: #{v.length}"
end
```

However, you should be careful to only use this pattern in single, simple blocks. In blocks of more than three lines, and when nesting block usage, it's better to choose longer and more descriptive variable names. Let's look at this code:

```
options.each do |k, v|
  k.each do |k2|
    v.each do |v2|
      p [k2, v2]
    end
  end
end
```

You may be able to figure that the `options` hash has keys and values that are both enumerable, and this prints out each key/value pair separately, but it's not immediately obvious. More intuitive variable naming in this case would be something like this:

```
options.each do |key_list, value_list|
  key_list.each do |key|
    value_list.each do |value|
      p [key, value]
    end
  end
end
```

In any case where you are using a gateless equivalent to a scope gate, such as using `define_method`, be extra careful with your local variable naming, so that you don't accidentally overwrite a local variable unintentionally.

One case where it can be a good idea to use a single letter or otherwise short variable name in a longer scope is when there is a defined convention in the library you are using. For example, in the Roda web toolkit, there is a convention that the request object yielded to blocks is always named `r`, and documentation around request methods always shows calls such as `r.path` or `r.get`. The reason for this convention is the request object is accessed very often inside blocks, and a variable name such as `request` or even an abbreviation such as `req` would make the code more taxing to read. However, in the absence of a library convention for single-letter or otherwise short variable names, you should use more descriptive variable names for longer scopes.

In this section, you've learned about Ruby's favorite variable type, the local variable. You've learned how to use local variables for safe optimizations, the issues with using scope gates, and important principles in local variable naming. In the next section, you'll learn how best to use instance variables.

Learning how best to use instance variables

Almost all objects in Ruby support instance variables. As mentioned in *Chapter 1, Getting the Most out of Core Classes*, the exceptions are the immediate objects: `true`, `false`, `nil`, integer, floats, and symbols. The reason the immediate objects do not support instance variables is that they lack their own identity. Ruby is written in C, and internally to Ruby, all Ruby objects are stored using the `VALUE` type. `VALUE` usually operates as a pointer to another, larger location in memory (called the Ruby heap). In that larger location in memory is where instance variables are stored directly, or if that isn't large enough, a pointer to a separate location in memory where they are stored.

Immediate objects are different from all other objects in that they are not pointers, they contain all information about the object in a single location in memory that is the same size as a pointer. This means there is no space for them to contain instance variables.

Additionally, unlike most other objects, conceptually there are no separate instances of immediate objects, unlike other objects. Say you create two empty arrays like the following:

```
a = []
b = []
```

Then a and b are separate objects with their own identity. However, Say you create two `nil` objects:

```
a = nil
b = nil
```

There is no separate identity for the `nil` objects. All `nil` objects are the same as all other `nil` objects, so instance variables don't really make sense for `nil` (and other immediate objects), because there are no separate instances.

In this section, you'll learn how to increase performance by using instance variables, about issues with instance variable scope, and how best to name instance variables.

Increasing performance with instance variables

Just as with local variables, you can increase performance by adding instance variables. The same principles for optimizing with local variables, in general, apply to instance variables. Most times where you have a method that is likely to be called multiple times and where the method is idempotent, you can store the result of the calculation in an instance variable to increase performance.

Let's assume you have an `Invoice` class that accepts an array of `LineItem` instances. Each `LineItem` contains information about the item purchased, such as the price of the item and the quantity of items purchased. When preparing the invoice, the total tax needs to be calculated by multiplying the tax rate by the sum of the total cost of the line items:

```
LineItem = Struct.new(:name, :price, :quantity)


class Invoice
  def initialize(line_items, tax_rate)
    @line_items = line_items
    @tax_rate = tax_rate
  end


  def total_tax
    @tax_rate * @line_items.sum do |item|
      item.price * item.quantity
    end
  end
end
```

If `total_tax` is only called once in the average lifetime of the `Invoice` instance, then it doesn't make sense to cache the value of it, and caching the value of it can make things slower and require increased memory. However, if `total_tax` is often called multiple times in the lifetime of an `Invoice` instance, caching the value can significantly improve performance.

In the typical case, it's common to store the results of the calculation directly in an instance variable:

```
  def total_tax
    @total_tax ||= @tax_rate * @line_items.sum do |item|
      item.price * item.quantity
```

```
      end
   end
```

In this particular case, this approach should work fine. However, there are a couple cases where you cannot use this simple approach. First, this approach only works if the expression being calculated cannot result in a `false` or `nil` value. This is due to the `||=` operator recalculating the expression if the `@total_tax` instance variable is `false` or `nil`. To handle this case, you should use an explicit `defined?` check for the instance variable:

```
def total_tax
  return @total_tax if defined?(@total_tax)
  @total_tax = @tax_rate * @line_items.sum do |item|
    item.price * item.quantity
  end
end
```

This will handle cases where the expression being cached can return `nil` or `false`. Note that it is possible to be more explicit and use `instance_variable_defined?`(`:@total_tax`) instead of `defined?(@total_tax)`, but it is recommended that you use `defined?` because Ruby is better able to optimize it. This is because `defined?` is a keyword and `instance_variable_defined?` is a regular method, and the Ruby virtual machine optimizes the `defined?` keyword into a direct instance variable check.

The second case where you cannot use this check is when the `Invoice` instance is frozen. You cannot add instance variables to frozen objects. The solution in this case is to have an unfrozen instance variable hash inside the frozen object. Because the unfrozen hash can be modified, you can still cache values in it. You can modify the `Invoice` class to make sure all instances are frozen on initialization but contain an unfrozen instance variable named `@cache`, and that the `total_tax` method uses the `@cache` instance variable to cache values:

```
LineItem = Struct.new(:name, :price, :quantity)

class Invoice
  def initialize(line_items, tax_rate)
    @line_items = line_items
    @tax_rate = tax_rate
    @cache = {}
    freeze
```

```
    end

  def total_tax
    @cache[:total_tax] ||= @tax_rate *
      @line_items.sum do |item|
        item.price * item.quantity
      end
  end
end
```

Like the instance variable approach, the previous example also has issues if the expression can return `false` or `nil`. And you can fix those using a similar approach, with `key?` instead of `defined?`:

```
  def total_tax
    return @cache[:total_tax] if @cache.key?(:total_tax)
    @cache[:total_tax] = @tax_rate *
      @line_items.sum do |item|
        item.price * item.quantity
      end
  end
```

The other issue with this approach, and with caching in general using instance variables, is that, unlike local variables, you probably do not have control over the entire scope of the instance. When caching in local variables, you know exactly what scope you are dealing with, and can more easily determine whether using the local variable as a cache is safe. If any of the objects in the expression being cached are mutable, there is a chance that the cached value could become inaccurate, as one of the objects in the expression could be changed.

In the previous example, the `Invoice` class does not offer an accessor for `line_items` or `tax_rate`. Since it is frozen, you can assume `tax_rate` cannot be changed, since it is probably stored as a numeric value, and those are frozen by default, even if they are not immediate objects. However, consider `line_items`. While `Invoice` does not offer an accessor for it, the values passed in could be modified after they are passed in and the total tax has been calculated:

```
line_items = [LineItem.new('Foo', 3.5r, 10)]
invoice = Invoice.new(line_items, 0.095r)
tax_was = invoice.total_tax
```

```
line_items << LineItem.new('Bar', 4.2r, 10)
tax_is = invoice.total_tax
```

With this example, tax_was and tax_is will be the same value, even though the Invoice instances line items have changed. To avoid this issue, there are a couple of approaches. The first approach is that Invoice could duplicate the line items, so that changes to the line items used as an argument do not affect the invoice:

```
def initialize(line_items, tax_rate)
  @line_items = line_items.dup
  @tax_rate = tax_rate
  @cache = {}
  freeze
end
```

This still allows someone to use instance_variable_get(:@line_items) to get the array of line items and modify it.

The second approach is freezing the line items:

```
def initialize(line_items, tax_rate)
  @line_items = line_items.freeze
  @tax_rate = tax_rate
  @cache = {}
  freeze
end
```

This is a better approach, except that it mutates the argument, and in general it is a bad idea for any method to mutate arguments that it doesn't control unless that is the sole purpose of the method. The safest approach is the combination of approaches:

```
def initialize(line_items, tax_rate)
  @line_items = line_items.dup.freeze
  @tax_rate = tax_rate
  @cache = {}
  freeze
end
```

This makes sure that the array of line items cannot be modified. However, there is still a way for the resulting calculation to go stale, and that is if one of the line items is modified directly:

```
line_items = [LineItem.new('Foo', 3.5r, 10)]
invoice = Invoice.new(line_items, 0.095r)
tax_was = invoice.total_tax
line_items.first.quantity = 100
tax_is = invoice.total_tax
```

Here you are modifying the quantity in the first line item, which should result in a change to the total tax. To avoid this issue, you need to make sure you can freeze the line items. One approach is to make all `LineItem` instances frozen:

```
LineItem = Struct.new(:name, :price, :quantity) do
  def initialize(...)
    super
    freeze
  end
end
```

However, if you don't want to take that approach, and only want to freeze line items given on the invoice, in the `Invoice#initialize` method, you can map over the list of line items, return a frozen dump of each item, and then freeze the resulting array:

```
def initialize(line_items, tax_rate)
  @line_items = line_items.map do |item|
    item.dup.freeze
  end.freeze
  @tax_rate = tax_rate
  @cache = {}
  freeze
end
```

You've now learned that in order to get the maximum benefit of caching inside objects, you need to be dealing with frozen objects, but where each frozen object has an unfrozen cache.

Handling scope issues with instance variables

Like local variables, instance variables have their own scopes, but unlike local variables, the scope of instance variables is not lexical. The scope of instance variables is always the same as the implicit receiver of methods, `self`. The scope gates that were discussed in *Handling scope gate issues*, `def`, `class`, and `module`, also change instance variable scope. However, the gateless equivalents of `define_method`, `Class.new`, and `Module.new` also change instance variable scope, since they have a new `self`.

One of the main issues to be concerned with when using instance variables is using them inside blocks passed to methods you do not control. Let's assume you were using the `Invoice` class from the previous section, but you want to add a method named `line_item_taxes` that returns an array of taxes, one for each line item. One way to implement this would be a map over the line items, with the total price of the line item multiplied by the tax rate of the invoice:

```
class Invoice
  def line_item_taxes
    @line_items.map do |item|
      @tax_rate * item.price * item.quantity
    end
  end
end
```

This would work in most cases, but there is a case where it would fail. In this example, you are assuming that `@line_items` is an array of `LineItem` instances. However, that doesn't necessarily have to be the case. Instead of a simple array, the passed-in `line_items` argument could be an instance of a separate class:

```
class LineItemList < Array
  def initialize(*line_items)
    super(line_items.map do |name, price, quantity|
      LineItem.new(name, price, quantity)
    end)
  end

  def map(&block)
    super do |item|
      item.instance_eval(&block)
    end
```

```
      end
   end
```

```
   Invoice.new(LineItemList.new(['Foo', 3.5r, 10]), 0.095r)
```

One reason to implement such a class is to make it easier to construct a literal list of
line items, by just providing arrays of name, price, and quantity to the `LineItemList`
initializer, and having it automatically create the `LineItem` instances. To make things
even easier for the user, the `LineItemList` class has a `map` method that evaluates the
block passed to it in the context of the item, in addition to passing the item as a variable
to the block. This allows for simpler code inside the block, as long as you are only
accessing local variables and methods of the current line item. For example, you can
generate an array of total costs for each line item more easily:

```
   line_item_list.map do
      price * quantity
   end
```

Instead of the following more verbose code:

```
   line_item_list.map do |item|
      item.price * item.quantity
   end
```

The trade-off in this case is that doing this changes the scope of the block from the
caller's scope to the scope of the line item. This breaks the example used earlier, because
the `@tax_rate` reference is no longer the tax rate of the invoice, but the tax rate of
the line item. As `LineItem` doesn't have a `@tax_rate` instance variable, the instance
variable access returns `nil`, and this likely results in `NoMethodError`:

```
   class Invoice
      def line_item_taxes
         @line_items.map do |item|
            @tax_rate * item.price * item.quantity
         end
      end
   end
```

You can work around this case by assigning the instance variable to a local variable before the block and accessing the local variable inside the block. As explained in *Increasing performance by adding local variables*, that's probably a good idea anyway, as it is likely to improve the overall performance. This is because accessing local variables is faster than accessing instance variables. Let's switch the example to store the instance variable in a local variable for better performance:

```ruby
class Invoice
  def line_item_taxes
    tax_rate = @tax_rate
    @line_items.map do |item|
      tax_rate * item.price * item.quantity
    end
  end
end
```

Issues like this are one reason why it's generally a bad idea for code to use methods such as `instance_eval` and `instance_exec` without a good reason. Using `instance_eval` or `instance_exec` on blocks that are likely to be called inside user code, as opposed to blocks used for configuration, can be a common source of bugs. In this particular case, the issue shows up with instance variable use, but it also occurs any place methods of the surrounding scope are called implicitly, or when `self` is used directly.

Naming considerations for instance variables

Like local variables, instance variables should be named with `@lower_snake_case` with all-ASCII characters. One exception to this is when using instance variables with anonymous classes and modules (generally when testing), in which `@ClassName` and `@ModuleName` are also acceptable. Like local variables, avoid emoji in instance variable names, and only use non-ASCII characters with localized names when the code is being maintained solely in that language.

Since instance variable scope is not lexical, you never know how long the scope will be, and therefore you should avoid single-letter or other very short instance variable names. However, because instance variables are internal to the object and easy to refactor later, you generally should not need to use long descriptive instance variable names.

Using the `TransactionProcessingSystemReport` example from *Naming considerations with local variables*, if you have to store a `TransactionProcessingSystemReport` instance in an instance variable, the fully descriptive name is probably too long:

```
@transaction_processing_system_report =
    TransactionProcessingSystemReport.new
```

You should probably use an abbreviated name:

```
@tps_report = TransactionProcessingSystemReport.new
```

Or even simpler if the object only deals with a single type of report:

```
@report = TransactionProcessingSystemReport.new
```

In this section, you learned how to use instance variables to improve performance, about issues with instance variable scope, and important principles in instance variable naming. In the next section, you'll learn that Ruby's constants are really variables in disguise.

Understanding how constants are just a type of variable

Ruby has constants, but unlike constants in most other languages, Ruby's constants are actually variables. It's not even an error in Ruby to reassign a constant; it only generates a warning. Say you try the following code:

```
A = 1
A = 2
```

Then you'll see it only generates two warnings:

```
# warning: already initialized constant A
# warning: previous definition of A was here
```

At best, Ruby's constants should be considered only as a recommendation. That being said, not modifying a constant is a good recommendation. In general, you shouldn't modify constants unless you have to, especially constants that are in external code such as libraries.

You can think of a constant in Ruby as a variable type that can only be used by modules and classes, with different scope rules. As both modules and classes are objects, they can both have instance variables in addition to constants. When a class or module needs to store information, you should consider whether an instance variable or a constant is more appropriate.

Handling scope issues with constants

Constant scope in Ruby is different than both local variable scope or instance variable scope. In some ways, it is lexical, but it's not truly lexical as the constant doesn't have to be declared in the same lexical scope in which it is accessed. Constant scope and resolution is one of the more involved parts of Ruby, and even many experienced Ruby programmers probably forget how it works in detail.

It's easiest to learn Ruby's constant scope rules by examples. You can start by defining class A, with constants W, X, Y, and Z. You can also define constants U and Y in Object, as it will be easier to learn constant resolution with them. As A does not specify a subclass, Ruby will make it a subclass of Object:

```
class A
  W = 0
  X = 1
  Y = 2
  Z = 3
end

class Object
  U = -1
  Y = -2
end
```

You can make a subclass of A named B, and define constants X and Z inside B:

```
class B < A
  X = 4
  Z = 5
end
```

If you open up the B class in a separate scope, you can check the value of each of U, W, X, Y, and Z to see how constant resolution works:

```
class B
  U # -1, from Object
  W # 0, from A
  X # 4, from B
  Y # 2, from A
  Z # 5, from B
end
```

We see X and Z use the value directly defined in B, while W and Y use the value from A (the superclass of B), and U uses the value from Object (the superclass of the superclass of B). From this example, you know that the class lookup will look first at the class or module for the constant, and only at superclasses of the class or module if the constant isn't found in the class directly, and if the superclass doesn't contain the constant, continue recursively up the ancestor chain.

For a single-class definition, that's all you need to worry about in regards to constant resolution. However, the situation gets significantly more complex when you have a class or module definition inside another class or module definition. To illustrate this, you can define another subclass of A named C that just defines a constant, Y:

```
class C < A
  Y = 6
end
```

You can also define a class, D, that defines a constant, Z:

```
class D
  Z = 7
end
```

And then a subclass of D named E that defines a constant, W:

```
class E < D
  W = 8
end
```

To further understand constant resolution, we will look at two different possible ways to nest constants. The first one is where class C is nested under class E. You need to use class ::C in this case so that you reopen the top-level C class and do not create an E::C class:

```
class E
  class ::C
    U # -1, from Object
    W # 8, from E
    X # 1, from A
    Y # 6, from C
    Z # 3, from A
  end
end
```

From these results, you can see that E takes priority over A (the superclass of C) because both E and A define the constant W, but the constant resolution of W inside C will find the constant in E before it finds the constant in the superclass of C. However, for the constant Z, it is defined in both D (the superclass of E) and A (the superclass of C), but the value used is from A and not D.

If you switch the nesting, you get different results:

```
class C
  class ::E
    U # -1, from Object
    W # 8 from E
    X # NameError
    Y # 6, from C
    Z # 7, from D
  end
end
```

Here, you get NameError for X but not for Z. X is defined in A, which is the superclass of C, while Z is defined in D, the superclass of E.

Just to make sure you get a more complete understanding, let's nest both C and E under B:

```
class B
  class ::C
    class ::E
      U # -1, from Object
      W # 8 from E
      X # 4, from B
      Y # 6, from C
      Z # 5, from B
    end
  end
end
```

Here you can see that X and Z now resolve to the constants in B. Because Z is defined in both D and B, you can see that the lexical nesting in B takes precedence over the superclass resolution in E.

From this example, you can probably guess Ruby's constant lookup algorithm:

1. Look in the current namespace (W in the previous example).

2. Look in the lexical namespaces containing the current namespace (X, Y, and Z in the previous example).

3. Look in the ancestors of the current namespace, in order (U in the previous example).

4. Do not look in ancestors of the lexical namespaces containing the current namespace.

Stated in four brief rules, the algorithm is not difficult to understand, but constant scope is still much trickier than class instance variable scope, which is always the same no matter the nesting:

```
class C
  @a # instance variable of C
end

class B
  class ::C
    @a # same instance variable of C
```

```
    end
  end
```

In this section, you've learned that constant scope in Ruby may not be intuitive, but it can be understood by remembering four simple rules. You also saw how constants and class instance variables differ in terms of scope. In the next section, you'll learn how constants and class instance variables differ in terms of visibility.

Visibility differences between constants and class instance variables

One significant difference between constants and class instance variables is that constants are externally accessible by default, whereas class instance variables are like all instance variables and not externally accessible by default. You can make constants not externally accessible using `private_constant`:

```
class A
  X = 2
  private_constant :X
end

A::X
# NameError
```

However, this error occurs only when getting the value of the constant; you can still set the value of the constant with only a warning:

```
A::X = 3
# warning: already initialized constant A::X
```

Note that reassigning the constant does not change the external visibility; you still get a `NameError` if trying to externally access the constant after reassigning the value:

```
A::X
# NameError
```

You have to explicitly set the constant as public using `public_constant` to make it externally accessible again:

```
class A
  public_constant :X
```

```
end
```

```
A::X # 3
```

For class instance variables, you can make them externally accessible similar to how you make instance variables accessible for regular objects, by calling `attr_reader` or `attr_accessor`. When making instance variables accessible for other objects, you generally make them accessible for all instances of the same class, so you define `attr_reader` or `attr_accessor` on the class itself.

However, you don't want to define accessors for class instance variables for all classes (all instances of the `Class` class); you only want to define accessors for instance variables for a specific instance of `Class`. In this case, you would do the same thing for a class as you would if you wanted to define accessors for only a specific instance of the class. You would define the methods on the singleton class of the object:

```
class A
  @a = 1

  class << self
    attr_reader :a
  end
end

A.a # 1
```

In this example, `attr_reader` is called on the singleton class of A, which makes the A.a method return the value of the @a class instance variable of A.

You'll learn about more differences between constants and class instance variables later in this chapter, where you'll learn about replacements for class variables.

Naming considerations with constants

The naming of constants depends on whether they are classes/modules or other objects. Classes and modules should use `CamelCase`. Other objects should use `ALLCAPS_SNAKE_CASE`. Ruby follows these conventions internally. You have class names such as `ArgumentError` and `BasicObject`, and other constant names such as `TOPLEVEL_BINDING` and `RUBY_ENGINE`.

Like local and instance variables, it's best to keep this to all-ASCII names. Avoid emoji in constant names, and only use non-ASCII characters with localized names when the code is being maintained solely in that language.

In general, it's best to keep class and module names long and descriptive. In cases where the entire class name becomes tedious to use, the class can be stored with a shorter name in a local variable, instance variable, or other constant.

Similar to local variable names, one case where constant names can be short is when there is a defined convention in the library being used for short constant names. For example, in the Sequel database library, the convention is to store the `Sequel::Database` instance in a constant named `DB`, since there is usually only one instance initialized in each application. All of the documentation for the library uses this convention, and users are strongly encouraged to follow it. However, in the absence of a library or application convention for short constant names for specific constants that are used constantly in the application, constant names should be long and descriptive.

In this section, you learned how constants are just a type of variable, how constant scope works, how constants differ from class instance variables in terms of scope, and important principles when naming constants. In the next section, you'll learn about Ruby's class variables, and what you should use instead.

Replacing class variables

There are a few features in Ruby you should never use, and class variables are one of them. Class variable semantics are bad enough that the Ruby core team now recommends against their use, and no longer considers it worth it to even fix bugs in how class variables are handled. This is a shame because class variables almost have behavior you want. However, class variable behavior is just different enough from what you want to not be useful.

At first appearance, class variables have desirable qualities:

- You can access them in the class itself.
- You can access them when reopening the singleton class in the class itself.
- You can access them in the class's methods.
- You can access them in all of these places in any of the class's subclasses.

Here's an example:

```ruby
class A
  @@a = 1

  class << self
    @@a
  end

  def b
    @@a
  end
end

class B < A
  @@a
end
```

So far, so good. However, what happens when you change the value of the class variable in B ?

```ruby
class B
  @@a = 2
end

A.new.b # 2
```

Changing the class variable in B doesn't affect just the class variable in B as you might expect, it changes the class variable in A as well. This is because class variables aren't really specific to a class but to a class hierarchy. Therefore, you can never safely define a class variable in any class that is subclassed or any module that is included in other classes, ruling out their safe usage completely in libraries.

That's weird and bad, but it gets worse. Let's say you have a class variable in B:

```ruby
class B
  @@b = 3

  def c
    @@b
```

```
      end
   end
```

```
B.new.c  # 3
```

Okay, that works as expected. What happens if, later, you try to access the class variable from A, the superclass of B?

```
class A
   @@b  # NameError
end
```

You get NameError. That's good, because you never defined the class variable in A, and surely you don't want the class variable to propagate up to superclasses?

What happens if, later, you define a class variable with the same name in A?

```
class A
   @@b = 4
end
```

Ruby doesn't complain about this; it doesn't even issue a warning. However, what if you later call that B#c method?

```
B.new.c
   # RuntimeError (class variable @@b of B is overtaken by A)
```

You get RuntimeError. RuntimeError is raised when the class variable is accessed, instead of when the class variable was overridden in the superclass. This RuntimeError may not occur when your application is loaded, only later when the method is called.

This means it is never safe to define a class variable in a subclass because if the same class variable name is added to a superclass, it will break the subclass.

Since you can't safely use a class variable in a subclass, and can't safely use a class variable in a superclass or module, there really isn't any way to use them safely. That plus the fact that modifying a class variable in a subclass changes the value of the class variable in the superclass means that there is no reason to use them.

There are at least three reasonable separate approaches for replacing class variables in Ruby, which you'll learn about in the following sections.

Replacing class variables with constants

One possible approach to replacing class variables is using constants instead. Constants have a nice property that they already operate more or less sanely in a class hierarchy:

```
class A
  C = 1
end

class B < A
  C # 1
end
```

Accessing a constant will use the constant defined in the superclass, as you saw in *Handling scope issues with constants* earlier in this chapter. What happens when you set the constant in the subclass?

```
class B
  C = 2
end

class B
  C # 2
end

class A
  C # 1
end
```

It only sets the constant value in the subclass; it does not propagate the change to the superclass. That's much better than class variable behavior.

What's the downside of using constants as a replacement for class variables? The main downside is that, as you learned in *Understanding how constants are just a type of variable*, Ruby warns you when you change the value of a constant:

```
class B
  C += 1 # warning
end
```

Also, while you can access a constant inside a method, you can't set a constant inside a method, at least not using the standard constant setting syntax:

```
class B
  def increment
    # would be SyntaxError, dynamic constant assignment
    # C += 1
  end
end
```

You have to use `Module#const_set`:

```
class B
  def increment
    self.class.const_set(:C, C + 1)
  end
end
```

This is still a poor approach as it warns on every call to the method.

Because a constant can refer to a mutable object, it is possible to allow reassignment behavior without actually reassigning the constant itself:

```
class B
  C = [0]
  def increment
    C[0] += 1
  end
end
```

Using a mutable constant to work around constant reassignment warnings is definitely a hack and not an implementation recommendation. It's a bad idea to use this approach, for the same reason it is bad to rely on globally mutable data structures in general.

For class variables that do not need to be modified, using a constant instead should work fine. However, in any case where you will be reassigning the value, it is a bad idea to use a constant, and you should use one of the next two approaches instead.

Replacing class variables with class instance variables using the superclass lookup approach

If you cannot replace your class variable with a constant because you are reassigning it, you should replace it with a class instance variable. However, like all instance variables, class instance variables are specific to the class itself and are not automatically propagated to subclasses. One approach to work around this fact is to look in the superclass if you don't find the instance variable in the current class, called the superclass lookup approach.

To implement this approach, let's continue with our example with class A and subclass B, but this time class A has an instance variable @c with a value of 1:

```
class A
  @c = 1
end

class B < A
end
```

Let's say you want to get the value of @c from B using the superclass lookup approach. This involves either a recursive or iterative approach to look in superclasses. Here's how you could code the iterative approach:

```
class B
  if defined?(@c)
    c = @c
  else
    klass = self
    while klass = klass.superclass
      if klass.instance_variable_defined?(:@c)
        c = klass.instance_variable_get(:@c)
        break
      end
    end
  end
end
```

If B already defines the instance variable, you just use the defined value. Otherwise, you look in the superclass of B and see whether it defines the instance variable, and if it is defined, then you use it, otherwise, you try the next superclass.

As you can see, this is a lot of code for every time you want to access the instance variable, so almost always this would be wrapped in a class method of the superclass so that it works for all subclasses:

```ruby
def A.c
  if defined?(@c)
    @c
  else
    klass = self
    while klass = klass.superclass
      if klass.instance_variable_defined?(:@c)
        return klass.instance_variable_get(:@c)
      end
    end
  end
end

A.c # 1
B.c # 1
```

It's still simple to set an explicit class instance variable value inside class B, and the iterative approach will pick it up:

```ruby
class B
  @c = 2
end

A.c # 1
B.c # 2
```

The recursive approach is similar to the iterative approach, it just uses recursion instead of iteration in the lookup method. This is actually a much simpler approach in terms of code, and it performs better as well, due to fewer and simpler method calls:

```ruby
def A.c
  defined?(@c) ? @c : superclass.c
end
```

One advantage of the superclass lookup approach is that if you change the class instance variable value in the superclass without changing it in the subclass, calling the lookup method in the subclass will reflect the changed value in the superclass. Another advantage is that the superclass approach uses minimal memory. The disadvantage is the variable lookup can take significantly more time, at least for deep hierarchies, especially if it is unlikely you'll be changing the value in subclasses. This is a classic processing time versus memory trade-off. The superclass lookup approach makes the most sense if reduced memory is more important than processing time.

Replacing class variables with class instance variables using the copy to subclass approach

The alternative to the superclass lookup approach when replacing class variables with class instance variables is copying each instance variable into the subclass when the subclass is created. This approach requires that you set up the support for it before creating subclasses.

In order to modify each subclass as soon as it is created, you use the `inherited` singleton method of the superclass. This method is called with each subclass created and can be used to modify the created subclass. In your `inherited` method, for each of the class instance variables you want to copy into the subclass, you call `instance_variable_set` on the subclass:

```
class A
  @c = 1

  def self.inherited(subclass)
    subclass.instance_variable_set(:@c, @c)
  end
end

class B < A
  @c # 1
end
```

This approach has the advantage that you can access the instance variables directly in subclasses without having to use a special method. This makes accessing the values in the subclass faster. The disadvantage is that if you change the value of the variable in A without having modified the value in B, looking up the value in B will reflect the initial value that was set when B was created, instead of the current value in A. Additionally, the subclass copy approach requires more memory, especially if you have a large number of instance variables you need to copy into the subclass and/or a large number of subclasses.

In this section, you learned that you should never use class variables and three approaches to replacing them. In the next section, you'll learn about Ruby's final variable type, the global variable.

Avoiding global variables, most of the time

Global variables are available in Ruby, but in general, their use is discouraged unless it is necessary. Some examples where it may make sense for you to use global variables are when you are modifying the load path:

```
$LOAD_PATH.unshift("../lib")
```

Or when you are silencing warnings in a block (assuming you actually have a good reason to do that):

```
def no_warnings
  verbose = $VERBOSE
  $VERBOSE = nil
  yield
ensure
  $VERBOSE = verbose
end
```

Or lastly, when reading/writing to the standard input, output, or error:

```
$stdout.write($stdin.read) rescue $stderr.puts($!.to_s)
```

These are all cases where you are using the existing global variables. It rarely makes sense to define and use your own global variables, even though Ruby does make it easy to use global variables since they are global and available everywhere.

The main issues with using global variables in Ruby are the same as using global variables in any programming language, in that it encourages poor coding style and hard-to-follow code. Additionally, because there is only one shared namespace for global variables, there is a greater chance of variable conflicts. Let's say you have code like the following:

```
class SomeObject
  def current_user
    $current_user
  end
end
```

And somewhere else in your application is the following:

```
$current_user = User[user_id]
```

It's probably going to be a pain to use parts of your application in a script that doesn't set $current_user. Global variables make this type of setup easy, but in general, this is a Faustian bargain, as you are trading to get convenient localized access in exchange for long-term architectural problems. This approach almost always results in significant technical debt as soon as it is committed.

As you'll learn, it's fairly easy to replace global variables, but using an approach that avoids global variables while keeping the same architecture does not fix anything. If you need information in a low-level part of your application that comes from a high-level part of your application, do not take the shortcut of using a global variable or any similar approach. Properly pass the data as method arguments all the way from the high level to the low level. Otherwise, you are just setting yourself up for long-term problems.

That being said, there are cases where you need a global value or some global state. For example, if you are writing a batch processing system for the invoices discussed earlier in the chapter and you want to print a period for every 100 invoices processed as a minimal form of progress indicator, you could use a global variable as a quick way to implement it. You could initialize your global variable at the start of your program:

```
$invoices_processed = 0
```

And then every time you process an invoice:

```
$invoices_processed += 1
if $invoices_processed % 100 == 0
  print '.'
end
```

To avoid the use of a global variable, it's possible to switch to a constant object with some useful helper methods:

```
INVOICES_PROCESSED = Object.new
INVOICES_PROCESSED.instance_eval do
  @processed = 0

  def processed
    @processed += 1
    if @processed % 100 == 0
      print '.'
    end
  end
end
```

And then when you process an invoice, you can use simpler code:

```
INVOICES_PROCESSED.processed
```

If you don't want to use a single constant with specialized behavior, you can also just add an accessor to an existing singleton, such as the `Invoice` class:

```
class Invoice
  @number_processed = 0
  singleton_class.send(:attr_accessor, :number_processed)
end
```

And then your invoice processing code can use similar code as was used for the global variable:

```
Invoice.number_processed += 1
if Invoice.number_processed % 100 == 0
  print '.'
end
```

About the only time to use a global variable instead of a singleton accessor method or a specialized constant is when you need the absolute maximum performance, as global variable getting and setting is faster than calling a method. In all other cases, defining your own global variables should be avoided.

Summary

In this chapter, you learned all about Ruby's different variable types. You learned how to use local variables whenever possible. You also learned how both local variables and instance variables can provide substantial performance benefits with intelligent caching.

Moving on, we covered that constants are just another type of variable and that both constants and class instance variables can replace the use of class variables. Finally, you learned about global variables and how to replace their usage with constants or accessor methods on singletons.

Most importantly, in this chapter, you learned when it is appropriate to use each of Ruby's variable types, and how to properly name them, which are two of the most important factors in writing Ruby programs that are easy to maintain.

In the next chapter, you'll build on this knowledge, and learn about methods and how best to use their many types of arguments.

Questions

1. Is it always a good idea to use long descriptive names for local variables?
2. When using instance variables for caching, why is it important that the object be frozen?
3. A constant named `SomeValue` probably contains an instance of what type of Ruby class?
4. When should you use class variables?
5. Should you always avoid using global variables?

Further reading

Numbered parameters: `https://docs.ruby-lang.org/en/3.0.0/Proc.html#class-Proc-label-Numbered+parameters`

4
Methods and Their Arguments

Methods are where almost all the logic is implemented in Ruby programs. Along with how you design your classes, how you design your methods makes all the difference between a library that is a joy to use and one that inspires dread. In this chapter, you'll learn how to design methods to inspire joy in the users of the methods, even if you are the only user. You'll learn how limiting the visibility of methods allows for easier refactoring down the line. You'll also gain a greater understanding of Ruby's object model by learning what class methods actually are.

In this chapter, we will cover the following topics:

- Understanding that there are no class methods, only instance methods
- Naming methods
- Using the many types of method arguments
- Learning about the importance of method visibility
- Handling delegation

By the end of this chapter, you'll have a better understanding of methods in Ruby, including how to name them, what types of arguments they should take, and whether you should make them public. With this, you'll be able to write libraries that are easier to use and applications that are easier to maintain.

Technical requirements

In this chapter and all chapters of this book, the code provided in code blocks was designed to be executed on Ruby 3.0. Many of the code examples will work on earlier versions of Ruby, but not all of them. The code for this chapter is available online at `https://github.com/PacktPublishing/Polished-Ruby-Programming/tree/main/Chapter04`.

Understanding that there are no class methods, only instance methods

Ruby programmers often refer to methods you can call on classes as *class methods*, and methods that you can call on modules as *module methods*. However, Ruby does not have class methods or module methods as separate concepts – it only has instance methods. Every method that you would think of as a class or a module method is just an instance method of the class or module's singleton class. That doesn't mean that you should stop using the terms class method or module method – it just means you should understand that these methods are not special and are just like all other methods.

You will often see class methods defined on classes in one of four ways. The most common way is to use `self` in front of the method, as shown here:

```ruby
class Foo
  def self.bar
    :baz
  end
end
```

This makes it obvious that the method being defined is a singleton method, because any method definition in Ruby that uses the def expression.name format defines a singleton method on the object returned by expression. The previous method definition is basically the same as the following:

```
class Foo
end

def Foo.bar
  :baz
end
```

The only difference between these two approaches is that the constant lookup in the Foo.bar approach would be different from the earlier self.bar approach, as it would not look in the Foo namespace for the constant.

Ruby is flexible in what expressions are allowed when you're defining a singleton method. You can provide any expression – it doesn't have to be self, a constant, or a variable. Please refer to the following code:

```
def (Foo = Class.new).bar
  :baz
end
```

The second way that you will commonly see class methods defined in Ruby is via the << self singleton class opening syntax:

```
class Foo
  class << self
    def bar
      :baz
    end
  end
end
```

The nice aspect of this approach is that this approach reflects what actually happens in Ruby, where bar is a regular instance method in the Foo singleton class.

You rarely see the singleton class opening syntax being used with an argument that is not `self`, but it is completely possible and works the same way:

```
class Foo
end

class << Foo
  def bar
    :baz
  end
end
```

The third way that you'll see singleton methods defined is when `instance_eval` is used on a class:

```
Foo.instance_eval do
  def bar
    :baz
  end
end
```

Unlike `class_eval`, which is very similar to opening a class with the standard `class Foo` syntax, `instance_eval` on a class is like `instance_eval` on any other object, wherein regular methods defined inside the block (without the `def expression. name` syntax) are defined on the object's singleton class.

As a general principle, it's a good idea to avoid `instance_eval` in cases where you don't need it. In general, it is probably best to use the explicit `self` method definition:

```
class Foo
  def self.bar
    :baz
  end
end
```

The main case where the `<< self` syntax makes more sense is if you are doing more advanced work in your class, such as modifying method visibility, or when aliasing or removing methods, as shown here:

```
class Foo
  class << self
```

```
    private

    def bar
       :baz
    end

    alias baz bar
    remove_method :bar
  end
end
```

You can do this without the `<< self` syntax, but it is more cumbersome:

```
class Foo
  def self.bar
     :baz
  end
  private_class_method :bar

  singleton_class.alias_method :baz, :bar
  singleton_class.remove_method :bar
end
```

The fourth way to implement class methods is to use `define_singleton_method`:

```
class Foo
  define_singleton_method(:bar) do
     :baz
  end
end
```

As you'll learn in *Chapter 8, Designing for Extensibility*, sometimes, it's best to skip the use of class methods completely and use modules that extend the class instead, as that approach tends to be more flexible.

In this section, you learned that Ruby does not have class methods as a separate concept. What it calls class methods are just a type of instance method. In the next section, you'll learn about the importance of proper method naming.

Naming methods

More than local variable naming, instance variable naming, and most constant naming, method naming is probably the most important naming in Ruby. The only other naming that is roughly as important is class and module naming. However, in general, there are significantly fewer classes and modules than methods, so you will be dealing with method naming more often.

The Ruby core team recognizes the importance of good method naming, and sometimes there are Ruby features that are considered desirable by the core team but are not accepted into the language, simply because a good method name has not been proposed for them.

One reason why method naming is so important is that method names are difficult to change without breaking backward compatibility, at least if the methods are public. Another reason is that method names have a large effect on the understandability and user-friendliness of the code, especially if they are called often.

In *Chapter 3*, *Proper Variable Usage*, you learned that one principle for naming local variables is that the length of a local variable name should be inversely proportional to the size of the scope of the local variable. There is a similar principle with method names, and that is that *the length of a method name should be inversely proportional to how often the method will be called.*

If a method is called very frequently, you want it to have the shortest possible understandable name. For example, the method to get the number of elements in an array is called very frequently, so it has a short name (`size` or `length`) as opposed to a longer, potentially more descriptive name such as `number_of_elements`. Getting the binary content of a string is so common in some cases that it has a single character method name, b. Likewise, debugging by printing an object's `inspect` output is so common in Ruby that it has a single-letter method name in all objects, p (and pp for a more nicely formatted `inspect`).

When using the `frozen-string-literal` magic comment to make all the strings in a file frozen, even `dup`, a three-letter method name, was considered too long, so they added the +@ unary operator on strings (+@ doesn't duplicate the string if it isn't frozen, but it is almost always used on frozen strings).

For methods that are not called frequently, or that you want to discourage users from calling frequently, it's good for them to have long, descriptive names. It's not recommended to poke around the instance variables of other objects, so `instance_variable_get` and `instance_variable_set` are used instead of something shorter, such as `iv_get` and `iv_set`, respectively. However, it is normal to get and set instance variables directly when writing C extensions, so the Ruby C API functions are named `rb_iv_get` and `rb_iv_set`. Getting a list of instance methods of a certain visibility for a class or module isn't a common need, so the method names that are used here are `private_instance_methods`, `protected_instance_methods`, and `public_instance_methods`.

For methods that should only be called once during application initialization for configuring applications, it's a good idea to give them very descriptive names. For example, the Rodauth authentication framework is configured using a domain-specific language, and the configuration methods that are used in it are very long and descriptive, such as `two_factor_modifications_require_password?` and `webauthn_duplicate_webauthn_id_message`. These long names are not a problem because, in general, these methods are only called once by the user in the application.

In this section, you learned about the importance of naming methods and how method name length should be inversely proportional to usage. In the next section, you'll learn about some special method names and why you should take extra care before defining methods with those names.

Special method names

There are a few methods that you will want to give extra consideration before you use the method's name.

One of these methods is `to_proc`. This is because `to_proc` is called when the `&` operator is used, so once you use `to_proc` for a method, that is how the object will always act when it's passed as a block. You want to be very sure that you know how the object should be used as a block before defining the `to_proc` method on it.

Another method is `call`. This is because the `call` method is called whenever the `.()` syntax is used on the object, and `call` is the method that most other objects will use if they expect a callable object. You should be sure about how you want the object to operate as a callable object before defining the `call` method.

Another of these methods is `===`. This is because `===` is called by `case when` expressions, and it controls which objects the receiver will match against. You should wait to define the `===` method until you are sure how you want the object to work as a matcher.

Finally, the `[]` method is probably the method you should give the most consideration before using, as it becomes the shortest way to invoke a method on the object (`.()` is one more character). While you commonly see this method in collection classes such as `Array` and `Hash`, it can be defined in any class, and intelligent use can result in a significant decrease in verbosity. The Sequel database library uses the `[]` method extensively for creating datasets from databases, returning single rows from datasets or models, and for wrapping Ruby objects in Sequel-specific objects that can be correctly literalized into SQL queries.

If you want the row from the database table, `b.a`, where the `id` column is `1`, you could use the following code in Sequel:

```
DB.from(Sequel.identifier(:a).qualify(:b)).
  first(:id=>1)
```

However, the idiomatic approach in Sequel is to use `[]` in these cases:

```
DB[Sequel[:b][:a]][:id=>1]
```

Such code may be less intuitive to new users of the library, so one consideration before defining the `[]` method is whether you want to give users the option for less verbose code. Allowing less verbose code benefits users who use the code extensively, since writing the code is less fatiguing. However, allowing less verbose code can hurt new users of the library as it tends to be less descriptive and thus less intuitive. You should consider that trade-off before defining the `[]` method on your objects.

In this section, you learned about the importance of good method naming. In the next section, you'll learn about the many different types of method arguments that Ruby supports, and when it is best to use each type.

Using the many types of method arguments

One of the great aspects of Ruby that makes it so flexible and fun to program in is the many types of method arguments that Ruby supports.

The first thing to consider is whether a method needs arguments at all. If you can get a method to work without arguments, that is great, because it eliminates a whole class of possible errors, and you don't even need to think about which types of method arguments to use. Additionally, the caller of the method doesn't have to worry about which types of arguments to pass. There's a whole bunch of complexity you can avoid if your method does not need an argument.

If you look at the public instance methods of `Object`, accepting no arguments is the most common case. 23 `Object` methods accept no arguments. The next most common cases are methods that require a single argument, and methods that take a variable number of arguments. 17 `Object` methods accept a single argument, and 17 `Object` methods accept a variable number of arguments. Here's an example of calculating these numbers:

```ruby
h = Hash.new(0)
o = Object.new
o.methods.
  each do |m|
    h[o.method(m).arity] += 1
  end
h
# => {0=>23, -1=>17, 1=>17, 2=>1}
```

Methods that do not accept arguments (zero arity methods) are the fastest for Ruby to execute, so if you don't need a method to have an argument, it's best to avoid it for performance reasons.

However, for many methods to work, they need to operate on objects other than the receiver of the method, so often, it's best to provide those objects as arguments. In this section, you'll learn about how to use Ruby's many types of arguments.

Positional arguments

Positional arguments are the default method argument types if you just use local variable names for the method definition:

```ruby
def method_name(positional_argument)
end
```

Other than the methods that do not accept arguments, methods that require a single positional argument are the next simplest. They are simple for the method writer because only a single variable is passed to the method. You can think of method arguments as local variables that are defined before the method code is executed. That is actually how Ruby implements method arguments.

After method arguments that require a single positional argument, methods that require two positional arguments are the next simplest. However, introducing a second argument adds a whole new dimension of complexity, and that is due to argument order. With methods that take a single argument, you don't have to worry about the order of arguments. However, for methods that accept more than a single argument, you need to think carefully about the arguments and what argument order makes sense.

For example, to rename a file in Ruby, you can use `File.rename`:

```
File.rename('file1', 'file2')
```

The big question here is, does this rename `file1` to `file2`, or `file2` to `file1`? On the command line, `mv file1 file2` renames `file1` to `file2`, and Ruby follows that design. However, even an example like this with a source first, destination second approach is not universal. `memcpy` is a famous C function that uses destination first and source second.

Ruby isn't even internally consistent here since it also has a common method that takes the destination as the first argument and the source as the second argument:

```
class C
  alias_method :destination_method, :source_method
end
```

The destination first, source second argument order from `alias_method` actually comes from Ruby's `alias` keyword, which operates the same way and can alias global variables in addition to methods:

```
alias $destination $source
```

Of the public methods that Ruby defines in the core classes, only about 2% require exactly two arguments. `Kernel#instance_variable_set` is available to all objects, and most of the other methods also set data and accept as arguments the data to set and the value to set. Some examples of the other methods are `Binding#local_variable_set`, `Module#const_set`, and `Module#class_variable_set`.

It's even rarer for Ruby core classes to require an exact number of more than two arguments. Only three methods do that, all of which take exactly three arguments and are very rarely used: `Process.setpriority`, `Process::Sys.setresuid`, and `Process::Sys.setresgid`.

One reason that Ruby avoids methods with many required arguments is that method ordering issues become even more complex. There are only 2 ways to order 2 elements, but 6 ways to order 3 elements and 24 ways to order 4 elements. If you are considering writing a method with many required arguments, strongly consider the argument ordering issues involved before doing so.

For example, consider a `Screen` class with a method named `draw_box` that takes in coordinates for the box:

```
class Screen
  def draw_box(x1, y1, x2, y2)
  end
end
```

This has a classic method argument issue since we don't know whether this should be x1, y1, x2, y2 or x1, x2, y1, y2.

One alternative to accepting many exactly required arguments is to accept a single object that has that many accessors, such as a `Struct` subclass. Please refer to the following code:

```
Box = Struct.new(:x1, :y1, :x2, :y2)

class Screen
  def draw_box(box)
  end
end
```

However, this type of design encourages class proliferation, which leads to higher cognitive overhead. Additionally, this approach requires object allocation, which, in general, is going to be bad for performance. Also, if you use the previous example, you will probably end up with the same issue, since callers would often change from this code:

```
screen.draw_box(0, 0, 10, 20)
```

To the following code:

```
screen.draw_box(Box.new(0, 0, 10, 20))
```

Now, this has the same method argument ordering issue. However, the separate-class approach does at least allow for a design that avoids this issue, as follows:

```
box = Box.new
box.x1 = 0
box.x2 = 10
box.y1 = 0
box.y2 = 20
screen.draw_box(box)
```

In general, the approach to creating a separate class for the argument only really makes sense if you will be passing instances of the class to multiple methods and not just a single method, or if there are methods that will be returning instances of the class. In other words, only create a separate class if creating a class makes sense in the domain model. Do not create a class just to avoid method argument ordering issues.

Another alternative to avoiding method argument ordering issues is to use required keyword arguments:

```
class Screen
  def draw_box(x1:, y1:, x2:, y2:)
  end
end
```

This has the advantage that it allows the user to explicitly name each method argument, which avoids the method argument ordering issues:

```
screen.draw_box(x1: 0, x2: 0, y1: 0, y2: 20)
```

However, it also forces the users who would like to use a shortcut to then use a more verbose method calling format. Is it possible to allow either calling format? Thankfully, as you have learned to expect from Ruby, yes, it is possible:

```
class Screen
  def draw_box(_x1=nil, _y1=nil, _x2=nil, _y2=nil,
               x1:_x1, y1:_y1, x2:_x2, y2:_y2)
    raise ArgumentError unless x1 && x2 && y1 && y2
  end
end
```

This requires a more verbose method definition, and it also requires manual error checking since you can omit both the positional and keyword arguments and Ruby won't raise an `ArgumentError` automatically. This approach allows us to follow both approaches:

```
screen.draw_box(0, 10, 0, 20)
screen.draw_box(x1: 0, x2: 0, y1: 0, y2: 20)
```

Unfortunately, the lunch is not free. This is down to two reasons. The first reason is that this approach also accepts the following:

```
screen.draw_box(5, 30, 15, 40,
                x1: 0, x2: 0, y1: 0, y2: 20)
```

This call makes no sense since the argument values conflict. However, the previous approach will not raise an `ArgumentError`. You can handle that and correctly raise an `ArgumentError` with a more involved method definition that doesn't have the keyword argument value default to the positional argument value, but in general, it's probably best to avoid doing so unless you really need to in order to preserve backward compatibility. *Left as an exercise for the reader*, as the saying goes.

The second reason there is no free lunch with this approach is that it performs substantially worse, so if performance is important, you may want to avoid it.

In terms of internal optimization, methods that only accept required positional arguments are also very easy for Ruby to optimize, so there is no reason to avoid them for performance reasons.

Optional positional arguments

So far, you've learned about issues with positional arguments, but most of the positional arguments shown in the previous examples are required positional arguments. As you are aware, and as the previous example showed, you can give any positional argument a default value, and that argument becomes optional. That's not completely accurate because, as it turns out, you can only make a subset of arguments optional. For example, you can surround an optional positional argument with two required positional arguments, as shown here:

```
def a(x, y=2, z)
  [x, y, z]
end
```

```
a(1, 3)
# => [1, 2, 3]
```

However, Ruby does not allow you to surround a required positional argument with two optional positional arguments:

```
eval(<<END)
  def a(x=1, y, z=2)
  end
END
# SyntaxError
```

Most Ruby programmers probably believe that there are only two types of positional arguments in Ruby: required positional arguments and optional positional arguments. However, internally, the reason that you can surround optional positional arguments with required positional arguments, but not surround required positional arguments with optional positional arguments, is that there are actually four types of positional arguments in Ruby (if you consider the rest argument a positional argument), and they must be given in this order:

1. Leading arguments

2. Optional arguments

3. Rest argument

4. Post arguments

Each argument type can have zero arguments, and there can be multiple arguments of each type, except for the rest argument (which you'll learn more about in the next section).

In the previous working example, we had the following:

```
def a(x, y=2, z)
end
```

The x argument is a leading argument, the y argument is an optional argument, and the z argument is a post argument.

In the previous syntax error example, we had the following:

```
eval(<<END)
  def a(x=1, y, z=2)
```

```
      end
    END
```

There are no leading arguments here; the x argument is an optional argument, the y argument is a post argument, and a SyntaxError is raised when parsing the = sign after the z argument. This is because Ruby's syntax does not expect a default argument value for post arguments.

In general, you rarely see methods in Ruby that have post arguments. If a method uses optional arguments, it will almost always be written as follows:

```
def a(x, y=nil)
end
```

It is fairly rare to define methods like so:

```
def a(x=nil, y)
end
```

The historical reason behind this is that post arguments were not supported before Ruby 1.9, and if a method supported required and optional positional arguments, the optional positional arguments were required to come after the required positional arguments. The other reason you rarely see this format is when you have a method that accepts a required argument:

```
def a(y)
end
```

Here, the callers of this method will use a format similar to the following:

```
a(2)
```

Let's say you add an optional argument to the front of the method:

```
def a(x=nil, y)
end
```

Here, your users need to add the argument to the start of the method call instead of the end:

```
a(1, 2)
```

In general, most users are not conditioned to add optional arguments to the front of the method. They are unlikely to complain about it, but it will probably seem strange to them. One reason this is strange is that other optional arguments that are added to methods, such as keyword arguments and blocks, come after the existing arguments instead of before. In general, it is best to avoid adding optional arguments before required arguments.

Is there ever a good reason to use optional and post arguments? Yes, but such cases are rare. One case is when you have a method that can either be called with one or two arguments, where if one only argument is given, it semantically represents what would happen if only the second of the two arguments were passed.

For example, in SQL, identifiers can be either qualified or unqualified. Qualified identifiers look like `table.column`, while unqualified identifiers look like `column`. If you represent this in Ruby, you could have a choice. The first looks like this:

```
def identifier(column, table=nil)
end
```

The second looks like this:

```
def identifier(table=nil, column)
end
```

Of these two cases, the second one makes more sense, because to create an identifier such as `foo.bar`, it is conceptually simpler to call `identifier("foo", "bar")`, than it is to call `identifier("bar", "foo")`, and know that the method will apply the second argument before the first argument in the generated SQL.

Methods that only accept lead arguments and optional arguments are also easy for Ruby to optimize. However, Ruby does not optimize methods that accept post arguments to the same degree, which is another reason to avoid using post arguments in most cases.

Rest arguments

Rest arguments in Ruby are only allowed, at most, once in a method definition, and take all the positional arguments in the method call that are not taken by the lead, optional, and post arguments as values. In addition to only being allowed once, they are also different from the other types of positional arguments in that the rest argument does not need a name:

```
def foo(bar, *)
end
```

This format can be used if you want to ignore arguments, but that's almost always a sign of poor method design. The only good use case for this is when you are calling `super` with no argument, which will implicitly pass the same arguments:

```
def foo(bar, *)
  bar = 2
  super
end
```

More accurately, `super` passes the same local variables given as arguments to the `super` method, which reflects the new values of the local variables. Internally, when you don't give the rest argument a name, Ruby gives it a name internally that you can't access so that it can be passed in a `super` call.

When you're considering whether a method should support a rest argument, you should always consider whether it is better to accept a single array argument instead. After all, Ruby will be internally generating an array for you if you use a rest argument. Let's consider the following:

```
def a(*bar)
end
```

Here, you should also consider whether it would be better to accept a single argument instead:

```
def a(bar)
end
```

This requires that the callers pass in an array. If you want to still allow calling without arguments, you could have the value default to the empty array, like so:

```
def a(bar=[])
end
```

This causes an allocation if an array is not provided, but that is not a black mark against it, as the rest argument allocates an array in all cases. If you want to avoid array allocation in all cases, you can use a frozen constant, as follows:

```
EMPTY_ARRAY = [].freeze
def a(bar=EMPTY_ARRAY)
end
```

With this approach, calling a never allocates an array. One difference between the two approaches is that when you're accepting a single array argument, you need to ensure that you do not mutate the argument:

```
EMPTY_ARRAY = [].freeze
def a(bar=EMPTY_ARRAY)
  bar << 1
end
```

This is because it is a bad idea for a method to mutate any arguments unless that is the purpose of the method. One advantage of using the frozen constant approach, as shown in the previous example, is that it isn't just a performance optimization – it also catches cases where you are accidentally mutating the method argument. This is because if no argument is passed, it will attempt to mutate the frozen constant, and that will result in the method raising a `FrozenError` exception. If you want to mutate the argument, you should dup it first:

```
EMPTY_ARRAY = [].freeze
def a(bar=EMPTY_ARRAY)
  bar = bar.dup
  bar << 1
end
```

The corollary to this is that if you are using the rest argument, you know you are dealing with a newly generated array object, so you should mutate it if you need to as there is no point in duplicating the array. Another way to look at this is that if you know you will need to modify the resulting array, there is no performance difference between the two approaches, so you should choose whichever provides the user with a nicer API.

So, which API is nicer, the rest argument or the single array argument? This depends on the method, and which arguments will be passed to the method. If the method is typically called with explicit arguments, the rest approach provides a nicer API:

```
a(:foo, :bar)
```

You can compare this to needing to wrap arguments manually in the single array approach:

```
a([:foo, :bar])
```

However, if most of the calls to the method deal with an existing array of arguments, the single array approach is actually nicer:

```
a(array)
```

You can compare this to the splat argument, which is required in the rest argument approach:

```
a(*array)
```

In addition to requiring an array allocation, Ruby does not optimize methods that accept an argument splat either, which is another consideration when you're thinking of using a rest argument.

As we mentioned in the previous section, you can combine rest arguments with other positional arguments. Most commonly, you will see just leading and rest arguments:

```
def a(x, *y)
end
```

In some cases, you will also see rest arguments and optional arguments:

```
def a(x, y=nil, *z)
end
```

This form is often a code smell. There are certain cases where it can make sense, but it's probably best to avoid doing this, unless you need it for backward compatibility. One strike against it is that you cannot pass values just to the rest argument without also providing a value for the optional argument.

You can combine rest arguments with post arguments:

```
def a(*y, z)
end
```

This form is fairly rare, but there are cases where it makes sense. One example is when you are trying to offer an API similar to the mv command. Usually, mv takes two arguments, the source and destination, but the other usage is an arbitrary number of arguments and a destination folder to put all of them into. You want to make sure that at least two arguments are provided in this case. You can mimic this API in Ruby by using a rest argument for additional sources and a post argument for the destination:

```
def mv(source, *sources, dir)
  sources.unshift(source)
  sources.each do |source|
    move_into(source, dir)
  end
end
```

This allows you to offer an API that works with two or more arguments:

```
mv("foo", "dir")
mv("foo", "bar", "baz", "dir")
```

While this does mirror the mv command nicely, it might be more friendly for the average Ruby programmer to use a required keyword argument, which you'll learn about in the next section.

Keyword arguments

Ruby supports a limited form of keyword arguments for calling methods, all the way back to at least Ruby 1.6. However, this support was limited to not requiring braces when passing a hash to a method, so Ruby would accept either of the following:

```
# Hash
foo({:bar=>1})
```

```
# Hash (without braces)
foo(:bar=>1)
```

In both these cases, Ruby would pass the argument as a single hash argument. In the method definition, the argument would be a normal positional argument:

```
def foo(options)
end
```

In most cases, the keyword arguments are optional, so it is common practice to make the default value of the argument an empty hash:

```
def foo(options={})
end
```

However, as you saw in the previous section on rest arguments, this causes a hash allocation on every call to the method when no options are provided. To optimize this case and avoid a hash being allocated to every method call without an options argument, you can take a similar approach as in the previous section and use a frozen hash constant:

```
OPTIONS = {}.freeze
def foo(options=OPTIONS)
end
```

With this approach, calling the method without options never allocates a hash. However, using the keyword syntax when calling the method always allocates a hash, because the hash is created before the method is called:

```
foo(:bar=>1)
```

The only way around the hash allocation on the caller side would be to also use a constant or some other shared object:

```
BAR_OPTIONS = {:bar=>1}.freeze
foo(BAR_OPTIONS)
```

This approach can only be used when the options do not vary per call to the method, and there are many cases where the options do vary per call, in which case it would not be possible to avoid the hash allocation.

The other issue with this approach for keyword arguments is that, by default, unrecognized keywords passed are ignored, instead of triggering an ArgumentError:

```
def foo(options=OPTIONS)
  bar = options[:bar]
end

# :baz keyword ignored
foo(:baz=>2)
```

This significantly complicates debugging if there is a typo in a keyword argument, which is a common error for programmers to make. This can be worked around by checking that there are no unexpected hash keys:

```
def foo(options=OPTIONS)
  options = options.dup
  bar = options.delete(:bar)
  raise ArgumentError unless options.empty?
end
```

However, this approach is fairly slow due to the additional hash allocation and extra logic, so it's quite cumbersome if it's used in every method that uses an options hash. This is one reason it is an uncommon approach.

As an alternative to this historical approach to handling keywords via a final positional hash argument, support for keyword arguments in method definitions was added in Ruby 2.0:

```
def foo(bar: nil)
end
```

This type of keyword argument has nice properties. It offers better performance because calling the method does not allocate a hash. Please refer to the following code:

```
# No allocations
foo
foo(bar: 1)

# This allocates a hash
hash = {bar: 1}

# But in Ruby 3, calling a method with a
# keyword splat does not allocate a hash
foo(**hash)
```

More importantly, passing an unrecognized keyword argument will trigger an error:

```
foo(baz: 1)
# ArgumentError (unknown keyword: :baz)
```

This makes debugging much simpler in case an unrecognized keyword is used, because you will get an immediate `ArgumentError`.

In Ruby 2, there were issues with using keyword arguments, because they were not fully separated from positional arguments. This especially affected methods that used optional arguments or rest arguments in addition to keyword arguments. In these cases, Ruby 2 would treat a final positional hash argument as keywords:

```ruby
def foo(*args, **kwargs)
  [args, kwargs]
end


# Keywords treated as keywords, good!
foo(bar: 1)
# => [[], {:bar=>1}]


# Hash treated as keywords, bad!
foo({bar: 1})
# => [[], {:bar=>1}]
```

In some cases, these issues were even worse than the issues with unrecognized keywords being ignored. Once you found the unrecognized keyword and fixed it, your code worked correctly. However, if this issue affected your code, there was no good workaround, since it was a problem with the language itself.

Thankfully, in Ruby 3, these issues have been resolved, and Ruby always separates positional arguments from keyword arguments:

```ruby
# Keywords treated as keywords, good!
foo(bar: 1)
# => [[], {:bar=>1}]


# Hash treated as positional argument, good!
foo({bar: 1})
# => [[{:bar=>1}], {}]
```

In Ruby 2, there were also more performance issues with keyword arguments compared to using a single positional argument with the default value of a frozen empty hash. These issues were reduced with Ruby 3, except that accepting arbitrary keywords still always allocates a hash:

```ruby
# Always allocates a hash
def foo(**kwargs)
end
```

If you are doing keyword argument delegation through multiple methods, this can add up as it allocates a hash per delegating method:

```ruby
def foo(**kwargs)
  bar(**kwargs)
end

def bar(**kwargs)
  baz(**kwargs)
end

def baz(key: nil)
  key
end

# 2 hash allocations
foo
```

When delegation is used, the positional argument with a default value still performs better since you can avoid hash allocation completely:

```ruby
def foo(options=OPTIONS)
  bar(options)
end

def bar(options=OPTIONS)
  baz(options)
end

def baz(options=OPTIONS)
```

```
    key = options[:key]
end


# 0 hash allocations
foo
```

It is possible to avoid hash allocations when using keywords, but only if you know which method you are delegating to, and which keywords the method accepts. This approach does not work for generic delegation methods, but it is the fastest option if it can be used:

```
def foo(key: nil)
  bar(key: key)
end

def bar(key: nil)
  baz(key: key)
end

def baz(key: nil)
  key
end

# 0 hash allocations
foo
```

The main issue with explicit keyword delegation is that it is significantly more difficult to maintain, especially with many keywords. If you add keywords to a lower-level method, you need to add the same keywords to all the methods that delegate to it. If you change the default value of a keyword in a lower-level method, you need to make the same change to the default value in every method that delegates to it. It looks ugly and does not bring joy to the programmer, so it should only be used if the absolute maximum performance is required. If the absolute maximum performance is required, you should prefer positional arguments as they are more optimized.

In most cases, for new code, it is best to use keyword arguments instead of an optional positional hash argument. One thing to consider for new methods is the use of the `**nil` syntax in method definitions, which marks the method as not accepting keyword arguments:

```
def foo(bar, **nil)
end
```

The reason for doing this is to avoid breakage if keywords are added to the method later. Let's say you don't use `**nil` and your method definition looks like this:

```
def foo(bar)
  bar
end
```

If it is valid to pass a hash to the method, the callers of this method can pass keyword arguments:

```
foo(bar: 1)
# => {:bar=>1}
```

Since the method does not accept keyword arguments, Ruby will convert the keywords into a positional hash argument for backward compatibility with historical code that accepts a positional argument. Let's say you add keywords to this method later:

```
def foo(bar, baz: nil)
  bar
end
```

By doing this, you break the callers of this method:

```
foo(bar: 1)
# ArgumentError (wrong number of arguments)
```

Because the `foo` method now accepts keyword arguments, Ruby no longer performs keyword to positional hash conversion, thereby breaking the caller. You can avoid this issue for new methods with the `**nil` syntax:

```
def foo(bar, **nil)
  bar
end
```

This indicates that no keywords are accepted, so you will never have callers break when adding keywords later. If the user tries to call the method with keywords before the keywords have been added, the method will raise an `ArgumentError`:

```
foo(bar: 1)
# ArgumentError (no keywords accepted)
```

For existing methods, the decision to add `**nil` to methods not currently accepting keywords is more difficult. If you are sure you don't have any callers that are using keywords, it can be added safely, but often, this isn't needed in those cases since keywords will only be used if the final positional argument can be a hash. If you have any callers that are using keywords as a final positional hash argument, it's definitely not desirable to add as it would break any existing code.

If you are maintaining Ruby code that uses positional arguments with default hash values as a replacement for keyword arguments, you should consider whether you want to convert them into keyword arguments. Outside of cases involving delegation, in general, switching to keyword arguments will improve performance since using explicit keyword arguments in a method call will not allocate a hash. The main issue with such a conversion is backward compatibility when unrecognized keys are used. While in simple cases this can be considered a bug, there are more complex cases where unrecognized keys are expected. For example, let's say you have a method that delegates the same options hash to multiple methods:

```
def foo(options=OPTIONS)
  bar(options)
  baz(options)
end

def bar(options)
  options[:bar]
end

def baz(options)
  options[:baz]
end
```

It can be tempting to replace this with keyword arguments, with `bar` and `baz` only defining the keywords they use, like so:

```
def foo(**kwargs)
  bar(**kwargs)
  baz(**kwargs)
end

def bar(bar: nil)
  bar
end

def baz(baz: nil)
  baz
end
```

Unfortunately, this simplistic approach completely fails if either `:bar` or `:baz` is provided as a keyword argument. This is because a `:bar` keyword argument will be rejected by `baz`, and a `:baz` keyword argument will be rejected by `bar`. There are a few approaches to handling this type of case. One is explicit keyword delegation, as shown here:

```
def foo(bar: nil, baz: nil)
  bar(bar: bar)
  baz(baz: baz)
end

def bar(bar: nil)
  bar
end

def baz(baz: nil)
  baz
end
```

This approach contains all the maintainability problems we discussed previously regarding explicit keyword delegation.

Another approach is to ignore the keyword arguments in `bar` and `baz`:

```
def foo(**kwargs)
  bar(**kwargs)
  baz(**kwargs)
end

def bar(bar: nil, baz: nil)
  bar
end

def baz(baz: nil, bar: nil)
  baz
end
```

This is a code smell and still has maintainability issues similar to explicit keyword delegation, just to a lesser degree. You don't need to worry about default value changes for keyword arguments, but you still need to add the same keywords to `bar` when adding them to `baz` and vice versa.

The third approach is ignoring all unrecognized keywords in `bar` and `baz`:

```
def foo(**kwargs)
  bar(**kwargs)
  baz(**kwargs)
end

def bar(bar: nil, **)
  bar
end

def baz(baz: nil, **)
  baz
end
```

This makes maintenance simpler but is bad for performance as it requires three hash allocations for each call to `foo`. In cases like this, it's probably best to keep to the original approach of using a positional argument with a default hash value.

When designing your method API, you often have a choice between keyword arguments and optional arguments. In most cases, it is better to accept a keyword argument than an optional argument as it allows more flexibility for future changes. If you have a method that takes no arguments and you want to add support for an optional `bar` argument, you could add an optional positional argument or a keyword argument:

```
# Positional
def foo(bar=nil)
end


# Keyword
def foo(bar: nil)
end
```

Let's say that you want to add support for an optional `baz` argument, which you think will be a lot more common to use than the `bar` argument. You can add it to both these cases:

```
# Positional
def foo(bar=nil, baz=nil)
end


# Keyword
def foo(bar: nil, baz: nil)
end
```

The problem with the optional argument approach is that if you want to pass the `baz` argument and not the `bar` argument, you can't really do this and you need to explicitly pass `nil` as the value of `bar`. This is unlike the keyword argument approach, where you can just pass the `bar` argument:

```
# Positional
foo(nil, 1)


# Keyword
foo(baz: 1)
```

This gets progressively worse when you keep adding arguments. Very few programmers want to pass four `nil` arguments before the one optional argument they need. If you want to add an optional argument to an existing method, unless you have a good reason to add it as an optional positional argument, it is better to add it as an optional keyword argument.

Block arguments

Blocks are considered by many Ruby programmers to be the best aspect of Ruby. The simplicity of the block syntax makes passing blocks to methods easy, and many core methods accept blocks. The flexibility of blocks is wonderful as blocks can be used for looping (for example, `Kernel#loop`), resource management (for example, `File. open`), sorting (for example, `Array#sort`), handling missing data (for example, `Hash#fetch`), and so many other purposes. The fact that blocks can return out of the calling scope using `return` or out of the block scope using `next` or `break` is another reason they are so flexible.

Because blocks are so important to the idiomatic usage of Ruby, and there can only be one block argument per method, you should give more thought to how a method should use a block than you should give to any other type of argument. Said another way, the block argument is the single most important argument that a method accepts. Why is that? This is because if you want to change the behavior of an existing method in a backward-compatible manner, it is easy to add an optional positional argument or optional keyword argument. However, once you have decided how a method will handle a block, you are committed to keeping the behavior of that block argument the same unless you want to break backward compatibility.

It is possible to change how the block behaves and still be backward compatible, but you must trigger the new behavior with another argument, such as a keyword argument. Let's say you have a method that yields the argument and the current value of one of the receiver's instance variables to the block:

```ruby
def foo(bar)
  yield(bar, @baz)
end
```

This allows callers to do the following:

```ruby
foo(1) do |bar, baz|
  bar + baz
end
```

Later, you determine that it would be more useful to also yield an additional value to the block, maybe from another instance variable:

```
def foo(bar)
    yield(bar, @baz, @initial || 0)
end
```

This still allows callers to do the following:

```
foo(1) do |bar, baz|
    bar + baz
end
```

This is because the block will ignore the extra argument that's been passed.

The previous method definition also allows the following block, which uses the extra argument:

```
foo(1) do |bar, baz, initial|
    bar + baz + initial
end
```

Unfortunately, the change that we made to the previous method definition is not completely backward compatible. It does work correctly for regular blocks, but it will break if you pass in a lambda proc that expects the previous block API:

```
adder = -> (bar, baz) do
    bar + baz
end


# Worked before, now broken
foo(1, &adder)
```

Because lambda procs are strict in regard to arity, it is never safe to modify the arity of what you are yielding to a block if users can pass a lambda proc as the block argument.

As we mentioned earlier, to handle this case safely, you must trigger the new behavior, and it's probably best to do that via a keyword:

```
def foo(bar, include_initial: false)
    if include_initial
        yield(bar, @baz, @initial || 0)
```

```
    else
      yield(bar, @baz)
    end
  end
```

This is a safe approach. However, it significantly increases complexity, both for the caller of the method and for the maintainer of the method. An alternative approach to handling block argument changes is to check the block's arity:

```
def foo(bar, &block)
  case block.arity
  when 2, -1, -2
    yield(bar, @baz)
  else
    yield(bar, @baz, @initial || 0)
  end
end
```

This approach can be easier on the caller, since they can provide a block that accepts additional arguments without passing a keyword argument. It will work correctly in most cases, but it will result in the third argument not being passed to a block that accepts an optional third argument. The advantage of the keyword argument approach is that the caller has full control over whether the additional argument is passed to the block. The disadvantage is that you need a keyword argument when just having the block accept an additional argument will work in most cases.

Whenever you would like to change the arguments that are being passed to the block, give strong consideration to defining a separate method with the new block arguments, instead of using either the keyword argument approach or the arity checking approach, as described previously.

Another consideration for block arguments is that there can be only a single block argument. What if you have a method where multiple block arguments would be useful? Well, only one can be the block argument; the other argument needs to be passed as a callable object in another type of argument (often, a keyword argument).

Let's say you have a method where you need to listen for a notification from a server. This involves telling the server you are listening for a notification, waiting for a notification to be received, then returning the value of the notification while making sure to tell the server you are no longer listening:

```
def listen
  server.start_listening
  server.receive_notification
ensure
  server.stop_listening
end
```

This method doesn't take any arguments or a block – you would just call it to get a notification:

```
notification = listen
```

After this method is in your library for a while, someone requests the ability to run arbitrary code after the server has started listening, but before a notification has been received. This is easy to implement with a block:

```
def listen
  server.start_listening
  yield if block_given?
  server.receive_notification
ensure
  server.stop_listening
end
```

This allows the user to pass a block, which they could use to measure the amount of time until a notification is received, but not including the time to start the listening process:

```
time = nil
notification = listen do
  time = Time.now
end
elapsed_seconds = Time.now - time
```

This block is used by relatively few users, but it is helpful to those users.

Later, a different group of users tells you they've been using this API, but it is inefficient because it only listens for a single notification, and they want to handle many notifications. They have been using the method in a loop:

```
while notification = listen
  process_notification(notification)
end
```

Worse than being inefficient, they have found that they have missed notifications because once the `listen` method returns, they are not listening for notifications until `listen` is called again. They think it would be much more useful to have `listen` yield each notification to a block with the following API:

```
listen do |notification|
  process_notification(notification)
end
```

You agree that this approach is much more useful, but unfortunately, because the block is already being used to run arbitrary code once the server has started listening, you can't use the block argument for that. The best you can do is add it as a keyword argument, as shown here:

```
def listen(callback: nil)
  server.start_listening
  yield if block_given?
  if callback
    while notification = server.receive_notification
      callback.(notification)
    end
  else
    server.receive_notification
  end
ensure
  server.stop_listening
end
```

This requires the caller to pass the argument as a keyword argument instead of a block, which is significantly uglier and does not make the average Ruby programmers happy:

```
listen(callback: ->(notification) do
  process_notification(notification)
end)
```

Hindsight being 20/20, you realize it would have been better to design your method like the following example, because far more users benefit from the looping construct than the callback after listening:

```
def listen(after_listen: nil)
  server.start_listening
  after_listen.call if after_listen
  if block_given?
    while notification = server.receive_notification
      yield notification
    end
  else
    server.receive_notification
  end
ensure
  server.stop_listening
end
```

The moral of this story is to think long and hard about how a method would best use a block, before adding support for a block to the method. Once you've decided on the block's behavior, you will be painting yourself into a corner, so make sure you like the corner first.

In this section, you learned about the different types of method arguments that Ruby supports. In the next section, you'll learn how to choose an appropriate visibility setting for your methods.

Learning about the importance of method visibility

While it is easy to develop code in Ruby without worrying about method visibility, neglecting to use method visibility wisely tends to result in more difficult long-term maintenance. If you never use one of Ruby's method visibility methods when developing, all the methods you define are public methods. When an object has a public method, it signals to the users of the object that the method is part of the object's supported interface, which, in general, should only change in a major update to the library containing the method. When a method is not public, it signals to the users of the object that the method is an implementation detail, and subject to change at any time.

Whether a method is a supported interface (public method) or an implementation detail (protected or private method) is critical to the long-term maintenance of a library. In general, the larger the supported interface for an object, the more difficult it is to maintain it. An object with 100 public methods basically requires that changes to the object do not change the desired behavior of 100 methods. Alternatively, an object with one public method and 99 private methods is much easier to maintain. This is because you only need to make sure the one public method has the same behavior; you can change the behavior or even remove any of the 99 private methods as needed.

Whenever you add a method to a class, one of the first questions you should ask yourself is, *Do I want to commit to supporting backward compatibility for this method, at least until the next major version is released, and potentially forever?* If the answer is yes, then it should be a public method. If not, in most cases, the method should be private.

This discussion of method visibility has an implicit assumption, which is that keeping backward compatibility for methods is very important. However, it's reasonable to question this assumption. Is keeping backward compatibility for methods actually important? Well, that depends on your point of view, but think of the code you currently maintain in Ruby. You are unlikely to only be using your own code – you are probably using a library. One day, a new version of the library is released, and unfortunately, it contains changes that break your code. Think about how that would make you feel, or if this has happened to you previously, how it made you feel.

The most common feelings people have when a library they are relying on breaks their code are betrayal and annoyance. Betrayal is a more common feeling for less experienced programmers, while annoyance is more common for more experienced programmers. Less experienced programmers feel betrayed because they trusted this code to make their jobs easier, and the library has betrayed that trust by giving them even more work to do. More experienced programmers have been betrayed by libraries enough times that they are used to it, so they only feel annoyance.

Certainly, breaking backward compatibility in major library releases is somewhat expected. However, any time you break backward compatibility in a library, even in a major version, you should have a good reason to. Even if their code breaks, the users of a library tend to feel less betrayed and annoyed when they can see that such a breakage was necessary for greater progress.

In general, you should only break backward compatibility in a library when the breakage is necessary, and when keeping the backward compatibility would significantly harm future development. Backward compatibility breakage is easier to stomach if the backward compatibility is small or in an infrequently used part of the library. It is also easier to stomach if the backward compatibility breakage is only by default, and you are offering an alternative approach that users can easily switch to if they would like to keep backward compatibility.

This brings us back to method visibility. Because backward compatibility is so critical when designing methods, you should do what you can to avoid breaking backward compatibility, and the best way to do that is to have as few public methods as possible. Only make a method public if it must be usable by users.

If you aren't sure whether a method should be public or private, make it private. Only make it public if you are sure it should be public. Later, you may get a request from a user to change the visibility of a method from private to public, and at that point, you can reevaluate whether the benefits of making the method public are worth the future maintenance costs.

What about protected method visibility? In general, you should probably avoid protected visibility except for one main use case. The main use case for protected visibility is when you're calling methods internally to the library, where the caller is another method in the same class, and where you want to avoid the performance overhead of calling `send`. The downside of protected visibility is that due to backward compatibility, protected methods show up in `Module#instance_methods` and `Kernel#methods`, even though you can't call the methods normally:

```ruby
class MethodVis
  protected def foo
    :foo
  end
end

MethodVis.instance_methods(false)
# => [:foo]
```

```
m = MethodVis.new
m.methods.include?(:foo)
# => true

m.foo
# NoMethodError
```

What about the visibility of constants? In general, it's best to use `private_constant` for any constant you do not want to expose to users. Only leave a constant public if there is a good reason for it to be public. It's almost always better to force external users to call a public method to get a constant value. This is because you can modify the method later if the internals of your library change. Once a constant is public, it's part of your library's interface, and you should treat changes that are made to the constant similar to changes that are made to any public method, so do your best to keep backward compatibility for it.

Fixing visibility mistakes

Let's say you've made a mistake in your library development and have made a method that should have been a private method public instead. Can this be handled in a way that doesn't break backward compatibility? Unfortunately, the answer is no, as such a change always breaks backward compatibility. However, there is a way to break backward compatibility gradually and warn others of upcoming method visibility changes.

Ruby doesn't provide a way for a method to know if it was called in a public context (`self.method_name`) or a private context (`method_name` or `send(:method_name)`). So, how can you implement this warning? Let's look at the previous example, where we called the protected method directly:

```
m.foo
# NoMethodError
```

Notice that it raised a `NoMethodError`, not a `MethodVisibilityError` (this is not a real exception class). This is not an accident; this is by design. What method in Ruby, by default, raises a `NoMethodError`? If you said `method_missing`, you are correct! When you call a private or protected method from a context that does not allow the method to be called, Ruby calls `method_missing` internally. It is possible to override `method_missing` to issue a warning that the visibility will be changing, and then call the method directly:

```
class MethodVis
  private def method_missing(sym, ...)
```

```
    if sym == :foo
      warn("foo is a protected method, stop calling it!",
           uplevel: 1)
      return foo(...)
    end
    super
  end
end


m.foo
# foo is a protected method, stop calling it!
# => :foo
```

Let's say you also made a mistake in your library development and left a constant public when you should have made it private. Can this be fixed in the same way? The good news is yes, you can fix it in a similar way. First, let's look at what happens when you access a private constant:

```
class ConstantVis
  PRIVATE = 1
  private_constant :PRIVATE
end


ConstantVis::PRIVATE
# NameError
```

Interestingly, you get a `NameError`, not a `ConstantVisibilityError` (again, this is not a real exception class). Similar to the method case, this is not an accident; this is by design. What method in Ruby raises a `NameError` by default? If you said `Module#const_missing`, you are correct! When you access a private constant from a context that does not allow constant access, Ruby calls `const_missing` on the module internally. It is possible to override `const_missing` to issue a warning that the visibility will be changing, and then return the value of the constant:

```
class ConstantVis
  def self.const_missing(const)
    if const == :PRIVATE
      warn("ConstantVis::PRIVATE is a private constant, " \
           "stop accessing it!", uplevel: 1)
```

```
      return PRIVATE
    end
    super
  end
end


ConstantVis::PRIVATE
# ConstantVis::PRIVATE is a private constant,
# stop accessing it!
# => 1
```

If you have a lot of methods and constants that are currently public and should be made private, it is a little tedious to do all this `method_missing` and `const_missing` overriding. In that case, you can use the `deprecate_public` gem to handle all the hard work for you:

```
require 'deprecate_public'

class MethodVis
  deprecate_public :foo
end

class ConstantVis
  deprecate_public_constant :PRIVATE
end
```

In this section, you learned about choosing the proper method visibility and how to change method visibility gradually. In the next section, you'll learn about the best approach for delegating method arguments.

Handling delegation

Delegation refers to taking the arguments that were passed to one method and passing those arguments to a different method. In Ruby, it's common to use delegation to wrap calls to other methods in order to add behavior around the method call. Handling delegation incorrectly can make debugging and refactoring more difficult, so it useful to learn how best to implement it.

Let's say you have a public method you want to rename:

```ruby
def foo(*args, **kwargs, &block)
  [args, kwargs, block]
end
```

Let's say you just rename the method, as follows:

```ruby
def bar(*args, **kwargs, &block)
  [args, kwargs, block]
end
```

Here, you break backward compatibility for users calling foo.

The best way to handle this is to re-add the same method you are renaming, have it issue a deprecation warning, and then forward all arguments to the renamed method:

```ruby
def foo(*args, **kwargs, &block)
  warn("foo is being renamed to bar", uplevel: 1)
  bar(*args, **kwargs, &block)
end
```

Delegating all arguments to another method is such a common pattern in Ruby that they added a shortcut for it in Ruby 2.7 by using . . . :

```ruby
def foo(...)
  warn("foo is being renamed to bar", uplevel: 1)
  bar(...)
end
```

In Ruby 2, it was recommended to not use explicit delegation of keywords arguments due to the lack of separation between positional arguments and keyword arguments, so it is common to see delegation like this in older Ruby code:

```ruby
def foo(*args, &block)
  warn("foo is being renamed to bar", uplevel: 1)
  bar(*args, &block)
end
```

This works fine in Ruby 3, but only if you are sure that the method you are delegating to does not accept keyword arguments. If you are not sure whether the method accepts keyword arguments, you should use explicit keyword delegation with `**kwargs`, or `...` to forward all arguments.

If you are maintaining code that must run correctly on both Ruby 2 and Ruby 3, you must use the old-style `*args` delegation in the method, and then mark the method using `ruby2_keywords`:

```ruby
def foo(*args, &block)
  warn("foo is being renamed to bar", uplevel: 1)
  bar(*args, &block)
end
ruby2_keywords(:foo) if respond_to?(:ruby2_keywords, true)
```

`ruby2_keywords` marks the method as passing through keywords, so that if keywords are passed to `foo`, they will be implicitly passed to `bar`. You can only mark methods with `ruby2_keywords` if they accept a rest argument and no keywords. Internally, Ruby will wrap the keywords that were passed in a specially flagged hash, and then when an array is splatted in a method call, if the final argument in the array is a specially flagged hash, the hash will be passed as keywords.

By using `respond_to?(:ruby2_keywords, true)` as a guard, the `ruby2_keywords(:foo)` method call will not happen on Ruby versions before 2.7. This is what makes the code backward compatible, even back to Ruby 1.8.

Delegating to other objects

Another common case for method delegation in Ruby is when you are delegating not to a different method in the same class, but to a different object. For example, let's say you have class A, which has an attribute, b:

```ruby
class A
  attr_accessor :b

  def initialize(b)
    @b = b
  end
end
```

Let's say you want to delegate `A#foo` to call `b.foo`. You can use either of the manual delegation approaches discussed previously, such as the explicit argument delegation approach:

```
class A
  def foo(*args, **kwargs, &block)
    b.foo(*args, **kwargs, &block)
  end
end
```

Alternatively, you can use the argument forwarding approach:

```
class A
  def foo(...)
    b.foo(...)
  end
end
```

Alternatively, you could use the backward-compatible approach with `ruby2_keywords`:

```
class A
  def foo(*args, &block)
    b.foo(*args, &block)
  end
  if respond_to?(:ruby2_keywords, true)
    ruby2_keywords(:foo)
  end
end
```

For a single method, any of these approaches works fine. However, if you must delegate lots of methods, it can get tedious to write them. Thankfully, Ruby includes a standard library named `forwardable` that handles method delegation. Ruby also includes a standard library named `delegate`, but that is for creating delegate objects, not for delegating method arguments.

Using the `forwardable` library, you can handle this method delegation without defining a method yourself:

```
require 'forwardable'

class A
  extend Forwardable
  def_delegators :b, :foo
end
```

`Forwardable` is fairly flexible since it also allows delegation to instance variables or constants:

```
class A
  extend Forwardable
  def_delegators :@b, :foo
  def_delegators "A::B", :foo
end
```

One of the main advantages of `forwardable` is that you can delegate a bunch of methods in a single call:

```
class A
  extend Forwardable
  def_delegators :b, :foo, :bar, :baz
end
```

`Forwardable` also includes additional ways to delegate methods, such as having A#foo call b.bar, or setting up delegations for multiple methods to multiple separate objects in a single method call. For details, see the `Forwardable` documentation.

In this section, you learned about some good approaches to implementing delegation, both to different methods in the same object and to methods in a different object.

Summary

In this chapter, you learned that Ruby doesn't have class methods – it only has instance methods on singleton classes. You learned that the length of a method name should be proportional to the inverse of the frequency of calling the method. You then learned about Ruby's many types of arguments, such as positional arguments, keyword arguments, and block arguments, and when it is best to use each. You also learned about method visibility and how important it is for backward compatibility. Finally, you learned how to implement method delegation in Ruby. With the knowledge you've gained, you'll be able to design better methods, which will make the libraries and applications you write easier to use and maintain.

In the next chapter, you'll learn how best to handle errors and other exceptional situations in your Ruby code.

Questions

1. If class methods are instance methods, what class contains those instance methods?

2. How are method call frequency and method naming related?

3. What's the best argument type to use for an argument that will rarely be used?

4. If you make a mistake with method or constant visibility, what gem helps you convert a public method or constant into a private one, while also issuing warnings if it's accessed via a public interface?

5. What's the best way to delegate all arguments to another method so that it works correctly in Ruby 2.6, 2.7, and 3.0?

5
Handling Errors

There are multiple ways to handle errors in your code. Most commonly in Ruby, errors are handled by raising exceptions, but there are other approaches used occasionally, such as returning `nil` for errors.

In this chapter, you'll learn about trade-offs in error handling, issues when handling transient errors with retries, and more advanced error handling such as **exponential backoff** and **circuit breakers**. You'll also learn how to design useful exception class hierarchies.

In this chapter, we will cover the following topics:

- Handling errors with return values
- Handling errors with exceptions
- Retrying transient errors
- Designing exception class hierarchies

By the end of this chapter, you'll have a better understanding of how best to handle errors in your Ruby programs.

Technical requirements

In this chapter and all chapters of this book, code given in code blocks is designed to execute on Ruby 3.0. Many of the code examples will work on earlier versions of Ruby, but not all. The code for this chapter is available online at `https://github.com/PacktPublishing/Polished-Ruby-Programming/tree/main/Chapter05`.

Handling errors with return values

In programming languages that do not support exceptions, errors are generally handled by using a return value that indicates failure. Ruby itself is written in **C**, and in C, functions that can fail will often use a return value that is zero on success, and non-zero on failure. While Ruby has exceptions, there are instances where methods can fail and this will occasionally return a value instead of raising an exception, even in cases where other programming languages raise an exception.

For example, in **Python**, if you have a hash (called a dictionary in Python), and you try to access a member in the hash that doesn't exist, you get an exception raised:

```
# Python code:
{'a': 2}['b']
# KeyError: 'b'
```

Ruby takes a different approach in this case, returning `nil`:

```
{'a'=>2}['b']
# => nil
```

This shows the two different philosophies between the languages. In Ruby, it is expected that when you are looking for a value in a hash, it may not be there. In Python, it is expected that if you are looking for a value in a hash, it should exist. If you want to get the Ruby behavior in Python, you can use `get`:

```
# Python code:
{'a': 2}.get('b', None)
# => None (Python equivalent of Ruby's nil)
```

Likewise, if you want to get the Python behavior in Ruby, you can use `fetch`:

```
{'a'=>2}.fetch('b')
# KeyError (key not found: "b")
```

Both Python and Ruby support similar behavior for retrieving data from hashes, but Ruby, in this case, is permissive, while Python, in this case, is strict.

In other cases, such as which objects are treated as false in conditionals, Python is permissive, and Ruby is strict. Ruby's permissiveness in either area can be considered a bug or a feature, depending on your point of view. Most programmers who prefer to use Ruby probably consider it a feature, since otherwise, they would probably prefer to use another language.

Ruby's permissiveness in the hash retrieval case is what allows for Ruby's very simple idiomatic memoization technique:

```
hash[key] ||= value
```

This is because this memoization construct is shorthand for the following code:

```
hash[key] || (hash[key] = value)
```

If hash[key] raised an exception in Ruby if key wasn't present in hash, this shorthand wouldn't work, and you would have to write a longer code that is more similar to the type of code needed in Python:

```
if hash.key?(key)
    hash[key]
else
    hash[key] = value
end
```

In general, the Ruby principle for data access via [] is that an exception is not raised if there is a way the access would work if the receiver included different data. You see this with arrays in the following code:

```
ary = [1, 2, 3]
ary[3]
# => nil

ary << 4
ary[3]
# => 4
```

Accessing the `ary` array with an index that is beyond the bounds of the array returns `nil`, because if the array is expanded later, the same call will be within the bounds of the array, and will return the value at that index.

You see this with hashes, shown in the following code:

```
hash = {1 => 2}
hash[3]
# => nil

hash[3] = 4
hash[3]
# => 4
```

Accessing `hash` with a key that does not currently exist in the hash returns `nil`, because if the key is added to the hash later, the same call will return the value associated with the key.

If you use the `OpenStruct` class in the standard library, you see that it operates the same way:

```
require 'ostruct'

os = OpenStruct.new
os[:b]
# => nil

os.b = 1
os[:b]
# => 1
```

As noted previously, the principle only applies if the receiver were to return an expected result if it included different data. If the call were to always fail regardless of which data the receiver included, Ruby will raise an exception. You can see this with a `Struct` subclass:

```
A = Struct.new(:a)
a = A.new(1)
a[:a]
# => 1
```

```
a[:b]
# NameError (no member 'b' in struct)
```

This is because no matter what kind of data the A instance contains, it will not have a b element, so this call will always fail.

There are two primary benefits of using return values to signal errors:

- First, this approach offers much better performance than using exceptions, with pretty much the same performance in a successful case, and unintuitively, sometimes much better performance for an unsuccessful case than a successful case.

- Second, if the error is common, it's easier for the user to deal with it instead of forcing them to rescue an exception.

Let's say you have a method that looks up a row in a database by the primary key of the row. In this case, the primary key is an integer column named id:

```
def pk_lookup(pk)
  database.first(<<-END)
    SELECT * FROM table where id = #{database.literal(pk)}
  END
end
```

Assuming database.first returns a hash or some other object when the row exists, and nil when the row does not exist, this is an example of a method that uses a return value to handle an error.

One issue with this method is that it will still run a query even if you know that the query will not return a row, such as when the value passed in is nil. Assuming that this is a case you want to optimize for, you can use this code:

```
def pk_lookup(pk)
  return unless pk
  database.first(<<-END)
    SELECT * FROM table where id = #{database.literal(pk)}
  END
end
```

The preceding code gives you the same behavior. However, it improves the performance of the case where the pk argument is nil, making it much faster than the success case since the database query is skipped.

The trade-off in this case is that every time you call pk_lookup, you cannot assume it will return a valid row. Code such as row = pk_lookup(1) will not raise an exception when pk_lookup is called if there is no matching row.

However, if row is used later and expected to be a hash or other object, the code will fail later, which may complicate debugging. In general, that's not a major issue, because if there is a problem due to not finding a row, you'll probably be alerted to it one way or another.

A more insidious case is when, in normal use of the method, you do not need the return value because the method is called for side effects. Consider the case where instead of looking up an object by primary key, you are updating the database. The following code demonstrates this:

```
def update(pk, column, value)
  database.run_update(<<-SQL)
    UPDATE table
    SET #{column} = #{database.literal(value)}
    WHERE id = #{database.literal(pk)}
  SQL
end
```

You can assume that database.run_update, in this case, returns the number of rows updated. In the general case, the return value of database.run_update is useful because an update can affect more than one row. However, because you are passing the primary key in this case, you are sure that it will never modify more than one row, and the return value may not be important. You may often call this method and ignore the return value by using this code:

```
update(self.id, :name, 'New Name')
```

The problem, in this case, is that if the database row with the current id doesn't exist, this method returns 0. However, since you aren't checking the return value, you don't know whether this code is making the expected changes.

This type of error can linger in code undetected for a long time, especially in code that is not commonly called. You may only find out months or years later that you have missed updates, and at that point, there may be nothing you can do to fix the previous cases affected by the error.

This is not a theoretical case; it can be a common problem when using a database library where a method such as save returns false for an unsuccessful save instead of raising an exception.

The principle here is to be especially wary of using return values to indicate errors when the caller of the code does not need to use the return value of the method. It is usually better to raise an exception in this case, which you'll learn more about in the next section.

In this section, you learned how to handle errors using return values, and the trade-offs in doing so. In the next section, you'll learn about the alternative approach, handling errors using exceptions.

Handling errors with exceptions

Raising exceptions is the most common way to handle errors in Ruby. All core methods in Ruby can raise an exception when called incorrectly. The easiest way to get a core method to trigger an exception is to pass it an incorrect number of arguments, as shown in the following code:

```
"S".length(1)
# ArgumentError (wrong number of arguments)
```

We can also get a core method to trigger an exception when passing the wrong type of argument:

```
'S'.count(1)
# TypeError (no implicit conversion of Integer into String)
```

In almost all cases, any unexpected or uncommon error should be raised as an exception, and not handled via a return value. Otherwise, as shown in the previous section, you end up with a case where the error is silently ignored. In the previous section, you saw an example where the update method using a return value to signal an error resulted in data loss. However, there are other cases where the results are even worse than data loss.

Consider a case where you are designing an authorization system. You have a class named Authorizer, and this has a singleton method named check that takes user and action, and should indicate whether user is authorized to perform an action. Here is a simple example of implementing such a class:

```
class Authorizer
  def self.check(user, action)
    new(user, action).authorized?
  end

  def authorized?
    return true if user.admin?
```

```
    return true if action == :view_own_profile
    false
  end
end
```

One way to use the `Authorizer` class would be as follows:

```
if Authorizer.check(current_user, :manage_users)
  show_manage_users_page
else
  show_invalid_access_page
end
```

Unfortunately, this has similar issues as seen in the previous section, where it can be misused. If a new programmer doesn't understand the API, they may assume from a method name such as `check` that it handles the error by raising an exception, and writes code such as the following:

```
Authorizer.check(current_user, :manage_users)
show_manage_users_page
```

This can be even worse than the data loss case described previously, and result in an elevation of privilege vulnerability in the application, or possibly even worse depending on which action is improperly allowed.

In this case, it's generally better for the `Authorizer.check` method to raise an exception:

```
class Authorizer
  class InvalidAuthorization < StandardError
  end

  def self.check(user, action)
    unless new(user, action).authorized?
      raise InvalidAuthorization,
        "#{user.name} is not authorized to perform #{action}"
    end
  end
end
```

By raising an exception, as the previous example does, you are forcing the user to handle the exception, avoiding the case where the failure is accidentally ignored. If `Authorizer.check` is implemented as in the previous example, and a new programmer doesn't understand the API, they may assume that it returns `true` to indicate that the action is authorized, and `false` to indicate that it is not. If they make that incorrect assumption, they would still have an issue. The following code demonstrates this:

```
if Authorizer.check(current_user, :manage_users)
   show_manage_users_page
else
   show_invalid_access_page
end
```

In the case where the action is authorized, the previous code works fine. However, in the case where the action is not authorized, an exception will be raised, instead of the invalid access page being shown. This is certainly a problem, but it's an easily fixable one.

There are two important principles here.

One of the principles is that when you are designing an API, you should not only design the API to be easy to use, but you should also attempt to design the API to be difficult to misuse. This is the principle of **misuse resistance**. A method that does not raise an exception for errors is easier to misuse than a method that raises an exception for errors.

Another of the principles at play is that of fail-open versus fail-closed design. In a **fail-open design**, if there is a problem with checking access, access is allowed. In a **fail-closed design**, if there is a problem with checking access, access is not allowed.

In most cases involving security, fail-closed is considered to be the superior model. In the example where `Authorized.check` returns `true` or `false`, misuse of the method results in the system failing open, and unauthorized access being allowed.

In the example where `Authorized.check` raises an `Authorizer::InvalidAuthorization` exception, misuse of the method results in the system failing closed, and unauthorized access not being allowed.

Now, there may be many cases where the user of `Authorizer` does need a `true` or `false` value for whether an action is authorized. For example, let's say you are showing a dashboard page and need to know whether to include a link to the page to manage users. You don't want to write the following code:

```
begin
  Authorizer.check(current_user, :manage_users)
rescue Authorizer::InvalidAuthorization
  # don't show link
else
  display_manage_users_link
end
```

The preceding code uses exceptions for flow control, which is, in general, a bad approach. In a case like this, it's usually better to have multiple methods. The `Authorizer.check` method should raise an exception, but if you want a `true` or `false` value, you can have a method such as the `Authorizer.allowed?` method, as shown in the following code:

```
class Authorizer
  def self.allowed?(user, action)
    new(user, action).authorized?
  end
end
```

Isn't this just the same as the first definition of the `check` *method?* Yes, it is. However, because the method name ends in `?`, it signals to the user that this method will return a `true` or `false` value, and a user is much less likely to misuse it. With a method name such as `check`, it is ambiguous as to whether the method will return `true` or `false` or raise an exception, so misuse is much more likely to happen.

One other advantage of using exceptions to handle errors is that in many cases, higher-level code wants to handle the same type of error the same way. So, instead of having one hundred different `if`/`else` expressions in your application that use `Authorizer.allowed?`, as shown in the following code:

```
if Authorizer.allowed?(current_user, :manage_users)
  show_manage_users_page
else
  show_invalid_access_page
end
```

You can use a much simpler approach with `Authorizer.check`, as shown in the following code snippet:

```
code:Authorizer.check(current_user, :manage_users)
show_manage_users_page
```

Then, in a single place in your application, you have the following code that rescues the `Authorizer::InvalidAuthorization` exception and shows an appropriate page:

```
begin
  handle_request
rescue Authorizer::InvalidAuthorization
  show_invalid_access_page
end
```

In this section, you learned about maintainability and usability considerations when handling errors with exceptions. In the following section, you'll learn that handling errors with exceptions has performance considerations as well.

Considering performance when using exceptions

One reason to prefer handling errors via return values instead of exceptions is that return values, in general, perform much better. For simple methods, there isn't a way to get the exception handling approach even close to the return value approach in terms of performance.

However, for methods that do even minimal processing, such as a single `String#gsub` call, the time for executing the method is probably larger than the difference between the exception approach and the return value approach. Still, for absolute maximum performance, you do need to use the return value approach.

One consideration when using exceptions is that they get slower in proportion to the size of the call stack. If you have a call stack with 100 frames, which is quite common in Ruby web applications, raising an exception is much slower than if you only have a call stack with 10 frames.

The reason for this is that when you raise an exception the normal way, Ruby has to do a lot of work to construct the backtrace for the exception. Ruby needs to read the entire call stack and turn it into an array of `Thread::Backtrace::Location` objects.

Constructing that array gets slower in proportion to the size of the call stack. In general, the time to construct the array of `Thread::Backtrace::Location` objects is much longer than executing the non-local return to the appropriate exception handler (the `rescue` clause that will handle the exception).

Is there a way in which you can speed up the exception generation process? Thankfully, yes, there is. Instead of raising the exception the way you would normally, as follows:

```
raise ArgumentError, "message"
```

You can include a third argument to `raise`, which is the array to use for the backtrace. If you want to make the exception handling as fast as possible, you can use an empty array:

```
raise ArgumentError, "message", []
```

Like an empty array in exception arguments, you can make this even faster if you use a shared frozen constant:

```
# Earlier, outside the method
EMPTY_ARRAY = [].freeze


# Later, inside a method
raise ArgumentError, "message", EMPTY_ARRAY
```

As shown in the preceding example, by using a frozen constant, you can skip the allocation of an array when raising the exception.

Ruby allows you to construct an exception object manually, using an approach as per the following example:

```
exception = ArgumentError.new("message")
raise exception
```

If you are using the preceding approach, you can add a call to `set_backtrace`, so that `raise` will not try to generate the backtrace, as shown in the following code:

```
exception = ArgumentError.new("message")
exception.set_backtrace(EMPTY_ARRAY)
raise exception
```

However, this performance benefit has an associated cost. Because the exception being raised has no backtrace, it is much more difficult to debug if you run into problems. In general, if you want to use this approach, it is best to only use it for specific exception types. You should also make sure that you are specifically rescuing those exception types at some level above any methods you are calling that could raise the backtraceless exceptions.

Because backtraceless exceptions make debugging much more difficult, you should avoid using them by default in libraries. If you do want to support backtraceless exceptions in libraries for performance reasons, you should make the use of backtraceless exceptions only enabled via an option or setting. For example, if you have a module named `LibraryModule` and want to add support for backtraceless exceptions, you could add a `skip_exception_backtraces` accessor, as shown in this example:

```
exception = ArgumentError.new("message")
if LibraryModule.skip_exception_backtraces
  exception.set_backtrace(EMPTY_ARRAY)
end
raise exception
```

In this section, you learned about dealing with performance issues when raising exceptions. In the next section, you'll learn how to retry transient errors, using both the return value approach and exception approach.

Retrying transient errors

It's a fact of life, at least for a programmer, that some things fail all the time, but other things only fail occasionally. For those things that fail all the time, there is no point in retrying them. For example, if you call a method and it raises `ArgumentError` because you are calling it with the wrong number of arguments, as shown here:

```
nil.to_s(16)
```

You probably don't want to retry the preceding code, unless you expect that something will be redefining the `NilClass#to_s` method to accept an argument.

However, in many cases, especially those involving network requests, it is very common to encounter transient errors. In these cases, retrying errors makes sense. When making a network request, there may be multiple reasons why it may fail. Maybe the program at the other end of the request crashed and is being restarted. Maybe a construction crew accidentally cut a network cable between your computer and the computer you are connecting to, and failover to an alternative route hasn't happened yet. There are a vast number of possible reasons why transient errors could occur.

Thankfully, Ruby has a built-in keyword for handling transient errors, which is the `retry` keyword. Let's say you are writing a program that downloads data from a server using HTTP, given here:

```ruby
require 'net/http'
require 'uri'


Net::HTTP.get_response(URI("http://example.local/file"))
```

The preceding program doesn't handle errors, so any exception raised when trying to download the file will result in an exception being reported and the program ending.

If one of the requirements for the program is that it absolutely must wait until the data is available, with no exceptions (*pun intended*), no matter how long it takes, and that if a failure happens, the download must be retried again as fast as possible, you could implement this with a `rescue`/`retry` combination, given here:

```ruby
require 'net/http'
require 'uri'

begin
  Net::HTTP.get_response(URI("http://example.local/file"))
rescue
  retry
end
```

In general, the preceding approach is a bad idea, for multiple reasons. One reason is that it is a bad idea to retry on every exception type that could be raised. *What happens if you make a typo in the protocol name, and it will not parse as a valid URI?*

Well, then you end up with an infinite loop without it ever even attempting network access. You should almost always limit the errors you are retrying to specific exception classes. At least in this case, it might be useful to rescue errors related to sockets, system calls, and bad HTTP responses. It's even better to eliminate possible issues in URI creation, by moving the URI creation out of the loop. That also increases performance in the case where `retry` is needed, as given in the following code:

```ruby
require 'net/http'
require 'uri'

uri = URI("http://example.local/file")
begin
  Net::HTTP.get_response(uri)
rescue SocketError, SystemCallError, Net::HTTPBadResponse
  retry
end
```

When combined, the changes to set the `uri` variable before the `begin` clause and only rescue specific exception classes make the preceding code better. However, it still has issues.

One issue is that just because `Net::HTTP.get_response(uri)` returns a value and doesn't raise an exception, it does not mean the value isn't an error. The HTTP protocol supports both client errors (*4xx* errors) and server errors (*5xx* errors), and the returned response could be one of those errors.

You can check whether the response is an error response by checking whether the response code is greater than or equal to `400`. It would be nice if you could retry this in this case here:

```ruby
require 'net/http'
require 'uri'

uri = URI("http://example.local/file")
begin
  response = Net::HTTP.get_response(uri)
  if response.code.to_i >= 400
    # retry # would be nice
  end
rescue SocketError, SystemCallError, Net::HTTPBadResponse
```

```
    retry
end
```

Unfortunately, if you uncomment the first `retry` line, you'll see that the code raises `SyntaxError`. Since the `retry` keyword is only valid inside `rescue` clauses, it is not valid in the `begin` clause. *That's a bummer.*

One way around this issue is to raise one of the exceptions you are rescuing, and then have `retry` in the `rescue` clause handling the retry, as shown in the following code:

```
require 'net/http'
require 'uri'

uri = URI("http://example.local/file")
begin
  response = Net::HTTP.get_response(uri)
  if response.code.to_i >= 400
    raise Net::HTTPBadResponse
  end
rescue SocketError, SystemCallError, Net::HTTPBadResponse
  retry
end
```

This does work, even if it seems like a code smell to use exceptions for flow control in this way.

What if your requirements change, and now you only want to retry on an HTTP client or server error, and not for other errors? In these cases, `Net::HTTP` does not raise an exception, so there is no reason to use a `begin/rescue` approach. One approach is a simple `while` loop, as shown in the following code:

```
require 'net/http'
require 'uri'

uri = URI("http://example.local/file")

while response = Net::HTTP.get_response(uri)
  break unless response.code.to_i >= 400
end
```

This works fine and causes no problems, but determining the intent of the code is much harder. This looks like a loop that will continuously request the page, not an approach for retrying on error.

It turns out that Ruby has something that allows retrying outside `rescue` clauses. Unfortunately, it has its own limitation, and that is the fact that it is only usable inside blocks.

The `redo` keyword is one of the least used keywords in Ruby. If you haven't used it before, it is similar to the `next` keyword, but instead of going to the next block iteration, it restarts the current block iteration. Because it is only usable in blocks, it's a little hacky to use it for retrying on an error, but it does a better job of showing intent.

The trick is, you need a block that will be called exactly once. Thankfully, you already know one way to tell a block to execute a given number of times by using `Integer#times`. The following code shows you how you could use the `redo` keyword to retry on error:

```ruby
require 'net/http'
require 'uri'

uri = URI("http://example.local/file")

response = nil
1.times do
  response = Net::HTTP.get_response(uri)

  if response.code.to_i >= 400
    redo
  end
end
```

The advantage of the preceding code is that it conveys intent much better. You can see that by default, the block will only be called once, and it will only rerun the block if the response code indicates an error. Note that it's also possible to create a **proc** or **lambda** and just call it, but that generally performs worse as it requires allocating an object, unlike the approach of passing a block to `Integer#times`.

In general, procs and lambdas (`Proc` instances) are among the more expensive object instances to create, at least compared to other core classes.

Understanding more advanced retrying

In general, retrying an infinite number of times is a bad idea. If that is one of the requirements you are given, you may want to push back and see whether you can determine a reasonable limit. For network operations, retrying 2 to 5 times is not uncommon. Even retrying 100 times is probably better than always retrying.

It's fairly easy to retry a given number of times in Ruby. If you are using the exception approach to retrying, you can add a local variable for the number of retries, increment it with each exception, and use `raise` instead of `retry` if the local variable is over a specified number. If you wanted to retry a maximum of three times, the code would look like this:

```ruby
require 'net/http'
require 'uri'

uri = URI("http://example.local/file")

retries = 0
begin
  Net::HTTP.get_response(uri)
rescue SocketError, SystemCallError, Net::HTTPBadResponse
  retries += 1
  raise if retries > 3
  retry
end
```

Similarly, if you are using the loop for retrying without exceptions, or the `1.times` block with `redo`, you should switch to using `Integer#times` for the number of retries you want to allow, plus one for the initial attempt. The following code demonstrates this:

```ruby
require 'net/http'
require 'uri'

uri = URI("http://example.local/file")

response = nil
4.times do
  response = Net::HTTP.get_response(uri)
```

```
    break if response.code.to_i < 400
  end
```

Both of the preceding approaches are unfortunately too simple for most production usage. In general, retrying immediately is unlikely to get useful results in real-world situations.

You are likely to get better results if you wait between each retry attempt. How long you should wait depends on the situation, but in many network situations, waiting a few seconds is considered reasonable. If you want to wait a fixed amount of time between retries, you can add a `sleep` call before the retry. For example, the following code shows the case when we want to wait 3 seconds between `retries`:

```
require 'net/http'
require 'uri'

uri = URI("http://example.local/file")

retries = 0
begin
  Net::HTTP.get_response(uri)
rescue SocketError, SystemCallError, Net::HTTPBadResponse
  retries += 1
  raise if retries > 3
  sleep(3)
  retry
end
```

This approach in general is still too simple. In most real-world situations, you increase the amount of time between each retry. This provides a happy medium between too short of a retry time and too long of a retry time.

You send the first retry quickly, just in case there is a simple reason for the transient failure. However, after every retry, it looks less and less likely that the request will succeed if retried, so you wait longer between each retry. One approach to doing this is to start at 3 seconds, but double the amount of time in each retry. You can calculate this by multiplying the number of seconds to initially wait by 2 to the power of the number of retries already performed. The following code demonstrates this:

```
require 'net/http'
require 'uri'
```

```
uri = URI("http://example.local/file")

retries = 0
begin
  Net::HTTP.get_response(uri)
rescue SocketError, SystemCallError, Net::HTTPBadResponse
  retries += 1
  raise if retries > 3
  sleep(3 * 2**(retries-1))
  retry
end
```

This approach is decent, but it can result in the times to sleep growing quickly. For only 3 retries, it's probably fine, since you are retrying after 3 seconds, 9 seconds, and 21 seconds. However, if you are retrying 10 times, you will be waiting for close to an hour before all retries fail.

For a larger number of retries, you may want to decrease the exponentiation base. It's also a good idea to add some amount of randomness to the process if you have multiple processes using the same algorithm, to prevent a related problem called the **thundering herd**, where a large number of processes are retrying at exactly the same time and overwhelming the server. The following code is a modified implementation of a **classic exponential backoff algorithm**:

```
require 'net/http'
require 'uri'

uri = URI("http://example.local/file")

retries = 0
begin
  Net::HTTP.get_response(uri)
rescue SocketError, SystemCallError, Net::HTTPBadResponse
  retries += 1
  raise if retries > 3
  sleep(3 * (0.5 + rand/2) * 1.5**(retries-1))
  retry
end
```

With this approach, even with 10 retries, all retries will complete within 3 minutes.

In this section, you learned about advanced approaches to retrying in the face of transient errors. In the next section, you'll learn about how to avoid trying code that has recently raised transient errors, using an approach called a circuit breaker.

Breaking circuits

One related problem to retrying exceptions is when you have code you want to run, but isn't critical to the success of the program.

For example, if you are running a payment processing service, the actual payment processing is critical to the success of your business, so you want to do everything you can to make that work. However, your application may be calling an external service to get recommendations for the user making a request, and an external service to get advertisements to display on the page, and you would not want a failure of either service to affect the processing of payments.

Let's say you have code that looks like this:

```
begin
    @recommendations = recommender_service.call(timeout: 3)
rescue
end
@ads = ad_service.call(timeout: 3) rescue nil
process_payment
```

In general, it's not a good idea to use `rescue nil`, but if you really don't care why a service failed if it has failed, it can be okay to use. In this example, if either `recommender_service` or `ad_service` is temporarily down, payment processing will take 3 additional seconds. That can significantly affect how many payments you can process per hour, which can put a large dent in your bottom line.

In cases like this, you probably do not want to call either `recommender_service` or `ad_service` if they have been failing recently. For example, if you get three failing requests within a minute, you may want to not try the service until a minute after the first failing request.

You can build a simple class to handle this, called `BrokenCircuit`. The pattern this class implements is called a **circuit breaker** due to its similarity to physical circuit breakers in electrical engineering. You can start by having the constructor take a number of failures, and the number of seconds to wait. It will also use an array to store the failure times, as shown in the following code:

```ruby
class BrokenCircuit
  def initialize(num_failures: 3, within: 60)
    @num_failures = num_failures
    @within = within
    @failures = []
  end
```

You can code the circuit breaker implementation by seeing whether the current number of failures is greater than the number of failures allowed. If it is allowed, then you get a cutoff time to remove older failures by subtracting the time to wait from the current time, and then removing any times from the `failures` array that are before the cutoff time.

Finally, you recheck whether the number of recent failures is still greater than the number allowed, and if so, you return without yielding to the block. If the number of recent failures is less than the number allowed, you yield to the block and rescue any exceptions. If there is an exception, you store the time of failure in the `failures` array, and return `nil`, as shown in this code here:

```ruby
  def check
    if @failures.length >= @num_failures
      cutoff = Time.now - @within
      @failures.reject!{|t| t < cutoff}
      return if @failures.length >= @num_failures
    end

    begin
      yield
    rescue
      @failures << Time.now
      nil
    end
  end
end
```

Then you can set up your circuit breakers in your application. These are generally singleton objects, usually implemented as constants:

```
RECOMMENDER_CIRCUIT = BrokenCircuit.new
AD_CIRCUIT = BrokenCircuit.new
```

Then you can use the circuit breakers in your code prior to payment processing:

```
@recommendations = RECOMMENDER_CIRCUIT.check do
  recommender_service.call(timeout: 3)
end
@ads = AD_CIRCUIT.check do
  ad_service.call(timeout: 3)
end
process_payment
```

Generally speaking, production circuit breaker design is more complex and involved than all of the preceding examples, and you should probably use one of the many circuit breaker gems for Ruby instead of trying to implement a circuit breaker in your own code.

In this section, you learned all about retrying transient errors, including the basics of implementing circuit breakers. In the next section, you'll learn about how to design useful exception class hierarchies.

Designing exception class hierarchies

In general, if you are writing a library and raising an exception in it, it is useful to have a custom exception subclass that you use. Let's say you are passing an object to your method, and the object has to be allowed, or an exception should be raised. Ruby allows you to do this by using the following code:

```
def foo(bar)
  unless allowed?(bar)
    raise "bad bar: #{bar.inspect}"
  end
end
```

However, this is a bad approach, as it raises `RuntimeError`. In general, it is better to raise an exception class related to your library, since that allows users of your library to handle the exception differently from exceptions in other libraries. So if you have a library named `Foo`, it's common to have an exception class named something like `Foo::Error` that you can use for exceptions raised by the library. The following code demonstrates this:

```
module Foo
  class Error < StandardError
  end

  def foo(bar)
    unless allowed?(bar)
      raise Error, "bad bar: #{bar.inspect}"
    end
  end
end
```

It's important that `Foo::Error` is a subclass of `StandardError` and not of `Exception`. You should only subclass `Exception` in very rare cases because subclasses of `Exception` are not caught by `rescue` clauses without arguments. Using `rescue` with no exception classes given only rescues descendants of the `StandardError` class.

In general, it is best to keep your exception class hierarchy as simple as possible. If your code never explicitly raises an exception, do not create an exception class. When your code first needs to raise an exception, create a general `Error` class, such as `Foo::Error`. Thereafter, in future cases when raising an exception, use the same general `Error` class.

When should you have multiple exception classes in your library? In general, the only reason to use a separate `exception` class is for a type of error that users are likely to want to handle differently from other types of errors. For example, let's say in your library that there are two types of errors that can occur, **permanent errors** and **transient errors**.

In case of a transient error, it's possible that the same request will succeed in the future. However, if it is a permanent error, this means the same request will always fail in the future.

In this case, it makes sense to create a `Foo::TransientError` class:

```
module Foo
  class Error < StandardError
  end
  class TransientError < Error
```

```
      end
  end
```

This way, users calling your library can rescue that particular `exception` class, and only retry in that case:

```
begin
   foo(bar)
rescue Foo::TransientError
   sleep(3)
   retry
end
```

How will you know which exceptions deserve separate exception classes and which exceptions do not? In many cases, you won't know. Unless you have a very clear idea that a particular exception should be treated differently, just use the generic exception class for your library when raising the exception.

Later, you may get reports for users that they want to treat a particular error case differently. The following code shows what users will often be doing in this case:

```
begin
   foo(bar)
rescue Foo::Error => e
   if e.message =~ /\Abad bar: /
     handle_bad_bar(bar)
   else
     raise
   end
end
```

When you get a report that a user would like a new exception class created, then you can reanalyze the situation. At that point, you may want to create a subclass of the library generic `exception` class for that particular error, as well as change the particular exception raising location to use the new `exception` class, as shown in the following code:

```
module Foo
   class Error < StandardError
   end
```

```
class TransientError < Error
end

class BarError < Error
end


def foo(bar)
  unless allowed?(bar)
    raise BarError, "bad bar: #{bar.inspect}"
  end
end
end
```

The advantage of using the preceding approach for adding exception classes is that it is backward-compatible. The previous example, which rescues Foo:Error and checks e.message, still works. In the future, the user can switch to rescuing Foo::BarError, similar to this example:

```
begin
  foo(bar)
rescue Foo::BarError
  handle_bad_bar(bar)
end
```

The principle when designing exception class hierarchies is similar to the principle of designing class hierarchies in general, which is, to avoid exception class proliferation, and create only the exception classes necessary for users to appropriately handle exceptions raised by your library.

Using core exception classes

Note that in some cases, it may be permissible to use one of the built-in exception classes. For example, if you only want to accept a certain type of argument, you could raise TypeError if the passed argument is of the wrong type:

```
def baz(int)
  unless int.is_a?(Integer)
    raise(TypeError,
          "int should be an Integer, is #{int.class}")
  end
```

```
    int + 10
end
```

While this is an appropriate use of the `TypeError` exception class, it results in unidiomatic Ruby code. In general, idiomatic Ruby code avoids defensive programming based on types, because in Ruby, what matters is what methods the object responds to and the objects returned by those methods.

In Ruby, it shouldn't matter what actual class the object uses. Except in special cases, it's best to avoid this type of programming, and just use the object without explicitly checking its type. In this example, we pass the object directly as an argument to `Integer#+`:

```
def baz(int)
    10 + int
end
```

If Ruby needs to deal with the object internally, where the underlying type actually matters, `Integer#+` will raise `TypeError` if int is not comparable to an integer. You don't generally need to do such `TypeError` checks, because Ruby does it for you.

Summary

In this chapter, you've learned how best to handle errors in your Ruby code. You've learned about handling errors using return values, handling errors with exceptions, and the trade-offs between the two approaches.

You've learned how to retry in the case of transient errors when using both approaches, and you've also learned about more advanced techniques, such as exponential backoff and circuit breakers. You've also learned how to properly design exception class hierarchies. Proper error handling is one of the more important aspects of programming, and now you are better prepared to implement errors properly in your application.

In the next chapter, you'll shift gears a little and learn how code formatting can affect maintenance.

Questions

1. What is the main advantage of using return values to signal errors?
2. What is the main advantage of using exceptions to signal errors?
3. Why is it important not to retry transient errors immediately?
4. When is a good time to add a subclass of an existing exception class?

6
Formatting Code for Easy Reading

How to format code can be a divisive topic, especially in a language designed for programmers' happiness. In this chapter, you'll learn about different mindsets for code formatting, the advantages of consistency, the disadvantages of arbitrary limits, and the trade-offs of code formatting enforcement. You'll also learn about Ruby's built-in code formatting checker.

We will cover the following topics in this chapter:

- Recognizing different perspectives of code formatting
- Learning how syntactic consistency affects maintainability
- Understanding the consequences of using arbitrary limits
- Checking basic code formatting with Ruby
- Realizing the actual importance of code formatting

By the end of this chapter, you'll understand better whether to enforce code formatting when using Ruby, and how best to do so if you decide to.

Technical requirements

In this chapter and all chapters of this book, code given in code blocks is designed to execute on Ruby 3.0. Many of the code examples will work on earlier versions of Ruby, but not all. The code for this chapter is available online at `https://github.com/PacktPublishing/Polished-Ruby-Programming/tree/main/Chapter06`.

Recognizing different perspectives of code formatting

You've probably realized that not everyone thinks alike. Everyone is different, and has different opinions on how things should be. Programmers are no different, and in general, for any decently sized module, if you give two programmers the same specification, you will usually get quite different implementations. This isn't a problem or a weakness, it is a strength.

There are many different ways to do almost anything in programming. Some may be objectively better than others, and some objectively worse, but in many cases, given two different implementations of the same requirements, one will be better than the other in some ways, and worse than the other in other ways.

The differences in two different implementations of the same requirements will often vary at every level, from the higher-level design such as class architecture to the lower-level design, such as which expressions are used. For example, consider simple conditional expressions, where you only want to execute `bar` if `foo` is `true`. The most idiomatic way in Ruby to do this would probably be as follows:

```
bar if foo
```

However, for a programmer who comes from another language, these postfix conditionals may be jarring, and just backward from how they are used to thinking. It's fairly common in programming to want to think about the condition before the action that depends on the success of the condition, and for many programmers, the following approach matches their thinking much better:

```
if foo
  bar
end
```

These two approaches aren't even the only way this conditional can be written. Ruby's syntax in many ways is based on **Perl**'s syntax, and for former Perl programmers, there is another common approach to this conditional:

```
foo and bar
```

This approach may look strange if you haven't seen it before, but it is logically equivalent. It has the terseness of the postfix conditional approach, but it puts the condition before the action that depends on the condition, which in some programmers' minds is the best of both worlds.

There are many similar cases to the previous example. Let's say you want to return unless condition is true. The most idiomatic Ruby expression for this is probably the following:

```
return unless condition
```

However, if condition is a long expression, it's probably more common to avoid the postfix conditional:

```
unless condition
  return
end
```

For a programmer with a background in a language that lacks the equivalent of an unless conditional, it's very common to use if and manually invert the conditional:

```
if !condition
  return
end
```

There is also the approach commonly used by former Perl programmers:

```
condition or return
```

Each programmer is going to have their own view about which one of these approaches is best, and there are libraries where the same programmer will use all of these approaches in different cases. Semantically, all of these approaches do exactly the same thing, so which approach is used has no effect on the program itself; it only has an effect on the programmer who has to maintain the code.

Some programmers are comfortable and even prefer writing and reading a wide variety of styles when programming. For these programmers, Ruby's syntactic flexibility is wonderful, as the subtle differences between the different programming styles allow an almost poetic use of language. For these programmers, reading or writing a library where every single construct looks exactly the same is bland, and they dislike bland code the same as a food critic may dislike bland food. For simplicity, we'll refer to these programmers as poets.

However, other programmers are the exact opposite. They value consistency, and think that every code construct that does the same thing should look the same way. If they come across a code construct that works the same way but looks different, it can be jarring to them, and affect their own productivity. For these programmers, **syntactic inconsistency** is as problematic as **semantic inconsistency**, and should be avoided to the same degree. For simplicity, we'll refer to these programmers as philosophers.

Most programmers fall somewhere on a spectrum between the poet and philosopher. They probably have a preferred style that they use most of the time, but they can still deal with code written in a different style, even if it has a minor adverse effect on their own productivity.

In this section, you learned how different types of Ruby programmers view syntactic consistency. In the next section, you'll learn how syntactic consistency can affect maintainability, depending on the type of programmer working on the code.

Learning how syntactic consistency affects maintainability

In general, if a single programmer is maintaining the code, whether the code is syntactically consistent or not does not matter. All that matters is that the programmer who wrote the code can read it. In general, programmers tend to write code in a way that makes the most sense to them, even if it may not make the most sense to other programmers. If you are the sole maintainer of the code, you should write the way that feels most natural to you, because that is probably the most productive approach.

However, when multiple programmers are working on the same code, syntactic consistency may become more important, depending on where on the poet-philosopher spectrum each programmer working on the code is. If all of the programmers working on the code lean more toward the poet side of the spectrum, syntactic consistency may still not be important.

However, if a significant portion of the programmers working on the code lean more toward the philosopher side of the spectrum, then a lack of syntactic consistency may have a significant negative effect on their productivity, and therefore a significant negative effect on the productivity of the team overall.

In such cases, it is often a good idea to enforce syntactic consistency. Enforcing syntactic consistency can increase the performance of philosophers. The poets may find such code boring and not as fun to work on, and it is likely that enforcing syntactic consistency will affect their enjoyment of working on the code, but it is unlikely that enforcing syntactic consistency will harm their productivity, as they are, in general, able to read and write a wide variety of styles.

So, how do you know what types of programmers work on the team? One of the easiest ways to determine this is to look at previous code reviews. If during a review of the following code:

```
if !condition
  return
end
```

The programmer reviewing it requests changing it to the following:

```
return unless condition
```

Or if you have a spec guard such as the following:

```
it "foo should be true" do
  foo.must_equal true
end if RUBY_VERSION >= '3.0'
```

A different reviewer requests changing this to the following:

```
if RUBY_VERSION >= '3.0'
  it "foo should be true" do
    foo.must_equal true
  end
end
```

Then, you may have philosophers on the team, and enforcing syntactic consistency could increase productivity in part by decreasing time spent requesting syntax changes during code review.

Alternatively, if you are not enforcing syntactic consistency and your code reviews do not have many requests for syntax changes, there is probably not a significant advantage in enforcing syntactic consistency, because you are only likely to decrease the enjoyment of the poets working on the code.

It can be hard for the poet to understand the philosopher's mindset and vice versa. The poet generally doesn't have a problem reading diverse styles, and may have difficulty understanding why a philosopher would object to the diversity of style. The philosopher sees value in things that work the same way looking the same way, and sees syntactic consistency as increased simplicity, and diversity of style as unnecessary complexity. It is important to recognize that neither viewpoint can be objectively right or wrong; both are subjective preferences. What is important is to know where in general, on the poet-philosopher spectrum, the programming team maintaining the code lies, so you can choose whether or not to enforce syntactic consistency in the library.

Enforcing consistency with RuboCop

If you do want to enforce syntactic consistency in Ruby, the most common approach to doing so is to use the `rubocop` gem. **RuboCop** can operate both as a linter to alert you of a syntax that goes against the style you want to enforce in the library, and in some cases as a tool to automatically rewrite code from a syntax that goes against the enforced style to syntax in compliance with the enforced style.

RuboCop implements many checks, called cops, and most of the cops are enabled by default, even those not related to syntax. It can be tempting to use the RuboCop defaults, since it is otherwise daunting to go through every cop enabled by default and decide whether you want to enforce it. Thankfully, RuboCop has a solution for this, which is the configuration parameter, `AllCops:DisabledByDefault`. Using this configuration parameter, you can only enable the syntax checks that you believe will be helpful for your library.

One approach to trying to satisfy the philosophers on the team without undue irritation to the poets is to start with all of RuboCop's cops disabled, except those related to syntax issues that have previously been complained about during code review. Then, as future code reviews happen, if one of the philosophers complains about a new syntax issue that is available as a RuboCop cop, you can consider enabling that cop. Using this approach, you avoid many unnecessary syntax checks, and focus on only the syntax checks that your team finds beneficial.

In this section, you learned how syntactic consistency can affect maintainability, and how best to enforce consistency when using RuboCop. In the next section, you'll learn how enforcing arbitrary limits on your Ruby code usually results in worse code.

Understanding the consequences of using arbitrary limits

One major issue with RuboCop's default configuration is that it enables all of the cops related to metrics. By default, RuboCop complains about the following:

- Classes longer than 100 lines

- Modules longer than 100 lines

- Methods longer than 10 lines

- Blocks longer than 25 lines

- Blocks nested more than three times

- Methods with more than five parameters, including keyword parameters

Enforcing these limits will always result in worse code, not better code. In general, in this book, there are few principles stated as absolutes. This is one principle that is an absolute, so to restate it for emphasis—enforcing the previous arbitrary limits on your code will make the code worse, not better.

The argument against arbitrary limits is simple: if there was a better approach that was within the limit, it would have already been used. The argument for arbitrary limits is also simple: the programmer is too stupid, ignorant, or inexperienced to know what the best approach is, and an arbitrary limit can reduce the possible damage, by forcing the programmer to restructure their code. A simple counterargument to that is *if the programmer is too stupid, ignorant, or inexperienced to do things correctly within the limit, why do we trust them to split the code intelligently into smaller parts to get around the limit?*

If you have a class that is 300 lines, splitting the methods in it into four separate modules, each being around 75 lines, and including the four modules in the class is not an improvement *a priori*. That doesn't mean it is never an improvement. If you are able to combine related methods that implement a behavior into a single module that is usable in other classes, that may be a good reason to create a module. However, splitting up a class purely to avoid an arbitrary limit is always bad. Do not rearrange the deck chairs.

Take the following code as an example. This implements a XYZPoint class where we assume that xs, ys, and zs are methods that return arrays of integers. The all_combinations method yields each combination of elements from xs, ys, and zs and the given array:

```
class XYZPoint
  def all_combinations(array)
```

```
xs.each do |x|
  ys.each do |y|
    zs.each do |z|
      array.each do |val|
        yield x, y, z, val
      end
    end
  end
end
```

It does absolutely no good to avoid the maximum block limit by adding a private each_xy method to yield each x and y combination:

```
class XYZPoint
  private def each_xy
    xs.each do |x|
      ys.each do |y|
        yield x, y
      end
    end
  end
```

Then, you rewrite your all_combinations method to use it:

```
def all_combinations(array)
  each_xy do |x, y|
    zs.each do |z|
      array.each do |val|
        yield x, y, z, val
      end
    end
  end
end
```

Again, that doesn't mean that adding the `each_xy` method is bad. If there is another method using the same nested `xs.each` and `ys.each` approach, and the `each_xy` approach can be used to reduce overall complexity, which is a good reason to add an `each_xy` method. However, that's a good reason without an arbitrary limit. If you are only adding the `each_xy` method to satisfy the RuboCop block nesting cop, you are rearranging the deck chairs, and sacrificing performance and code locality for no benefit.

Let's say you have a method such as `CSV.new` in the standard library, which accepts one positional argument and over 20 keyword arguments to allow very flexible behavior. You can use this flexibility to parse many different types of files:

```
CSV.new(data,
        nil_value: "",
        strip: true,
        skip_lines: /foo/)
# or
CSV.new(data,
        col_sep: "\t",
        row_sep: "\0",
        quote_char: "|")
```

It does absolutely no good to switch to an API where a single `options` object is passed as an optional argument:

```
options = CSV::Options.new
options.nil_value = ""
options.strip = true
options.skip_lines = true
CSV.new(data, options)
# or
options = CSV::Options.new
options.col_sep = "\t"
options.row_sep = "\0"
options.quote_char = "|"
CSV.new(data, options)
```

One argument for the `options` object approach is that you can reuse the options in multiple calls:

```
options = CSV::Options.new
options.nil_value = ""
options.strip = true
options.skip_lines = true
csv1 = CSV.new(data1, options)
csv2 = CSV.new(data2, options)
```

However, you can already do this with the approach that `CSV.new` currently uses, without hurting the usability in the common case:

```
options = {nil_value: "", strip: true, skip_lines: /foo/}
csv1 = CSV.new(data1, **options)
csv2 = CSV.new(data2, **options)
```

Again, *is it necessarily a bad idea to use an* `options` *object as opposed to many keyword arguments?* No, it is not necessarily a bad idea.

However, it is always a bad idea to change from an API that uses many keyword arguments to an API that uses an `options` object for the sole purpose of satisfying RuboCop's arbitrary limits. As mentioned previously, RuboCop will warn by default when a method accepts more than five arguments, whether keyword or positional.

In short, don't assume that RuboCop knows better than you do and keep the default arbitrary limits. Use your judgment on what API makes sense for your library. Do not refactor a method to reduce the number of lines it contains because RuboCop complains about it. Only refactor it if you can identify shared code that is usable in other cases and makes sense on its own merits. Observe the following code and check whether you ever see a method with numbered private methods for the order in which they are called in another method:

```
def foo(arg)
  bar, baz = _foo_1(arg)
  val = _foo_2(bar)
  _foo_3(val, baz)
end
```

Then, there's a good bet it was to work around arbitrary method length limits, and is less readable, harder to maintain, and performs worse than the original definition of `foo`, which may have had 20 lines or more.

In this section, you learned the problems with enforcing arbitrary limits in your Ruby code. In the next section, you'll learn that Ruby comes with basic code format checking built-in, and how to use it.

Checking basic code formatting with Ruby

You may not have seen an example of it, but Ruby actually ships with a built-in syntax checker that will warn about syntax that is almost universally considered problematic. It can catch issues such as the following:

- Unused variables:

```
def a
  b = 1 # b not used
  2
end
```

- Unreachable code:

```
def a
  return
  2 # not reachable
end
```

- Mismatched and possibly misleading indentation:

```
if a
  if b
    p 3
end # misleading, appears to close "if a" instead of "if b"
end
```

- Unused literal expressions:

```
def a
  1 # unused literal value
  2
end
```

- Duplicated keyword arguments and hash keys:

```
a(b: 1, b: 2) # duplicate keyword argument
 {c: 3, c: 4} # duplicate hash key
```

- Using `meth *args` when `meth` is a local variable (which is parsed as `meth.*(args)` instead of `meth(*args)`)

- Using `if var = val` conditionals, where `val` is a static value such as a number or string (as `==` was probably intended)

- Using `a == b` expressions when the result is not used

- Use of `x > y > z` syntax (common for former **Python** programmers)

- Using regular expressions that have a `]` without a matching `[`

These are a large portion of actually useful syntax checks. Some are purely related to formatting, such as the mismatched indentation warning, but most exist to highlight code that has objective problems that should be fixed.

So, how do you use this built-in format checker? You combine two separate Ruby options. One option is `-w`, which turns on **verbose warnings**. Verbose warnings are not limited to syntax warnings (warnings emitted during Ruby program compilation, before the code is executed), but many other warnings as well, such as method redefinition warnings. However, by using the other option (`-c`), you will limit the warnings to syntax warnings. The `-c` option is used to turn on **syntax checking mode**.

By default, when you use `ruby -c file`, Ruby will parse `file` and either print the `Syntax OK` string to the standard output if it has valid syntax, or will print any syntax errors it encounters to the standard error output. However, when combining `-w` and `-c`, such as `ruby -wc file`, Ruby will parse the error and print syntax warnings to the standard error output, in addition to either printing `Syntax OK` to the standard output or syntax errors to the standard error output.

You can use `ruby -wc` even without a file. For small snippets of code, you can use `ruby -wce "ruby code here"`. For larger code snippets, you can run just `ruby -wc`, in which case Ruby will wait for code to be entered on standard input. You can either type the code in or paste the code. After typing or pasting the code in, you can either hit *Ctrl + D* on the keyboard or enter `__END__` on a line by itself to have Ruby stop parsing the code and exit. An alternative approach to setting the `-wc` option in each call to `ruby` is to use the `RUBYOPT` environment variable.

In this section, you learned how to use Ruby itself to check code formatting. In the next section, the final section in *Section 1* of the book, you'll gain some additional perspective on code formatting in Ruby.

Realizing the actual importance of code formatting

While code formatting is definitely part of programming, and can definitely affect how maintainable your code is; in most cases, the actual formatting of code matters far less than you would initially expect. Outside of egregious cases, you'll probably be able to read two different pieces of code formatted differently, and determine that they accomplish the same thing. On the flip side, there's definitely code that is difficult to understand regardless of how it is formatted.

Focus on the understandability of your code, not the formatting of your code. The main time you should worry about your code formatting is when it negatively impacts the understandability of your code. The other time is when you are formatting for artistic effect:

```
def      fed
( p      p )
p?a      a?p

q=  p q  =p
p %%.....%% q
dne      end
```

Since it is unlikely you are formatting for artistic effect, you should focus far more on the understandability of your code than on how your code is formatted.

Summary

In this chapter, you've learned that Ruby programmers are a diverse group, with different code formatting preferences. You've learned that some Ruby programmers place great value on syntactic consistency, whereas syntactic consistency leads to bland code in the eyes of other Ruby programmers.

Importantly, you've learned that enforcing arbitrary limits on your code style is always a bad idea. You've learned that Ruby comes with a built-in way to check for common syntactic and semantic problems that are considered objectively bad, and how to use it. Finally, you've learned that code formatting is ultimately one of the least important aspects of your programming, and is it much more important to focus on the understandability of your code. With all you've learned, you are now better able to make decisions regarding code formatting for your libraries and applications.

We'll now move to *Section 2* of the book, which focuses on higher-level programming principles. In the next chapter, you'll learn you'll learn important principles for designing libraries.

Questions

1. Do all Ruby programmers want to enforce syntactic consistency?

2. If you are using RuboCop to enforce syntactic consistency, what's one RuboCop configuration parameter you should definitely use?

3. Why does enforcing arbitrary limits usually result in worse code?

4. What Ruby command-line option allows you to check a file for common formatting issues?

5. When should you worry about code formatting?

Section 2: Ruby Library Programming Principles

The objective of this section is to have you learn about principles involved in maintaining larger bodies of code, such as designing libraries and applications.

This section comprises the following chapters:

7
Designing Your Library

Designing a useful library is hard work, requiring consideration of many important decisions. In this chapter, you'll learn how to design useful libraries by focusing on the user experience, deciding how large the library should be, and deciding whether to have fewer, more complex methods or simpler, more numerous methods.

In this chapter, we will cover the following topics:

- Focusing on the user experience
- Determining the appropriate size for your library
- Handling complexity trade-offs during method design

By the end of this chapter, you'll have a better understanding of the principles of a good Ruby library design.

Technical requirements

In this chapter and all chapters of this book, code given in code blocks is designed to execute on Ruby 3.0. Many of the code examples will work on earlier versions of Ruby, but not all. The code for this chapter is available online at `https://github.com/PacktPublishing/Polished-Ruby-Programming/tree/main/Chapter07`.

Focusing on the user experience

The most important aspect when designing a Ruby library is to understand how the user will be using it, and trying to simplify that usage as much as possible. Making your library easy to use actually starts even before the user uses the library. It starts when the user first hears about the library and wants to learn more about it. In order to learn about the library, the first thing they'll probably do is search for it using the library name.

Library naming

It may be unfortunate, but one of the most important aspects of your library is its name. Ideally, the name should be short and easy to pronounce and spell, not be used by any other Ruby library, and ideally not be used in other remotely popular technology. If your library name is long or difficult to spell, users may give up looking for it even before they try it.

If your library name is used by another Ruby library, you won't have any issues creating a repository, but when the time comes to publish your gem, you may not be able to use the gem name you want, in which case users will not be able to easily use it. Before deciding on a library name, always make sure to check `https://rubygems.org` and make sure that the gem name you want is available first.

If you forget to check `https://rubygems.org` first, and it turns out the gem name you want is already taken, it isn't a huge deal. However, you shouldn't announce a library until it is available in gem form for people to easily use. If there is a conflict, you just need to go through your library and rename it before you announce it. This process is tedious, but not difficult. In general, the process for renaming is easy to automate using search and replace. Make sure you check that the new gem name is available before renaming.

That also looks complex, but now you are feeling like there must be a pattern here. You decide to implement the final method, which based on the name is probably the most complex. Refer to the following code:

```
def first_n_matching_records_starting_at_offset(n, o)
  reset
  o.times{next_record}
  ary = []

  while record = next_record
    if yield record
      ary << record
      break if ary.length >= n
    end
  end

  ary
end
```

Well, you've figured it out now. It looks like all of the methods that deal with offsets are the same as the methods that don't deal with offsets, with the only difference being that the methods that deal with offsets use this code to skip all records until we reach the desired offset:

```
o.times{next_record}
```

In this section, you learned about implementing multiple methods that are less complex internally. In the next section, you'll learn about the alternative approach, implementing fewer methods that are more complex internally.

Fewer but more complex methods

Armed with this knowledge, you decide to combine methods:

```
def first_record(offset: 0)
  reset
  offset.times{next_record}
  next_record
end
```

You use a keyword argument `offset` for an optional offset. You can default the offset to 0, since performance isn't the primary concern, and it makes the code simpler. With this approach, the method for getting the first record or the record at offset O both use the same implementation. If for compatibility you still need the `record_at_offset` method, you can implement it by calling this method:

```
def record_at_offset(o)
  first_record(offset: o)
end
```

This keeps the API for the `record_at_offset` method the same as the initial implementation shown in the previous section, but internally uses the `offset` keyword argument to `first_record` to simplify the implementation.

Similarly, returning the first N records or the first N records starting at offset O looks mostly the same:

```
def first_n_records(n, offset: 0)
  reset
  offset.times{next_record}
  ary = []

  n.times do
    break unless record = next_record
    ary << record
  end

  ary
end
```

You can see how the other two methods will be combined. This leads to the following questions. First, as a library maintainer, *which implementation approach would you prefer to maintain?* Second, as a library user, *which interface would you prefer to use?* The answers to those questions can be different. Some programmers prefer the more explicit method names, while others prefer to use the same method name with different types of arguments. As you can see with the `record_at_offset` method calling the `first_record` method with the `offset` keyword argument, it's possible to give both users the interface they want, as long as you are comfortable maintaining the extra methods.

In terms of maintenance, there is a clear advantage in combining each method requiring an offset and method not allowing an offset into a method that accepts an optional offset. This is because one case is completely handled by the other, since the offset not allowed case is the same as providing an offset of 0. However, the next question becomes more interesting, which is *do you stop here?*

Consider the `first_n_records` and `first_n_matching_records` methods. We can ponder on whether it makes sense to combine them into a single method as shown here:

```
def first_n_records(n, offset: 0)
  reset
  offset.times{next_record}
  ary = []

  while record = next_record
    if !block_given? || yield(record)
      ary << record
      break if ary.length >= n
    end
  end

  ary
end
```

In this case, it looks like it may make sense to combine them, because the matching case is the same as the case where a matcher isn't provided, as that is the same as the matcher always being true.

Similarly, does it make sense to combine the two methods that return a single record, `first_record` and `first_matching_record`, into one method? It turns out you can apply exactly the same approach:

```
def first_record(offset: 0)
  reset
  offset.times{next_record}

  while record = next_record
    if !block_given? || yield(record)
      return record
    end
  end

  nil
end
```

This approach has a lot more code than the initial `first_record` approach, but since performance is not a primary concern, it doesn't matter. If this is a network service, the time spent calling `next_record` and `reset` will be way more than the time spent calling the other methods.

The final question is, now that you only have two methods instead of eight, *do you want to combine these two methods?* If you want to do that, you need to make sure that `first_record` or equivalent returns a single record or `nil`, and `first_n_records(1)` or equivalent returns an array with at most one record. Well, *what would that look like?* Something like this:

```
def first_n_records(number: (only_one = 1), offset: 0)
  reset
  offset.times{next_record}
  ary = []

  while record = next_record
    if !block_given? || yield(record)
      ary << record
      break if ary.length >= number
    end
  end
end
```

```
    only_one ? ary[0] : ary
end
```

This uses one of the awesome features of Ruby, which is that default argument values can be arbitrarily complex expressions and define their own local variables. If you call `first_n_records` with a number keyword argument, the `only_one` local variable will not be set, and you will always get an array. However, if you call `first_n_records` without a keyword argument, to get the value for the number keyword argument, it will evaluate the expression, which will set the `only_one` local variable to 1 in addition to setting the number keyword argument to 1. In the last line of the method, the `only_one` local variable being set to 1 will be treated as a `true` value by the ternary operator, so that the method will return the first element of the array instead of the array itself.

The only issue with the previous approach is that it looks odd to call `first_n_records` when you only need the first record, so you may want to consider adding a separate `first_record` method:

```
alias first_record first_n_records
```

This does allow you to call `first_record(number: 1)` and have it return an array, or `first_n_records` without arguments and have it return a single record. If either of those possibilities is problematic, you should probably rename `first_n_records` to a private method such as `_first_n_records`, and then implement wrapper methods:

```
def first_record(offset: 0, &block)
  _first_n_records(offset: offset, &block)
end
```

```
def first_n_records(number, offset: 0, &block)
  _first_n_records(number: number, offset: offset, &block)
end
```

This does require duplicating explicit keyword arguments, but considering the limited number of keyword arguments, that isn't a problem in this case. More advanced cases may want to use `**kwargs`:

```
def first_record(**kwargs, &block)
  kwargs.delete(:number)
  _first_n_records(**kwargs, &block)
end
```

```
def first_n_records(number, **kwargs, &block)
  kwargs[:number] = number
  _first_n_records(**kwargs, &block)
end
```

Looking back on the methods you've written, implementation-wise you could get away with a single method, `first_n_records`. However, because it looks weird to call `first_n_records` without arguments to get a single record instead of an array of records, you added an alias named `first_record`. However, there is another possible way to fix this, and that is to rename the `_first_n_records` method to `first`, so calls look like this:

```
first
first(number: 3)
first{|rec| rec.id == 10}
first(number: 9){|rec| rec.name == 'Ruby'}
first(offset: 7)
first(number: 3, offset: 1)
first(offset: 14){|rec| rec.id == 29}
first(number: 7, offset: 4){|rec| rec.name == 'Knight'}
```

The alternative approach would be to have the eight methods originally defined, each of which took mandatory arguments, and then internally call the `_first_n_records` method with the appropriate arguments. The only consideration here is that block arguments in Ruby are optional and not required by default. Calling `first_n_matching_records_starting_at_offset` without a block in the original case would result in an exception being raised (`LocalJumpError`). However, with the refactored implementation, just do as shown here:

```
def first_n_matching_records_starting_at_offset(n, o, &blk)
  _first_n_records(number: n, offset: o, &blk)
end
```

Then, calling `first_n_matching_records_starting_at_offset` without a block would now be valid and treated as a call to `first_n_records_starting_at_offset`. That may be what you want, but if it isn't and you want an exception to be raised, you have to raise it manually:

```ruby
def first_n_matching_records_starting_at_offset(n, o, &blk)
  raise ArgumentError, "block required" unless blk
  _first_n_records(number: n, offset: o, &blk)
end
```

In this section, you learned about complexity trade-offs when designing methods.

Summary

In this chapter, you've learned many principles of good library design. You've learned that you should focus on the user experience when designing your library. You've learned how to decide how large a library you want to design, and the trade-offs between defining many simpler methods compared to fewer, more complex methods.

In the next chapter, you'll learn about designing extensible libraries using plugin systems.

Questions

1. What should you focus on when first designing the library?

2. If you currently don't have a need for flexibility in your library, is it a good idea to increase the size of your library to add flexibility?

3. What is the main issue with having many similar methods with minor differences in behavior?

8
Designing for Extensibility

Most decent-sized libraries benefit from being designed upfront for extensibility. The larger the library, the more it benefits from extensible design. In this chapter, you'll learn how to make your libraries extensible, with a full discussion on implementing a plugin system to do so. You'll also learn how restricting mutability can result in more maintainable libraries that are easier to understand.

In this chapter, we will cover the following topics:

- Using Ruby's extensibility features
- Designing plugin systems
- Understanding globally frozen, locally mutable design

By the end of this chapter, you'll be close to an expert in plugin system design.

Technical requirements

In this chapter and all chapters of this book, code given in code blocks is designed to execute on Ruby 3.0. Many of the code examples will work on earlier versions of Ruby, but not all. The code for this chapter can be found here, `https://github.com/PacktPublishing/Polished-Ruby-Programming/tree/main/Chapter08`.

Using Ruby's extensibility features

One of the great aspects of Ruby is that even if you don't explicitly design your library for extensibility, the language itself offers ways to make the library extensible. Using the built-in language features directly makes it possible to extend a library, even if the library itself wasn't designed for extensibility.

Ruby has many ways to modify the behavior of objects. Other than the immediate objects, which we discussed in *Chapter 1, Getting the Most out of Core Classes*, and objects that are frozen and cannot be modified, all Ruby objects support extension by modifying the object's singleton class.

Commonly, libraries will define methods in classes. Let's say you are designing a Ruby library to manage books and users for physical libraries (those that lend out books such as this book). The physical library has many users, most of whom check out books on a regular basis. For each user, you want to track the books they have checked out, and for each book, you want to know to whom the book is checked out. We'll name this library `Libry`, since that is nice and short, and as of the time of writing, is not yet used:

```ruby
class Libry
  class User
    def initialize(id)
      @id = id
      @books = []
    end
    attr_accessor :books
  end

  class Book
    def initialize(name)
      @name = name
    end
    attr_accessor :checked_out_to
  end
end
```

In the previous example, you start with the basics for the library user, giving each user an ID and an array to track the books. For `books`, you want to track the name of the book.

When a user checks out a book, doing so updates the book to keep track of who has checked the book out, and it updates the list of books the user has checked out:

```ruby
class Libry
  class User
    def checkout(book)
      book.checked_out_to = self
      @books << book
    end
  end
end
```

Books are returned to the library via a mail slot. You implement book return, or check-in, using the following:

```ruby
class Libry
  class Book
    def checkin
      checked_out_to.books.delete(self)
      @checked_out_to = nil
    end
  end
end
```

When a book is checked in, it is removed from the list of books checked out to the user, and then the book is updated to show that it is not checked out to any user.

This is a fairly simple Ruby library design, with no features designed for extensibility. However, if you want to modify the behavior of a particular book, you can always just define a method on the Libry::Book instance as shown here:

```ruby
book = Libry::Book.new('name')

def book.checked_out_to=(user)
  def user.checkout(book)
    nil
  end

  nil
end
```

The `checked_out_to=` method internally creates a singleton class for the `book` instance and an instance method in the singleton class. Maybe this book is cursed and checking it out will curse the user who checks it out. `Libry` doesn't support cursing users yet, but you can have the curse make it so the user cannot check out another book.

Let's confirm that a user cannot check out a book after checking out a book that has been cursed:

```
user = Libry::User.new(1)
user.checkout(Libry::Book.new('x'))
user.checkout(book)
user.books.length
# => 2
```

In the preceding example, the user has checked out two books, and everything is working as expected. However, because the user checked out the cursed `book` instance, attempts to check out another book should fail. Let's try that:

```
user.checkout(Libry::Book.new('y'))
user.books.length
# => 2
```

The number of books the user has checked out has not increased, showing the user is now cursed.

This approach does work, and you can extend your library to support book and user cursing this way, but it's considered a bit of a code smell to manually define singleton methods on objects, at least if you are defining the same method on multiple objects. The more idiomatic approach in Ruby is to use modules, as shown here:

```
module Cursed
  module Book
    def checked_out_to=(user)
      user.extend(User)
      super
    end
  end

  module User
    def checkout(book)
      nil
```

```
      end
    end
  end
```

In the preceding code, we first design the `Cursed` module that just acts as a namespace, with `Cursed::Book` and `Cursed::User` modules nested underneath for modifying the behavior of `Libry::Book` and `Libry::User`.

Cursing a book is now as simple as extending the book with the `Cursed::Book` module. We can check that after a user checks out the cursed book, they can no longer check out any additional books, as follows:

```ruby
user = Libry::User.new(3)
user.checkout(Libry::Book.new('x'))

book = Libry::Book.new('name')
book.extend(Cursed::Book)
user.checkout(book)
user.books.length
# => 2

user.checkout(Libry::Book.new('y'))
user.books.length
# => 2
```

As you can see, Ruby offers the ability to easily extend classes and objects, even if the classes were not designed with extensibility in mind. However, *what if you design the classes with extensibility in mind? Can you make the extensibility easier?* The answer is yes, you can, and you'll learn how to do this in the next section on designing plugin systems.

Designing plugin systems

Having a defined plugin system for a library can be a huge advantage. Libraries that do not have a plugin system usually handle extensions to the library in an ad hoc manner that differs per extension. With a plugin system, extensions to the library operate in a uniform manner for each extension. This has the following advantages for everyone involved:

- The library creator can create the plugin system that works best for their library, allowing extensibility in the parts that should be extensible, and not allowing extensibility in parts that do not need to be extensible.

- The plugin creator can review the plugin system to determine how the library should be extended, such as which extension points exist. They probably also have many other examples of extensions to the library that they can review, which makes the process of building their plugin much easier.

- The library user knows how to use the plugin system for all of the library's extensions, they do not have to review the documentation for each extension in order to determine how to properly use the extension.

Probably the biggest advantage of designing a plugin system for a library is that the library itself can be built out of plugins. Only the core part of the library that is essential needs to be loaded by default. All other optional features can be built as optional plugins to the library that the library user can choose to load. This approach to building libraries has important advantages.

The first advantage is that in most cases, the core of the library turns out to be a small part of the library, and only loading that core by default makes things significantly simpler. For a new user using a monolithic library for the first time, even knowing where to focus in terms of using the library can be a daunting proposition. Documentation can definitely help in such cases, but there is simply so much more code available that the new user is often overwhelmed. A library based on a plugin system, even if the library itself is quite large, will generally have a small enough core that a new user can read through the core of the library within a few hours and have a good idea about how it works.

The second advantage is that, at least by default, libraries designed around plugin systems tend to be significantly faster. The startup time for libraries that only load the core of the library by default is often significantly faster than startup times for monolithic libraries. Large monolithic libraries can take seconds to load, whereas large libraries designed around plugin systems often load in fractions of a second. Additionally, it's not just startup times that are faster, but performance is often significantly improved. Very few users use more than a small portion of a large library. However, a large monolithic library has to have each feature assume that all other features may be in use and account for them. With a library designed around a plugin system, the core doesn't need to assume any plugins are in use and can be written to be as fast as possible. Features that may slow the core down can be implemented as separate plugins, each of which only overrides the part of the core that it needs in order to function.

That leads to the next advantage. By moving each separate feature into its own plugin, each user only has to load the plugins they need for their application, and doesn't have to pay the startup cost of loading any of the other plugins, or the runtime cost of the code related to the other plugins. This is a good basic principle of library design, which is to only make the user pay for the features they are using, and not make them pay for features they are not using.

Hopefully this section has persuaded you to consider designing a plugin system in a future library. In the next section, you'll learn how to design a plugin system that delivers these advantages.

Designing a basic plugin system

The first thing you need to decide when designing a plugin system is which objects in your library you would like to be extensible. In the previous example, we were managing a library with books (`Libry::Book`) and users (`Libry::User`). Let's redesign `Libry` to use a plugin system.

The first decision point when designing a plugin system is to decide whether you want to use an include-based or prepend-based plugin system. With an include-based plugin system, all methods are in modules that are included in the classes in the library, and the classes themselves are empty. With a prepend-based plugin system, methods are defined inside classes, and plugins contain modules that are prepended to the classes.

In general, an include-based plugin system is better. With an include-based system, a user of the library can add normal instance methods to the class and call `super` to get the default behavior. With a prepend-based system, methods a user defines directly in the class may have no effect, and that can be quite confusing to users. With a prepend-based system, users must prepend a module to the class with the method they want to define after they have already loaded all of the system plugins, or otherwise loading a plugin can override the user's custom methods. The rest of this section will focus on include-based plugin systems.

With an include-based plugin system, the basics of `Libry` may look something like this, with empty `Libry::Book` and `Libry::User` classes:

```
class Libry
  class Book; end
  class User; end
```

The core of the library will itself be a plugin. Usually, you will have a defined namespace for the plugins, and each plugin will be a module inside that module. So, we'll have a `Libry::Plugins` module to hold plugins, and the `Libry::Plugins::Core` module for the core plugin:

```
module Plugins
  module Core
```

In the case of `Libry`, we probably want to allow plugins to modify both `Libry::Book` and `Libry::User`. We'll put the methods for `Libry::Book` in a `BookMethods` module:

```ruby
module BookMethods
  attr_accessor :checked_out_to

  def initialize(name)
    @name = name
  end

  def checkin
    checked_out_to.books.delete(self)
    @checked_out_to = nil
  end
end
```

We'll put the methods for `Libry::User` in a `UserMethods` module:

```ruby
module UserMethods
  attr_accessor :books

  def initialize(id)
    @id = id
    @books = []
  end

  def checkout(book)
    book.checked_out_to = self
    @books << book
  end
end
  end
end
```

Now, all we need is a method that loads plugins to wire everything up. We'll add the
`Libry.plugin` method for this:

```
def self.plugin(mod)
  if defined?(mod::BookMethods)
    Book.include(mod::BookMethods)
  end
  if defined?(mod::UserMethods)
    User.include(mod::UserMethods)
  end
end
```

The `plugin` method will accept a plugin module and include the plugin's `BookMethods`
module in `Libry::Book` and the plugin's `UserMethods` module in `Libry::User`,
assuming the plugin defines those modules. Finally, you can load the core plugin into the
library, so that the core behavior is available by default:

```
  plugin(Plugins::Core)
end
```

Then, you can check that the plugin-based system works as you expect:

```
book = Libry::Book.new('b')
user = Libry::User.new 1
user.books.size
# => 0

user.checkout(book)
user.books.size
# => 1

book.checkin
user.books.size
# => 0
```

If you haven't worked with a plugin system before, it may look like this added complexity instead of removed complexity. If you only have a single plugin, that will always be the case. There is some cognitive overhead inherent in a plugin system, and in general, you should only implement a plugin system in cases where the benefit of the plugin system is worth the extra cognitive overhead. Most libraries are small enough not to need a plugin system, after all.

What's the advantage of this plugin system? Well, say you want to offer a book cursing feature, but most libraries don't need or want to support book cursing. You can design book cursing as a separate plugin:

```ruby
class Libry
  module Plugins
    module Cursing
      module BookMethods
        def curse!
          @cursed = true
        end

        def checked_out_to=(user)
          user.curse! if @cursed
          super
        end
      end
```

In the previous example, we added a `curse!` method that marks the book as cursed. We also overrode the `checked_out_to=` method to curse the user if the book is cursed.

For the user side of book cursing, if the `curse!` method is called on a user, they are cursed and no longer able to check out a book:

```ruby
      module UserMethods
        def curse!
          @cursed = true
        end

        def checkout(book)
          super unless @cursed
        end
      end
```

```
      end
    end
  end
```

Users of `Libry` that don't want to support book cursing wouldn't load this plugin. For users of `Libry` that want to support this plugin, they can load it:

```
Libry.plugin(Libry::Plugins::Cursing)
```

After loading the plugin, you can check whether book cursing works:

```
book = Libry::Book.new('a')
cursed_book = Libry::Book.new('b')
cursed_book.curse!
user = Libry::User.new 2

user.checkout(cursed_book)
user.books.size
# => 1

user.checkout(book)
user.books.size
# => 1
```

In the preceding code, after a user checks out a cursed book, we can see that the user cannot check out additional books.

The value proposition of the plugin system from the user perspective is high. With a single line of code:

```
Libry.plugin(Libry::Plugins::Cursing)
```

The user has loaded the feature. They don't need to worry about which modules need to be included in which objects. They just need to load the plugin with one line of code, and the plugin system takes care of the rest.

For the plugin author, the advantages are just as high. They don't need to monkey patch a class to alias and modify a method or prepend a module to a class and risk overriding the user's code. They can write regular instance methods as needed, just inside an appropriately named module. If they are overriding an existing method, they can call `super` to get the default behavior of the method. Alternatively, if they want to explicitly not allow the default behavior, as in the example of a cursed user attempting to check out a book, they can just avoid calling `super` in that case.

Handling changes to classes

The plugin system designed in the previous section works well, but it is simpler than one designed for production use. Thankfully, it doesn't take much additional work to build on the existing design and add all the features needed for a large library.

What if you want to add a plugin to keep track of all books or users? This isn't related to a particular `Libry::Book` or `Libry::User` instance, it's really a class-level concern. For tracking class-level information, you wouldn't want to include a module in `Libry::Book` and `Libry::User`, you would want to extend the `Libry::Book` and `Libry::User` classes with a module for that behavior.

Let's start by modifying the `Libry.plugin` method to support extending the classes with a module in addition to including a module in the classes. The start of the method remains the same. Then you add the support for extending the classes if the plugin includes the appropriately named modules:

```
class Libry
  def self.plugin(mod)
    # same as before

    if defined?(mod::BookClassMethods)
      Book.extend(mod::BookClassMethods)
    end
    if defined?(mod::UserClassMethods)
      User.extend(mod::UserClassMethods)
    end
  end
end
```

This checks whether the plugin module contains the `BookClassMethods` or `UserClassMethods` modules for defining class-level behavior, and if so, extends the appropriate classes.

That was pretty easy. It's almost the same code in both cases, just changing from `include` to `extend` and using a different module name. Next, you can add a plugin that will track created books and users, named `Tracking`. The good thing about this tracking support is that it is fairly generic, since you aren't tracking anything specific to books or users, just that they were created:

```ruby
module Libry::Plugins::Tracking
  module TrackingMethods
    attr_reader :tracked

    def new(*)
      obj = super
      (@tracked ||= []) << obj
      obj
    end
  end

  BookClassMethods = TrackingMethods
  UserClassMethods = TrackingMethods
end
```

This adds a `TrackingMethods` module to the `Tracking` plugin. It adds an attribute reader named `tracked` and overrides new to call `super`. It then takes the created instance and adds it to the array of tracked objects, initializing the `@tracked` instance variable to the empty array if it doesn't already exist. Then, it aliases the `TrackingMethods` module to `BookClassMethods` and `UserClassMethods`. This way, the `Libry.plugin` call will add this tracking support to books and users.

Then you can test that it works:

```ruby
Libry.plugin(Libry::Plugins::Tracking)

Libry::Book.new 'a'
Libry::Book.new 'b'
Libry::Book.tracked.size
```

```
# => 2
```

```
Libry::User.tracked.size
# NoMethodError
```

Well, that worked fine for books, but not users, as you can see that checking the number of tracked users raised `NoMethodError`. *Why is that?* This is because you hadn't created a user yet, so the tracking attribute for the `Libry::User` class hadn't been initialized to the empty array yet. You'll learn how to fix this issue in the next section.

Plugin modifications to classes

In order to fix the previous issue, the plugin system needs to be able to run code after the plugin modules have been loaded into the appropriate classes. One way to do that is to have the `Libry.plugin` method call a singleton method on the plugin module. Since this is used for running code after loading the plugin, you can call it `after_load`. You can first update the `Libry.plugin` method to support this:

```
class Libry
  def self.plugin(mod)
    # same as before
    mod.after_load if mod.respond_to?(:after_load)
  end
end
```

Then you can modify your `Tracking` plugin to support the `after_load` method, setting the instance variable in each class to the empty array:

```
module Libry::Plugins::Tracking
  def self.after_load
    [Libry::Book, Libry::User].each do |klass|
      klass.instance_exec{@tracked ||= []}
    end
  end
end
```

This makes the definition of the new method easier, since you can assume the @tracked instance variable is already set:

```
module TrackingMethods
  def new(*)
    obj = super
    @tracked << obj
    obj
  end
end
```

Then you can test that you get the correct results:

```
Libry.plugin(Libry::Plugins::Tracking)

Libry::Book.new 'a'
Libry::Book.new 'b'
Libry::Book.tracked.size
# => 2  # or 4

Libry::User.tracked.size
# => 0
```

Success! You get 0 as the size of the tracked users, instead of NoMethodError. You'll either get 2 or 4 for the books, depending on whether you were still in the same Ruby process as when you ran the previous example. This is because the after_load method did not override an existing array of tracked objects. You should always design your plugin after_load hook to be idempotent if possible.

Maybe after working on this, you find out your Cursing plugin is a hit, but now you have requests for an AutoCurse plugin that will automatically curse every newly created book after the plugin is loaded, and will curse all books currently possessed by the user when the user is cursed. The plugin itself seems easy enough to design:

```
module Libry::Plugins::AutoCurse
  module BookMethods
    def initialize(*)
      super
      curse!
```

```
      end
    end

    module UserMethods
      def curse!
        super
        books.each(&:curse!)
      end
    end
  end
```

In the previous example, you curse the book in `initialize`, since `initialize` is called for each newly created book. You can override the `curse!` method for users to call `super` for the default behavior, and then call `curse!` on each book they possess. Let's try using this plugin:

```
Libry.plugin(Libry::Plugins::AutoCurse)

Libry::Book.new('a')
# NoMethodError: undefined method `curse!'
```

Assuming you are running this as a process that didn't already load the `Cursing` plugin, you end up with `NoMethodError`, because when you create a book, it calls `curse!` on the book, but the `Cursing` plugin hasn't been loaded, so the `curse!` method is not defined on `Libry::Book`. Here you have a situation where the `AutoCurse` plugin depends on the `Cursing` plugin. *How do you fix this?* The best to fix it is to add support for plugin dependencies to the plugin system.

Supporting plugin dependencies

The best way to support plugin dependencies is to make sure the dependencies of the plugin are loaded before the plugin (loading the dependencies after the plugin will cause load order issues). One way for you to fix it is to modify the `Libry.plugin` method to support a `before_load` hook in addition to the `after_load` hook:

```
class Libry
  def self.plugin(mod)
    mod.before_load if mod.respond_to?(:before_load)
    # same as before
```

```
    end
  end
```

Then you can define a `before_load` method in your `AutoCurse` plugin:

```
module Libry::Plugins::AutoCurse
  def self.before_load
    Libry.plugin(Libry::Plugins::Cursing)
  end
end
```

Then you can test that cursing works correctly without explicitly loading the `Cursing` plugin before the `AutoCurse` plugin:

```
user = Libry::User.new 1
book = Libry::Book.new 'a'
user.checkout(book)

Libry.plugin(Libry::Plugins::AutoCurse)

user.curse!
```

This plugin system is getting closer to being production-ready! The next change that would be helpful is to make it easier for the user to load plugins.

Making plugin loading easier

As the plugin system is currently designed, to load a plugin, you have to manually load the plugin code, often by requiring a file, and then pass the plugin module object to the `Libry.plugin` method. In general, it's easier on users if they can just pass a symbol specifying the plugin to load and have the plugin system find the file containing the plugin, load the file, and then find the plugin module and use that.

Implementing the aforementioned is a multi-step process:

1. The first step is to offer a way to register plugins by symbol. This you can do using a hash constant, and a singleton method for registering plugins:

    ```
    class Libry
      PLUGINS = {}
    ```

```
    def self.register_plugin(symbol, mod)
      PLUGINS[symbol] = mod
    end
  end
```

2. The second step is registering plugins, which is usually done inside the definition of the plugin. To register a `Libry` plugin, such as `AutoCurse` or `Cursing`, the plugin needs to call `Libry.register_plugin` with the first argument being the symbol to use, and the second argument being the plugin module. For example, the `AutoCurse` plugin would have code similar to the one shown here (the `Cursing` and `Tracking` plugins would have something similar, using `:cursing` and `:tracking` as the symbol):

```
module Libry::Plugins::AutoCurse
  Libry.register_plugin(:auto_curse, self)
end
```

3. For the third step, you would store this plugin in a specific place under the Ruby library path. So, if the `lib` directory is in the Ruby load path, you would place the `Libry::Plugins::AutoCurse` module definition in `lib/libry/plugins/auto_curse.rb`.

4. The final step is modifying the `Libry.plugin` method to support a symbol being passed. If a symbol is passed instead of a module, the related file under `libry/plugins` in the Ruby library path is required. After requiring the file, the symbol is used to look into the `Libry::PLUGINS` hash to find the related module:

```
class Libry
  def self.plugin(mod)
    if mod.is_a?(Symbol)
      require "libry/plugins/#{mod}"
      mod = PLUGINS.fetch(mod)
    end

    # same as before
  end
end
```

After all of those previous steps, users of `Libry` can now load the `AutoCurse` plugin more easily:

```
Libry.plugin(:auto_curse)
```

Allowing loading of plugins using symbols makes things much easier on the user, since the user no longer needs to worry about loading the plugin file manually, and doesn't have to worry about passing the full plugin name to the `plugin` method.

So far, we've been assuming that our plugin system only deals with a single class, `Libry`. However, in many cases, it is helpful for plugin systems to deal with subclasses. We'll learn how to do that in the next section.

Handling subclasses in plugin systems

What if you want to make a subclass of `Libry`, *and want to be able to load plugins into the subclass, without affecting* `Libry` *itself?* Since plugins affect `Libry::Book` and `Libry::User`, you cannot do this currently. So, the first order of business is to make sure that subclasses of `Libry` use their own subclasses of `Libry::Book` and `Libry::User`. You can override the `Libry.inherited` method to implement that support:

```ruby
class Libry
  def self.inherited(subclass)
    subclass.const_set(:Book, Class.new(self::Book))
    subclass.const_set(:User, Class.new(self::User))
  end
end
```

Then you need to modify the `Libry.plugin` method to only modify constants under the receiver. The first part of the method focused on loading the plugin from the file system remains the same:

```ruby
class Libry
  def self.plugin(mod)
    if mod.is_a?(Symbol)
      require "libry/plugins/#{mod}"
      mod = PLUGINS.fetch(mod)
    end
```

The `before_load` method needs to be modified to accept the subclass loading the plugin as an argument:

```
mod.before_load(self) if mod.respond_to?(:before_load)
```

The references to the `Book` and `User` constants in the `plugin` method need to be qualified to the receiver of the method (`self`), instead of found using the normal constant lookup. This is important, because without the `self::` qualification, Ruby's constant lookup will always result in an unqualified reference to `Book` meaning `Libry::Book`, not the `Book` constant for the `Libry` subclass (there's a similar issue for `User`):

```
if defined?(mod::BookMethods)
  self::Book.include(mod::BookMethods)
end
if defined?(mod::UserMethods)
  self::User.include(mod::UserMethods)
end
```

Handling the plugin modules that extend the classes works similarly:

```
if defined?(mod::BookClassMethods)
  self::Book.extend(mod::BookClassMethods)
end
if defined?(mod::UserClassMethods)
  self::User.extend(mod::UserClassMethods)
end
```

The `after_load` method also needs to be modified to accept the subclass loading the plugin as an argument:

```
mod.after_load(self) if mod.respond_to?(:after_load)
  end
end
```

With this new approach, the `Tracking` plugin's `after_load` method would need to be modified to take the subclass as an argument and use the subclass to qualify constant references:

```
module Libry::Plugins::Tracking
  def self.after_load(libry)
    [libry::Book, libry::User].each do |klass|
      klass.instance_exec{@tracked ||= []}
    end
  end
end
```

The `Tracking` plugin also needs to make sure that it handles class instance variables for subclasses. Options here are either copying the values from the parent class into the subclass or setting initialized values in the subclass:

```
module TrackingMethods
  def inherited(subclass)
    subclass.instance_variable_set(:@tracked, [])
  end
end
end
```

As shown in the previous example, it's probably best for subclasses to have their own list of tracked books, so you can set the list of tracked objects to the empty array.

You also need to modify the `before_load` method in the `AutoCurse` plugin to take the subclass, and only load the `Cursing` plugin into that subclass:

```
module Libry::Plugins::AutoCurse
  def self.before_load(libry)
    libry.plugin(:cursing)
  end
end
```

You can now test that loading the plugin into a subclass works:

```
libry = Class.new(Libry)

user = libry::User.new 1
book = libry::Book.new 'a'
user.checkout(book)

libry.plugin(:auto_curse)

user.curse!
```

You can also test that this doesn't affect the superclass:

```
user = Libry::User.new 1
user.respond_to?(:curse!)
# => false
```

We have almost completed the design of the plugin system. One final useful feature for the plugin system is to allow for configuration.

Configuring plugins

While some plugins do not require any configuration, many plugins need to be configured with user-specific values in order to be useful. The easiest way to allow for plugin configuration is to allow the user to pass arguments when loading the plugin. For example, maybe you want to allow the Tracking plugin to accept a block that is yielded each tracked object. You could use this to automatically check out a book to each user when the user is created.

To implement this feature, you can have the Libry.plugin method accept arguments and pass them to the before_load and after_load methods:

```
class Libry
  def self.plugin(mod, ...)
    # plugin loading code

    if mod.respond_to?(:before_load)
      mod.before_load(self, ...)
    end
```

```
    # include/extend code

    if mod.respond_to?(:after_load)
      mod.after_load(self, ...)
    end
    nil
  end
end
```

In your Tracking plugin, you can update the after_load method to save a passed block:

```
module Libry::Plugins::Tracking
  def self.after_load(libry, &block)
    [libry::Book, libry::User].each do |klass|
      klass.instance_exec do
        @tracked ||= []
        @callback = block
      end
    end
  end
end
```

You'll also want to set the callback when subclassing Book and User:

```
module TrackingMethods
  def inherited(subclass)
    callback = @callback
    subclass.instance_exec do
      @tracked = []
      @callback = callback
    end
  end
```

Additionally, you'll want to make sure that the class `new` method calls the block used when loading the plugin, if a block was passed when loading the plugin:

```
    def new(*)
      obj = super
      @tracked << obj
      @callback&.(obj)
      obj
    end
  end
end
```

Now you can use this feature to automatically check out a book to users that you know they will cherish forever:

```
book = Libry::Book.new('Polished Ruby Programming')
Libry.plugin(:tracking) do |obj|
  if obj.is_a?(Libry::User)
    obj.checkout(book)
  end
end
```

After loading the plugin with this block, you can test to see whether it works. Only at the end here does it look like it would have been useful to add `attr_reader` for the book's name:

```
user = Libry::User.new 1
user.books.map do |book|
  book.instance_variable_get(:@name)
end
# => ["Polished Ruby Programming"]
```

In this section, you learned all about designing useful plugin systems for libraries. In the next section, you'll learn about globally frozen, locally mutable design, and how to achieve it in Ruby.

Understanding globally frozen, locally mutable design

You learned in *Chapter 3*, *Proper Variable Usage*, about the benefits of frozen objects with an unfrozen internal cache. It is usually a good idea to freeze an object you do not plan to modify. This principle extends not just to regular objects, but to classes and modules as well.

In general, when you first load a library, you don't want it to be frozen, because then you cannot modify it. When Ruby starts up, it doesn't have any frozen classes; it allows the programmer to modify every class. This flexibility is very important during application setup. During application setup, before you start accepting user input, you generally want to have complete control to modify any part of the program.

However, in general, after application setup, this flexibility is unnecessary and can be actively harmful. In most cases, you don't want the classes or modules in your application to be modified at runtime. Modifying instances of those classes may be fine if the class does not use frozen instances, but you generally don't want your application code adding or removing methods from classes at runtime, except possibly to define singleton methods on instances.

As a user of a library, it's a good idea to freeze classes after you have completed the setup. Using the `Libry` example from the previous section, that could be as simple as freezing after setup:

```
class MyLibry < Libry
  # application setup/plugin loading
  plugin(:tracking)

  Book.freeze
  User.freeze
  freeze
end
```

However, for libraries that are not prepared for this, doing so can break the library. If you want your library to be compatible with globally frozen, locally mutable design, you need to analyze all of the classes in your library and see how they should handle `freeze`. If the class doesn't have any constants or instance variables, it probably doesn't need changes. However, for every constant and instance variable, you need to analyze how it should be handled if the class is frozen.

This also extends to plugins that add instance variables to the class, such as the `Tracking` plugin. The `Tracking` plugin adds `@tracked` and `@callback` instance variables to the related `MyLibry::Book` or `MyLibry::User` constants. In this case, `@tracked` is an array of all instances created. If you freeze the `@tracked` array, you will no longer be able to create new instances of `MyLibry::Book` or `MyLibry::User`. That's probably not what you want, so you probably shouldn't freeze it. `@callback` is either `nil` or a `Proc` instance, and in either case, it's already immutable, so it doesn't need to be frozen either. After performing the analysis, it looks like the `Tracking` plugin doesn't need changes after all. That's good.

However, there may be good reasons to freeze a `MyLibry::Book` or `MyLibry::User` instance, but freezing those instances does not work correctly. This is because a frozen user can still check out a book:

```
user = MyLibry::User.new(1)
user.freeze
user.checkout(MyLibry::Book.new('b'))
```

That should probably fail because it modifies the books the user has checked out. Make sure to define `freeze` methods appropriately in your classes, and if you are building plugins and the plugins add instance variables, they should probably also define a `freeze` method to handle the instance variables appropriately, then call `super` to get the default behavior.

This issue doesn't just affect your library classes, it also potentially affects any class or module in Ruby. Let's say you are using a library that uses `autoload`:

```
class Foo
  autoload :Object, 'foo/object'
end
```

None of your code references `Foo::Object`, except this rarely used case in an error condition, which unfortunately you don't have covering tests for. Also, unfortunately, `Foo::Object` is itself not tested well by the library author, because almost nobody uses it. The `foo/object.rb` file it loads looks like this:

```
Foo.class_eval do
  class Object
    def initialize(object)
      @object = object
    end
```

```
    def method_missing(meth, ...)
        @object.send(:run, meth, ...)
    end

    def respond_to_missing?(meth)
        true
    end
  end
end
```

Unfortunately, when `Foo::Object` is referenced, the autoload triggers, `foo/object.rb` is loaded, a few warnings are printed, and then everything stops. The intent of the code was to define a `Foo::Object` class, but because `Foo.class_eval` doesn't change the current module nesting, the `class Object` definition inside modifies the `::Object` class. Modifying `Object#initialize`, `Object#method_missing`, or `Object#respond_to_missing` can cause an infinite loop, which is why everything stops.

One approach to handling this case is to freeze all core classes. That way, if someone makes a mistake like this during application runtime, `FrozenError` will be raised, which is certainly better than an infinite loop. You can do this manually:

```
Object.freeze
Kernel.freeze
# ...
```

However, there are a lot of core classes and modules (over 300), at least if you are using Rubygems, so this approach is probably not desired. Thankfully, there is a gem named `refrigerator` that handles freezing all core classes, and you can use that:

```
require 'refrigerator'
Refrigerator.freeze_core
```

Using `refrigerator` in your application may be difficult if you are using libraries that modify the core classes at runtime. Thankfully, `refrigerator` has support for skipping those core classes, assuming you really do need to modify them.

Using globally frozen, locally mutable design can improve the robustness of your library, especially in cases where your library will be used by multiple threads in the same process.

Summary

In this chapter, you've learned how to design libraries for extensibility, and you are probably close to an expert on plugin system design. You've also learned about globally frozen, locally mutable design, and how to properly freeze your libraries and runtime environment. With your knowledge of these topics, you are now much better able to design flexible and robust libraries.

In the next chapter, you'll learn about metaprogramming, and when an appropriate time to use it is.

Questions

1. What is the idiomatic way to add behavior to an individual object in Ruby?

2. If you have a medium or large library, what's the advantage of designing a plugin system for it?

3. What is the advantage of freezing the core classes when running a Ruby application?

9
Metaprogramming and When to Use It

Ruby has powerful metaprogramming capabilities, which is a double-edged sword. In the hands of a principled programmer, metaprogramming capabilities result in simpler, less verbose code. However, when misused, metaprogramming can result in code that is difficult to work with and hard to debug.

In this chapter, you'll learn about principles of responsible metaprogramming, so you can put metaprogramming to appropriate use in your libraries.

We will cover the following topics:

- Learning the pros and cons of abstraction
- Eliminating redundancy
- Understanding different ways of metaprogramming methods
- Using `method_missing` judiciously

By the end of this chapter, you'll have a better understanding of Ruby metaprogramming and how best to take advantage of it.

Technical requirements

In this chapter and all chapters of this book, code given in code blocks is designed to execute on Ruby 3.0. Many of the code examples will work on earlier versions of Ruby, but not all. The code for this chapter is available online at `https://github.com/PacktPublishing/Polished-Ruby-Programming/tree/main/Chapter09`.

Learning the pros and cons of abstraction

Unlike in many other programming languages, metaprogramming in Ruby isn't that much different than regular programming. Many other programming languages implement metaprogramming with a preprocessor before compilation or a macro processor during compilation, and there are things you can do in the metaprogramming environment that you cannot do in the runtime environment and vice versa. Thankfully, Ruby has no such restrictions on its metaprogramming. You use the same syntax for metaprogramming that you use for regular programming, and you can do metaprogramming at any time.

The main difference between programming and metaprogramming in Ruby is conceptual. Conceptually in Ruby, metaprogramming operates at a higher realm of abstraction than regular programming. If regular programming in Ruby uses classes to create objects and modify the data in those objects, metaprogramming in Ruby creates new classes and modifies the methods in those classes. Looking at metaprogramming this way, you could say that simply defining a class or a method is metaprogramming. Refer to the following code:

```
class A
  def b
    nil
  end
end
```

However, normal class definition is not really thought of as metaprogramming, even though it is equivalent to something like the following, which would generally be considered metaprogramming:

```
def_class = ->(sym, method_hash) do
  c = Object.const_set(sym, Class.new)
  method_hash.each do |meth, val|
    c.define_method(meth){val}
  end
end


def_class.call(:A, b: nil)
```

So why is a normal class definition not considering metaprogramming, when the equivalent approach using `Class.new`, `const_set`, and `define_method` is considered metaprogramming? The main difference between the two cases is that one is a concrete approach and one is an abstract approach. With a normal class definition, inside the class, you know exactly what class you are dealing with, and inside the method, you know what method you are defining. With the `def_class` approach, inside the lambda, you do not know what class is being defined, since that depends on the arguments. You don't know what methods you are defining.

In the example, `method_hash` is a hash, but it could be any object that responds to `each`, and that could involve reading a file, or a network call, or getting input from the user.

Abstraction has both advantages and disadvantages. Consider a class definition such as the following:

```
class MetaStruct
  def self.method_missing(meth, arg=nil, &block)
    block ||= proc{arg}
    define_method(meth, &block)
  end
end
```

This use of `method_missing` can make defining simple methods less verbose, shown as follows:

```
class A < MetaStruct
  b
  foo 1
  bar{3.times.map{foo}}
end

A.new.b
# => nil

A.new.foo
# => 1

A.new.bar
# => [1, 1, 1]
```

This programing does **DRY** (short for **Don't Repeat Yourself**) up the method definitions, but at what cost? Calling a method on the class that the class does not respond to now results in a method being defined instead of `NoMethodError` being raised, which is almost assuredly going to be the source of confusing bugs. This is an abstraction, but it's an abstraction that adds negative value to your code.

While there are negative uses of abstractions, there are many positive uses of abstractions. For example, if you want to write a method caching abstraction, you could have a module named `Memomer` that prepends a module to a class that extends `Memomer`, and keeps track of that module. Refer to the following code:

```
module Memomer
  def self.extended(klass)
    mod = Module.new
    klass.prepend(mod)
    klass.instance_variable_set(:@memomer_mod, mod)
  end
```

The module can have a memoize method that will define a method in the module that is prepended to the class. The memoize method will see whether a cached value is already set, and return it if so. If not, it will call super to get the value, and cache it, as shown in the following code block:

```
def memoize(arg)
    iv = :"@memomer_#{arg}"
    @memomer_mod.define_method(arg) do
        if instance_variable_defined?(iv)
            return instance_variable_get(iv)
        end
        v = super()
        instance_variable_set(iv, v)
        v
    end
  end
end
```

You can also use this with your previous class of A, as follows:

```
class A < MetaStruct
    extend Memomer
    memoize :bar
end
```

This will cache calls to bar, even if the definition of foo changes:

```
a = A.new
a.bar
# => [1, 1, 1]

A.foo 2

A.new.bar
# => [2, 2, 2]

a.bar
# => [1, 1, 1]
```

As you can see, there are both good and bad uses of abstraction, and you can use both in the same class. The goal is to be able to see the difference between two cases, and in the real world, the difference may not be as obvious.

In this section, you learned about the pros and cons of implementing abstractions in your Ruby programs using metaprogramming. In the next section, you'll learn about one of the best reasons to use metaprogramming in Ruby, which is to eliminate redundant code.

Eliminating redundancy

One of the best reasons to use metaprogramming is to eliminate redundancy. No Ruby programmer wants to write the same or similar code over and over, after all, unless they are getting paid by the line. Imagine programming in Ruby without `attr_accessor`, as shown in the following example:

```ruby
class Foo
  def bar
    @bar
  end

  def bar=(v)
    @bar = v
  end

  def baz
    @baz
  end

  def baz=(v)
    @baz = v
  end
end
```

It would definitely suck to have to define accessor methods this verbosely. It's hard to believe, but there are programming languages where you still have to do that, even some that were originally released after Ruby. Ruby realizes that no programmer likes that sort of repetitive coding, and being designed around programmer happiness, Ruby includes `attr_accessor` and similar methods so you can just do the following:

```ruby
class Foo
  attr_accessor :bar, :baz
end
```

Pretty much anytime you see yourself writing repetitive methods, see whether there is a way you can eliminate the redundancy via metaprogramming. For example, imagine you were storing data in an internal hash like this:

```ruby
class FooStruct
  def initialize(**kwargs)
    @values = kwargs
  end
```

And you wanted to write accessors that read and write common data to the hash:

```ruby
  def bar
    @values[:bar]
  end

  def bar=(v)
    @values[:bar] = v
  end

  def baz
    @values[:baz]
  end

  def baz=(v)
    @values[:baz] = v
  end
end
```

Since all of these accessor methods are the same, try to metaprogram them. If this is the only place you are using methods like this in your library or application, it's best to metaprogram directly in the class to avoid unnecessary indirection and keep the definitions local to the class (keeping the same `initialize` method as defined previously):

```ruby
class FooStruct
  %i[bar baz].each do |field|
    define_method(field) do
      @values[field]
    end

    define_method(:"#{field}=") do |v|
      @values[field] = v
    end
  end
end
```

You can then test that this works correctly, as follows:

```ruby
foo = FooStruct.new
foo.bar = 1
foo.baz = 2

foo.bar
# => 1

foo.baz
# => 2
```

However, if you plan on needing methods like these in multiple classes, it's best to move the metaprogramming code into a module. Maybe different classes need different instance variables, so you need to accept the instance variable to use as an argument:

```ruby
module HashAccessor
  def hash_accessor(iv, *fields)
    fields.each do |field|
      define_method(field) do
        instance_variable_get(iv)[field]
```

```
        end

        define_method(:"#{field}=") do |v|
          instance_variable_get(iv)[field] = v
        end
      end
    end
  end
end
```

Then you can extend your class with the module, and then define the methods similarly to how attr_accessor works (again, using the initialize method for FooStruct given previously):

```
class FooStruct
  extend HashAccessor
  hash_accessor :@values, :bar, :baz
end
```

You can then test that this works correctly:

```
foo = FooStruct.new
foo.bar = 1
foo.baz = 2

foo.bar
# => 1

foo.baz
# => 2
```

The advantage of extracting this feature is that you can use it in multiple places. Let's say you are writing a Bar class that keeps its data in a class instance variable, as follows:

```
class Bar
  @options = {:foo=>1, :baz=>2}
end
```

Let's say you want to add class-level accessors for `Bar`, so that you can change the values of the `:foo` and `:baz` options. Can you use your `HashAccessor` module to do that? Yes, you can. However, if you use the same approach as you did for `FooStruct`, it won't work correctly. Refer to the following code:

```
class Bar
  extend HashAccessor
  hash_accessor :@options, :foo, :baz
end

Bar.foo
# NoMethodError
```

This is because `hash_accessor` defines instance methods in the receiver. In this case, you don't want to define instance methods in `Bar`, you want to define methods you can call on `Bar` itself (class/singleton methods). Therefore, you need to operate on the singleton class of `Bar`:

```
class Bar
  singleton_class.extend HashAccessor
  singleton_class.hash_accessor :@options, :foo, :baz
end
```

Then you can test that this works:

```
Bar.foo = 1
Bar.baz = 2

Bar.foo
# => 1

Bar.baz
# => 2
```

The most interesting part here is how this line of metaprogramming works:

```
Bar.singleton_class.extend HashAccessor
```

If you remember that `extend` is shorthand for `singleton_class.include`, what this code is actually doing is the following:

```
Bar.singleton_class.singleton_class.include HashAccessor
```

This code includes a module in the `singleton` class of the singleton class of `Bar`, so that it can use metaprogramming in the singleton class of `Bar` in order to define methods you can call on `Bar` itself. This is one of the only cases where you need singleton classes of singleton classes, but Ruby will support as many levels of singleton classes as you need for your metaprogramming.

In this section, you learned about eliminating redundant code using metaprogramming. In the next section, you'll learn how there are different approaches to metaprogramming methods in Ruby, and the trade-offs of each approach.

Understanding different ways of metaprogramming methods

There are two separate approaches to metaprogramming in Ruby. The two separate approaches each have advantages and disadvantages, so the most appropriate one to use depends on the specific situation.

So far in this chapter, you've seen examples of using `define_method`, which is one of the methods used in **block-based metaprogramming**. There are other block-based metaprogramming methods, such as `Class.new`, `Module.new`, and `Kernel#define_singleton_method`:

```
Class.new do
  # class-level block metaprogramming
end

Module.new do
  # module-level block metaprogramming
end

define_singleton_method(:method) do
  # singleton-method defining block metaprogramming
end
```

Summary

In this chapter, you learned about metaprogramming and when to use it. You learned about the pros and cons of abstraction, and how to use metaprogramming to eliminate redundancy. You learned about the block-based and `eval`-based approaches to metaprogramming, and when to use each. You also learned about the trade-offs involved in deciding whether to use `method_missing` or `define_method`.

In the next chapter, you'll use this metaprogramming knowledge to design useful domain-specific languages.

Questions

1. When is it a bad idea to implement an abstraction via metaprogramming?

2. What is the most common reason to deal with singleton classes of singleton classes?

3. When should you use `eval`-based metaprogramming instead of block-based metaprogramming?

4. When should you use `method_missing`?

10
Designing Useful Domain-Specific Languages

Ruby makes it easy to implement **domain-specific languages** (**DSLs**), and many popular libraries offer DSLs to improve their usability.

In this chapter, you'll learn how to design and implement a DSL, which problems are handled well by DSLs, and both the advantages and disadvantages of using DSLs in your libraries.

We will cover the following topics:

- Designing your DSL
- Implementing your DSL
- Learning when to use a DSL

By the end of the chapter, you'll have a better understanding of not only how to design a DSL, but why it may or may not be a good idea to do so.

Technical requirements

In this chapter and all chapters of this book, code given in code blocks is designed to be executed on Ruby 3.0. Many of the code examples will work on earlier versions of Ruby, but not all. The code for this chapter is available online at `https://github.com/PacktPublishing/Polished-Ruby-Programming/tree/main/Chapter10`.

Designing your DSL

The most important thing to think about when designing a DSL is to focus on how the DSL will be used. Some DSLs are designed to configure a library. Some DSLs are used for making specific changes using the library. Some DSLs exist purely to reduce the verbosity of the code. Sometimes the library exposes a DSL as its only interface, and the library and DSL are basically the same thing. Let's focus first on DSLs designed for configuring a library.

Configuration DSLs

DSLs designed to configure libraries are often referred to as **configuration DSLs**. They are often initiated from a singleton method on the library's main module or class, often straightforwardly named `configure`. RSpec, a popular Ruby library for testing, uses a configuration DSL like this:

```ruby
RSpec.configure do |c|
  c.drb = true
  c.drb_port = 24601

  c.around do |spec|
    DB.transaction(rollback: :always, &spec)
  end
end
```

RSpec uses this DSL to configure itself. It passes in a configuration object, and you call methods on the configuration object to configure the library, in this case setting it to use drb (short for **distributed Ruby**, a standard library) on port 24601. It also calls the around configuration method with a block, which is yielded a proc (named spec in this example), which is passed as a block to DB.transaction for wrapping the entire test case in a database transaction that is always rolled back.

This type of configuration DSL is very helpful for users because it gives the user a single place to look for configuring the library. This is instead of the user looking through all of the RSpec documentation to determine how to configure settings such as the following:

```
RSpec::Core::DRbRunner.new(port: 24601)
```

```
RSpec::Core::Hooks.register(:prepend, :around) do |spec|
  DB.transaction(rollback: :always, &spec)
end
```

The user now has a single place they can look—the configuration DSL documentation—to determine all of the supported ways to configure the libraries. This makes configuration much easier. If your library has significant configuration options, strongly consider adding a configuration DSL for it. You don't necessarily have to use a separate method that takes a block.

For many libraries, the DSL can be as simple as singleton methods you can call on the library's main module. For example, if RSpec used this approach, a possible configuration DSL would be the following:

```
module RSpec
  self.drb = true
  self.drb_port = 24601

  around do |spec|
    DB.transaction(rollback: :always, &spec)
  end
end
```

This simpler approach has some disadvantages compared to the block-based approach, though. First, you need to know whether RSpec is a module or class because using module RSpec when RSpec is a class will result in a TypeError exception being raised. Second, writer methods (methods ending in =) are more awkward to call with this approach since they require an explicit self.

Suppose that you forget the explicit self, and you do the following:

```
module RSpec
  drb = true
  drb_port = 24601
end
```

Then you end up defining unused local variables, and this has no effect on the library. The general principle here is to avoid writer methods in cases where you will naturally call them on `self`. In these cases, it may be better to offer aliases such as `set_drb` and `set_drb_port`:

```
module RSpec
    set_drb true
    set_drb_port 24601
end
```

An alternative to this is having multipurpose `drb` and `drb_port` methods, which when called without arguments act as reader methods, but when called with one argument act as writer methods. Refer to the following code block:

```
module RSpec
    drb true        # Set the value
    drb_port 24601 # Set the value
end
RSpec.drb
# => true
RSpec.drb_port
# => 24601
```

Any of these approaches for configuration will work fine, the important principle is to make sure that you have a simple and well-documented way to configure your library, assuming your library is complex enough to require configuration.

In this section, you learned about DSLs for configuring a library, using a real-world example from `RSpec`. In the next section, you'll learn about DSLs for making complex changes using a library.

DSLs for making specific changes

For libraries that need to make complex changes atomically, there are three common approaches. The first is passing arrays or hashes or some nesting of the arrays or hashes to a single method, often with keyword arguments to influence the command. Refer to the following code:

```
Foo.process_bars(
    [:bar1, :baz2, 3, {quux: 1}],
    [:bar2, :baz4, 5],
```

```
  # ...
  skip_check: ->(bar){bar.number == 5},
  generate_names: true
)
```

This type of API is often hard for users to use. Manually making sure each of the arrays or hashes being passed in is the right format can be challenging by itself. It's best to avoid defining methods that require users to pass many complex objects if you can, as such methods are more difficult for users to use correctly.

Another approach is creating objects and individually attaching them to a command object, which is passed in. You often see this pattern in less powerful and expressive languages, where objects are explicitly instantiated and then passed to methods:

```
bar1 = Bar.new(:bar1, :baz2, 3, quux: 1)
bar2 = Bar.new(:bar2, :baz4, 5)

command = ProcessBarCommand.new
command.add_bar(bar1)
command.add_bar(bar2)
# ...
command.skip_check{|bar| bar.number == 5}
command.generate_names = true

Foo.process_bars(command)
```

This approach is better than the previous approach in most cases, as it is easier for users to use. However, it is a bit verbose, and not idiomatic Ruby. For this type of command, an idiomatic approach in Ruby would be to use a DSL inside a block, such as the following code:

```
Foo.process_bars do |c|
  c.bar(:bar1, :baz2, 3, quux: 1)
  c.bar(:bar2, :baz4, 5)
  # ...
  c.skip_check{|bar| bar.number == 5}
  c.generate_names = true
end
```

This retains the benefits of the command object approach but decreases the verbosity. Unlike the command object approach, it contains the logic for the command processing inside the block, which is an important conceptual difference. It also makes things easier for the user, as the user doesn't need to reference other constants manually, they just need to call methods on the yielded object.

Note that there are cases when the command object approach is probably better, and that is when you are passing the object to multiple separate methods. While you can pass blocks to methods using the & operator, it's probably not a good general approach, because the block will get evaluated separately by each method. With the command object approach, the command can be self-contained and you do not need to recreate the command every time you are calling a method. When using the command object approach, it is often a good idea for the command object initializer to use a DSL, shown as follows:

```ruby
command = ProcessBarCommand.new do |c|
  c.bar(:bar1, :baz2, 3, quux: 1)
  c.bar(:bar2, :baz4, 5)
  # ...
  c.skip_check{|bar| bar.number == 5}
  c.generate_names = true
end

Foo.process_bars(command)
```

With some extra work, you can have your library support the same configuration block both directly passed to `Foo.process_bars` and when using the command object approach with `ProcessBarCommand.new`. This gives you the best of both worlds. You'll learn how to implement this technique in a later section.

In this section, you learned about DSLs for making complex changes in a library. In the next section, you'll learn about using DSLs to reduce the verbosity of code.

DSLs for reducing the verbosity of code

`Sequel`, a popular database library for Ruby, uses a DSL designed purely for reducing the verbosity of code. If you want to express an inequality condition in one of your database queries, you can use a long approach such as the following:

```ruby
DB[:table].where(Sequel[:column] > 11)
# generates SQL: SELECT * FROM table WHERE (column > 11)
```

In this case, `Sequel[:column]` returns an object representing the SQL identifier, which supports the > method. This type of usage occurs very often in `Sequel`, so often that it is desirable to have a shortcut. `Sequel` has multiple shortcuts for this, but the one enabled by default uses a simple DSL:

```
DB[:table].where{column > 11}
```

This uses an `instance_exec` DSL, where methods inside the block are called on an object different than the object outside the block. Inside the block, methods called without an explicit receiver return `Sequel` identifier objects, so `column` inside the block is basically translated to `Sequel[:column]` (which itself is a shortcut for `Sequel::SQL::Identifier.new(:column)`). One issue with this approach is that if users are not familiar with the method and do not know the block is executed using `instance_exec`, they may do something like the following:

```
@some_var = 10
DB[:table].where{column > @some_var}
```

This doesn't work because the block is evaluated in the context of a different object. The need to reference methods or instance variables in the surrounding scope is common enough that the DSL also supports this approach, by yielding an object instead of using `instance_exec` if the block accepts an object:

```
@some_var = 10
DB[:table].where{|o| o.column > @some_var}
```

In this section, you learned about DSLs designed to reduce code verbosity, using a real-world example from `Sequel`. In the next section, you'll learn about libraries implemented purely as DSLs.

Libraries implemented as DSLs

Some libraries are implemented purely as DSLs, in that the expected use of the library is only via the DSL, and you as a user are never expected to manually create the library's objects. One library designed like this is `minitest/spec`, which is another popular Ruby library for testing.

With `minitest/spec`, all use of the library is via a DSL. You use `describe` to open a block for test examples. Inside the block, `before` is used for the code run before every example, and `after` for the code run after every example. You use `it` to define test examples. Notice in the following example, you never create any `minitest` objects:

```ruby
require 'minitest/autorun'

describe Class do
  before do
    # setup code
  end

  after do
    # teardown code
  end

  it "should allow creating classes via .new" do
    Class.new.must_be_kind_of Class
  end
end
```

Another library implemented as a DSL is **Sinatra**, which was the first Ruby web framework showing you could implement a web application in a few lines of code, and an inspiration for many minimal web frameworks in Ruby and other languages. With Sinatra, after requiring the library, you can directly call methods to handle HTTP requests. This simple web application will return `Index page` for GET requests to the root of the application and `File Not Found` for all other requests, as shown here:

```ruby
require 'sinatra'

get "/" do
  "Index page"
end

not_found do
  "File Not Found"
end
```

This type of DSL is not for every library. It is best left for specific environments, such as testing for `minitest/spec`, or for simple cases, such as only handling a few routes in Sinatra. For both `minitest` and Sinatra, there is an alternative API that is not a pure DSL, where classes are created in the standard Ruby way.

In this section, you learned about designing different types of DSLs. In the next section, you'll learn how to implement the DSLs you learned about in this section.

Implementing your DSL

One of the best aspects of Ruby is how easy Ruby makes it to implement a DSL. After programmer friendliness, probably the main reason you see so many DSLs in Ruby is the simplicity of implementation. There are a few different DSL types you learned about in the previous sections, and you'll learn how to implement each in this section.

The first type is the most basic type, where the DSL method accepts a block that is yielded as an object, and you call methods on the yielded object. For example, the `RSpec` configuration example could be implemented as follows:

```
def RSpec.configure
  yield RSpec::Core::Configuration.new
end
```

In this case, the configuration is global and always affects the `RSpec` constant, so the `RSpec::Configuration` instance may not even need a reference to the receiver.

For the `Foo.process_bars` example given previously, assuming the `ProcessBarCommand` uses the `add_bar` method and the DSL uses the simpler `bar` method, you need to implement a wrapper object specific to the DSL. Often the name of this object has DSL in it. Since the `skip_check` and `generate_names` methods are the same in both cases, you can cheat and use `method_missing`, though it is often better to define actual methods, as you learned in *Chapter 9, Metaprogramming and When to Use It*. In this example, we'll use the `method_missing` shortcut:

```
class ProcessBarDSL
  def initialize(command)
    @command = command
  end

  def bar(...)
    @command.add_bar(...)
```

```
  end

  def method_missing(...)
    @command.send(...)
  end
end
```

With the `ProcessBarDSL` class created, you can implement `Foo.process_bars`
by creating the `ProcessBarCommand` object, and yielding it wrapped in the
`ProcessBarDSL` instance. After the block completes processing, you can implement
the internal processing of the bars by calling a private internal method, here named as
`handle_bar_processing`:

```
def Foo.process_bars
  command = ProcessBarCommand.new
  yield ProcessBarDSL.new(command)

  handle_bar_processing(command)
end
```

If you want to support an API where you can either pass a block to `Foo.process_bars`
or pass an already created `ProcessBarCommand` object, that is also easy to implement.
Refer to the following code block:

```
def Foo.process_bars(command=nil)
  unless command
    command = ProcessBarCommand.new
    yield ProcessBarDSL.new(command)
  end

  handle_bar_processing(command)
end
```

For the `Sequel` example with the `where` method, because it allows both the
`instance_exec` approach and the `block` argument approach, it's slightly tricky. You
need to check the `arity` of the block, and if the block has `arity` of 1, then the block
expects an argument, and you yield the object to it. If the block does not have `arity` of
1, the block doesn't expect an argument, and you evaluate the block in the context of the
object with `instance_exec`. Refer to the following code:

```
def where(&block)
  cond = if block.arity == 1
    yield Sequel::VIRTUAL_ROW
  else
    Sequel::VIRTUAL_ROW.instance_exec(&block)
  end

  add_where(cond)
end
```

The `Sequel::VIRTUAL_ROW` object uses a `method_missing` approach since all
methods are treated as column names. Simplified, it is similar to the following code,
though the actual implementation is more complex at it also supports creating a SQL
function object if arguments are passed:

```
Sequel::VIRTUAL_ROW = Class.new(BasicObject) do
  def method_missing(meth)
    Sequel::SQL::Identifier.new(meth)
  end
end.new
```

In the `minitest/spec` example, the `describe` method is added to `Kernel`. It creates
a class, sets a name for the class based on the argument, and passes the block given to
`class_eval`. Simplified, it looks as follows:

```
module Kernel
  def describe(name, *, &block)
    klass = Class.new(Minitest::Spec)
    klass.name = name
    klass.class_eval(&block)
    klass
```

```
      end
  end
```

The `before` and `after` methods inside the `describe` block both define methods. `before` defines `setup` and `after` defines `teardown`. Simplified, they could be implemented by code as follows:

```
class Minitest::Spec
  def self.before(&block)
    define_method(:setup, &block)
  end

  def self.after(&block)
    define_method(:teardown, &block)
  end
end
```

The `it` method is similar, but the method it defines starts with `test`, and includes the description given. It also includes an incremented number so that two specs with the same description end up defining different test methods. It's a very common mistake to copy an existing test, modify the copy to test an additional feature, and forget to change the name. With a manual test name definition, that results in the second test method overriding the first. This can be caught if running tests in verbose warning mode (the `ruby -w` switch), as in that case Ruby will emit method redefinition warnings, but otherwise, it is easy to miss and results in you not testing everything you think you are testing.

Simplified, the `it` method could be implemented with an approach such as the following:

```
class Minitest::Spec
  def self.it(description, &b)
    @num_specs ||= 0
    @num_specs += 1
    define_method("test_#{@num_specs}_#{description}", &b)
  end
end
```

One issue with the `minitest/spec` implementation of `describe` is that it adds the method to `Kernel`, so it ends up being a method on every object. You can call it inside other classes and methods. This adds to the flexibility, and it's probably a good choice for `minitest/spec`, but it may not be the best decision for DSLs in general.

The Sinatra DSL works differently. It doesn't want to define methods such as `get` and `not_found` on every object, but it still wants you to be able to call them at the top level, outside of any classes and methods. It does this by calling `extend` in the top-level scope with a module. The top-level scope runs in the context of an object called `main`, and just like any other object, if you extend `main` with a module, the methods in the module are only added to `main` and not any other object. A simplified version of the Sinatra DSL is similar to the following:

```ruby
module Sinatra::Delegator
  meths = %i[get not_found] # ...

  meths.each do |meth|
    define_method(meth) do |*args, &block|
      Sinatra::Application.send(meth, *args, &block)
    end
  end
end

extend Sinatra::Delegator
```

In this section, you've learned the basics of implementing a variety of different types of DSLs. In the next section, you'll learn about which use cases lend themselves to DSL usage, and which use cases don't.

Learning when to use a DSL

There are some use cases in Ruby where using a DSL makes a lot of sense, and other cases where using a DSL increases complexity and makes the code worse instead of better. The best cases for DSL use in Ruby are where using the DSL makes the library easier to maintain and makes it simpler for a user to use the library. If you find yourself in that situation, then a DSL definitely sounds like the right choice. However, in most cases, a DSL is a trade-off.

In most cases, you design a DSL to make things easier in some way for the user, but it makes the internals more complex and makes your job as the maintainer of the library more difficult. It is possible but less likely for the opposite to be true, where you design a DSL to make your life as a maintainer easier, but the DSL makes the use of the library more difficult.

Of the DSL examples given previously, the `RSpec` configuration example may be an example of the best case for a DSL. It definitely makes it easier for the user to configure the library since they only need to look in one spot for configuration. Implementation of the DSL is fairly simple, and having all configurations run through a single configuration object may make it easier to maintain the library.

For the `Foo.process_bars` example, the DSL is definitely more idiomatic Ruby code, and likely to be easier for the user to use than the alternatives. In this case, it definitely adds maintenance work, since it requires creating a class specifically for the DSL. However, the DSL should be reasonably easy to maintain, so it's probably a good trade-off.

For the `Sequel` example with the `where` method that takes a block and either yields an object or uses `instance_exec`, it's definitely questionable whether the benefits outweigh the costs. This DSL only saves a little bit of typing for the user, and the fact that it can yield an object or use `instance_exec` is often a source of confusion, especially for users not familiar with the library. In general, using `instance_exec` for short blocks often results in user confusion, since most Ruby programmers are used to calling methods with blocks and using instance variables of the surrounding scope inside the blocks, and breaking that is often a bad idea.

In regards to the `Sequel` virtual row DSL, the DSL was designed back when the alternative approach was much more verbose (`Sequel::SQL::Identifier.new(:column) > 11`) than the current alternative approach (`Sequel[:column] > 11`), so the benefit of the DSL was higher back then than it is now. However, since the DSL is now widely used, it must continue to be supported. The principle to remember here is you will often need to support any DSL for a long time, so implementing a DSL just to reduce code verbosity is often a bad idea. Try hard to think of alternative approaches to using a DSL if you are using it just to reduce code verbosity.

For `minitest/spec`, the benefit of using the DSL is huge. For basic usage, you don't need to know about any `minitest` specific classes, you only need to know about four methods, `describe`, `before`, `after`, and `it`. This greatly simplifies the interface for the user and is one reason `minitest/spec` is such a pleasure to use. This does have an implementation cost, as `minitest/spec` has extra complexity on top of `minitest` itself, so there is a significant amount of maintenance involved. However, this is another case where the benefit outweighs the cost.

In the Sinatra case, the DSL is really what showed how simple web applications could be if you focused only on what was absolutely necessary to implement them. The actual DSL implementation in terms of extending `main` doesn't add much maintenance effort, so it is also a case where the benefit outweighs the cost.

As you have learned, there are some situations where implementing a DSL can be useful, and other situations where implementing a DSL can make a library worse.

Summary

In this chapter, you've learned that focusing on how the DSL will be used is the key to designing a good DSL. You've seen many examples of DSL usage from a user perspective, and how to implement each of these possible DSLs. Finally, you've learned when it is a good idea to implement a DSL, and when it may not be a good idea. With all you've learned in this chapter, you are better able to decide when a DSL makes sense for your library, and if you decide it does make sense, how better to design and implement it.

In the next chapter, you'll learn all about testing your Ruby code.

Questions

1. What is the main advantage of using a DSL for configuring libraries?

2. How can you implement a DSL that works both as a normal block DSL and an `instance_exec` DSL?

3. Of the various reasons given in this chapter for using a DSL, which is the most likely to cause problems for the user and the least likely to add value?

11
Testing to Ensure Your Code Works

Testing is more critical in Ruby than in most other programming environments, partly because of the power and flexibility Ruby offers, and also because of Ruby's dynamic typing. With proper testing, you can have confidence that your code works the way you expect, which is critical whenever you are making changes to it.

In this chapter, you'll learn that there are a lot of important considerations when testing, such as at what levels you want to test, how much abstraction should be used in your tests, and how thorough your tests need to be.

We will cover the following topics in this chapter:

- Understanding why testing is so critical in Ruby
- Learning different approaches to testing
- Considering test complexity
- Understanding the many levels of testing
- Realizing that 100% coverage means nothing

By the end of this chapter, you'll have a better understanding of testing in Ruby, and be better able to choose appropriate tradeoffs when designing your tests.

Technical requirements

In this chapter and all chapters of this book, code given in code blocks is designed to execute on Ruby 3.0. Many of the code examples will work on earlier versions of Ruby, but not all. The code for this chapter is available online at `https://github.com/ PacktPublishing/Polished-Ruby-Programming/tree/main/Chapter11`.

Understanding why testing is so critical in Ruby

Testing is critical to ensure proper behavior in every programming language, but it is especially critical in Ruby. In many other programming languages, the programming language has a type system that will catch errors related to improper use of types when the program is compiled, before the program is run. Ruby uses a dynamic type system, so it will not catch many errors related to the improper use of data types. Ruby programs are also generally not compiled until you try to run them, so even simple syntax errors will not be caught unless you try to load the related code. Combined, these two qualities make testing in Ruby more critical than in many other programming languages.

When talking about testing, the lack of type checking is often considered a missing feature. However, one of the best things about Ruby is that it doesn't require you to specify types for variables and methods. Unlike most languages, Ruby doesn't focus on the types of objects, only on what methods the objects respond to. That flexibility is what makes Ruby such a joy to program in.

Similarly, not having a separate compilation step before running Ruby code is one of the qualities that makes Ruby easy to use. Ruby does ship with the ability to just compile programs and not actually run them, it's just not commonly used. This feature is very useful with large libraries if you just want to check that there are no syntax errors in any of the source files. You can access this feature using the `-c` command-line option, such as `ruby -c file_name`.

If you want to do this for all `.rb` files under a given directory, you can find all files under a given directory using `Dir.[]`, then run `ruby -c` on each of the resulting files. In this case, it's a very good idea to use the `--disable-gems` flag in addition to the `-c` flag, because a huge part of Ruby startup time is spent loading `rubygems`, and you don't need `rubygems` at all if you are just checking syntax. Here's an example of how you could syntax check all Ruby files:

```
Dir['/path/to/dir/**/*.rb'].each do |file|
  print file, ': '
```

```
    system('ruby', '-c', '--disable-gems', file)
end
```

This is useful, but it could be better. The previous example prints one line for every file, but it would better if it just reported files with invalid syntax. That's not a hard change to make. We'll print a period for each file as a simple way to indicate progress, and if a file has a syntax error, we'll print the error. We don't actually need to print the filename when printing the error because syntax errors generally include the filename at the start of the error message:

```
Dir['/path/to/dir/**/*.rb'].each do |file|
  read, write = IO.pipe
  print '.'
  system('ruby', '-c', '--disable-gems', file,
         out: write, err: write)
  write.close
  output = read.read
  unless output.chomp == "Syntax OK"
    puts
    puts output
  end
end
```

This book was developed using `ruby -c` to check all source code examples. All source code in this book should at least have valid syntax.

For other programming languages that have a separate compilation step, in addition to compilation errors showing you that you have a problem in your code, there are often compilation warnings, showing things that may be wrong, but are not technically errors and do not stop the compilation process. This is basically the compiler being your friend, trying to point out things that may be wrong even if the compiler isn't sure. Thankfully, Ruby has something similar.

As we learned in *Chapter 6*, *Formatting Code for Easy Reading*, Ruby has a verbose warnings feature that prints additional warnings about cases that are not technically errors but still look wrong. You can enable this support using the `ruby -w` flag, and even better, you can combine it with the `ruby -c` flag to check source files for both syntax errors and compilation warnings. When used in this mode, the `-w` flag will only print compilation warnings, it won't print warnings for questionable behavior that can only be caught at runtime. Still, it's useful to include the `-w` flag whenever you are scanning code for syntax errors. You can update the previous example code to include reporting warnings instead of just reporting errors. Since files with warnings are still going to print `Syntax OK` at the end of the output, you need to remove that from the output before printing the output:

```
Dir['/path/to/dir/**/*.rb'].each do |file|
  read, write = IO.pipe
  print '.'
  system('ruby', '-wc', '--disable-gems', file,
         out: write, err: write)
  write.close
  output = read.read
  unless output.chomp == "Syntax OK"
    puts
    puts output.sub(/Syntax OK\Z/, '')
  end
end
```

Scanning all files with `ruby -wc` is a great idea, but it only does some fairly basic checks on the file. To actually verify whether your code works the way you expect, you need to test it, and you'll learn different approaches to doing that in the next section.

Learning different approaches to testing

There are many approaches to testing in Ruby. It's possible to use any of them or potentially all of them successfully on the same project, though most Ruby projects stick to a single approach.

One approach to testing is manual testing. This is where you just run the program or use the library, and make sure the results are as expected. It was common in older software for this to be the only method of testing. Applied vigorously enough, with strict checklists on everything in the system that had to be tested, manual testing can result in high-quality software. There were entire careers based not on writing software, but only manually testing software that was written by others.

While it is possible to be successful purely with manual testing, it is very labor-intensive to manually test code, compared to having a computer automatically test code. Back when programs were much simpler, programming took much longer, and software releases were years apart, having a separate quality assurance department manually testing software before release was a reasonable approach.

Times have changed since then, and it's almost always a bad idea to rely purely on manual testing. However, that doesn't mean that manual testing has no place. For some software, there may be small parts that are too complex or unreliable to test automatically, and you have to rely on manual testing for those. For example, if you are writing a Ruby program to generate pleasing music to listen to, you may be able to automatically test most of the pieces that make up the software. However, automatically testing whether the generated music is actually pleasing to listen to is probably harder to write than the software to generate pleasing music. For situations like that, incorporating manual testing into your testing approach is critical.

Other than manual testing, there are three major approaches to testing in Ruby. One approach is called **test after development** (sometimes abbreviated **TAD**). With this approach, you develop the code first without any automated tests. After you have the software mostly working the way you want, you then go back and add tests for it. This is probably the most popular form of testing, and it generally works well, even though proponents of other automated testing approaches often look down on it.

Another approach is called **test-driven development** (often abbreviated **TDD**). With TDD, you write the tests for your code before you write the code itself. How does this work? Well, first you write a test for a simple piece of code. Then you run the test and it fails. Then you write just enough code to make the test pass. Then you write another test for new behavior. You run the tests again and the first test passes and then the new test fails. Then you write just enough code to make the second test also pass, without breaking the first test. Then you refactor any code as needed while still keeping all tests passing. You repeat this process until the tests cover all desired functionality.

The third approach is called **behavior-driven development** (often abbreviated **BDD**). With BDD, the tests (called *specs*) are written in a reduced form of English, often by a non-programmer, possibly even a project manager. Then a programmer writes code to transform this reduced form of English into executable Ruby code that can be used for testing. Then the programmer implements the features needed to get that executable Ruby test code to pass. Then the cycle repeats, writing additional specs in the reduced form of English, having that translated into executable Ruby code, and then writing the code to make sure the tests pass.

All three approaches have different tradeoffs. With both TDD and BDD, you might end up with tests that are infeasible to implement, either because they are too difficult or the tests or specifications have bugs and it is actually impossible to have correct answers returned due to missing input. With TAD, since the tests are written after the library is developed, and the programmer is usually doing basic manual testing as they are writing the library, you end up writing fewer tests that you don't need.

For an example of this, say the project manager has worked all week on learning the BDD syntax, which sort of reads like English but is far less flexible. Near the end of the week, they are thrilled that they are finally able to submit a valid specification such as the following:

```
bdd_specification = <<END
Feature: Check whether program finishes

  Scenario: User submits program
    Given the User submits a program with a "loop"
    When the User clicks a button to check
        whether the program will finish
    Then the system outputs whether the program will finish
END
```

The junior programmer in charge of maintaining the testing infrastructure gets this feature, then writes the necessary code to translate this sort-of English into executable Ruby code, which takes another week. Then this shows up on the feature board for another junior programmer to work on. After a week of working on it, the junior programmer has a partially working implementation, but it still has a lot of bugs they cannot fix. They decide to ask for help from their team leader, who looks at the specification, tries to stifle his laughter, and tells the junior programmer not to worry about it, and that he'll talk with the project manager. Then the tech lead has to have a difficult conversation with the project manager about how their seemingly simple request is actually a restatement of the halting problem, which is provably unsolvable.

The previous example is, hopefully, an exaggeration of what could happen in the real world. In general, the only way to know whether it is possible to implement a complex feature is to try to implement it. If it is impossible to implement the feature, or infeasible due to an unexpected difficulty that was discovered during development, any time spent on testing the feature is wasted. In the previous example, two of the three weeks involved getting the testing set up, and one week was spent on implementation, so using a TAD approach, only one week would have been wasted instead of three weeks.

TAD is not without its problems. The main issue with TAD is you can end up implementing a feature that works, but the interface to use it is hard to use or testing it is difficult. If you use a TAD approach, you need to realize this while you are writing the feature, and constantly remind yourself to think of how the user will use the feature, make sure to keep that usage as simple as you can and avoid unnecessary complexity. Otherwise, it is common for code developed using the TAD approach to be implemented in a manner that makes the implementation as easy as possible, but that makes testing difficult.

With TDD, you can have the opposite problem. Because you are writing the test code first, you tend to design interfaces that are very easy to test but may be difficult to implement. Additionally, the needs when testing, especially when using mocked or stubbed objects, are often quite different than the needs of the average user of the library, so the interface you end up with when using a TDD approach might be easy for the use cases of the testing system, but not optimized for common user actions.

Let's see an example of that. Let's say you are writing a method that times the execution of two different callable objects and returns whichever callable object is faster. With a TAD approach, you may design the code similar to the following example. This adds a `faster_one` method, which will time the calls to both the first argument and the second argument, and return the argument that takes the least time to call:

```
class WhichFaster
  def faster_one(callable1, callable2)
    t1 = time{callable1.call}
    t2 = time{callable2.call}
    t1 > t2 ? callable2 : callable1
  end
  private def time
    t = clock_time
    yield
    clock_time - t
  end
  private def clock_time
    Process.clock_gettime(Process::CLOCK_MONOTONIC)
  end
end
```

This is a reasonably simple implementation, but testing it is quite challenging, mostly because of the usage of `Process.clock_gettime(Process::CLOCK_MONOTONIC)`. Testing the implementation robustly probably requires mocking at least the `clock_time` method, which means it isn't actually testing what happens inside that method. Alternatively, you could just pass in two callable objects, and you are sure that one is faster than the other. However, that approach is less robust, because which callable object is faster may change depending on time and the execution environment.

When using TDD, the test code is written first, and maybe written in the way simplest for testing. For testing, it's probably easier to create an object to set the callable objects as attributes of the object, and then provide a couple of implementations for the timer, calling it with each timer implementation to make sure that the returned callable matches the one with the lowest time. Refer to the following code:

```
describe WhichFaster do
  it "returns faster callable" do
    which = WhichFaster.new
    c1 = which.callable1 = ->{a}
    c2 = which.callable2 = ->{b}

    which.timer = {c1=>1, c2=>2}
    _(which.faster_one).must_equal c1

    which.timer = {c1=>2, c2=>1}
    _(which.faster_one).must_equal c2
  end
end
```

This is super simple to test. The implementation turns out to be much simpler as well. Just have attributes for the callable objects and the timer, get the times for each callable, and return the faster callable object. Check out the following code:

```
class WhichFaster
  attr_accessor :callable1, :callable2, :timer

  def faster_one
    t1 = timer[callable1]
    t2 = timer[callable2]
    t1 > t2 ? callable2 : callable1
```

```
      end
  end
```

While both the tests and implementation are simple, this is much more difficult to use. The complexity is removed from the library and forced onto to the user, who now has to do the following:

```
which = WhichFaster.new
which.callable1 = callable1
which.callable2 = callable2
which.timer = ->(callable) do
   t = Process.clock_gettime(Process::CLOCK_MONOTONIC)
   callable.call
   Process.clock_gettime(Process::CLOCK_MONOTONIC) - t
end
which.faster_one
```

This is much more complex compared to the TAD approach. This is likely because the TAD approach focused on implementing a design, and not simply on passing a test. Just as you need to focus on the user experience and not just use the easiest implementation approach with TAD, you need to focus on the user experience and not just use the easiest testing approach with TDD.

Another advantage of TAD is that since you've already implemented the library, you know where the most complex and error-prone sections of the implementation are, and you can focus on extra testing in those areas. With TDD, you are designing tests mostly around the proper use of the library, without knowing where the complex parts of the implementation will be. This makes it difficult to correctly expand the testing so that the most complex parts of the implementation have the appropriate testing. By writing tests up front, you can end up over-testing the simpler parts of the implementation and under-testing the more complex parts. Make sure if you use a TDD approach that you also review the implementation after it is finished, and make sure to add extra tests for more complex implementation areas, which you may not have known were needed originally.

In deciding whether to use BDD, the primary consideration will be whether non-programmers will be assisting the programming team in writing specifications and the quality of the generated specifications. If non-programmers will not be assisting the programming team by writing specifications, BDD generally ends up being mostly wasted effort. Similarly, even if the non-programmers are writing specifications, if the specifications are buggy or are taking significant time for the programming team to automatically translate into executable Ruby code, the costs of BDD may exceed the benefits.

In this section, you've learned about different approaches to testing. In the next section, you'll learn about test complexity, and the tradeoffs involved with making the tests more complex.

Considering test complexity

When programming, you tend to reach for abstractions to simplify code and reduce complexity. Since automated testing is just another form of programming, there is a natural tendency to use the same approach when writing tests. However, with abstraction comes indirection, and often complexity. For example, you may have three tests that do similar things, like in the following code snippet:

```ruby
describe Foo do
  it "should have bar return a Bar instance" do
    _(Foo.new.bar).must_be_kind_of(Bar)
  end

  it "should have baz return a Baz instance" do
    _(Foo.new.baz).must_be_kind_of(Baz)
  end

  it "should have quux return a Quux instance" do
    _(Foo.new.quux).must_be_kind_of(Quux)
  end
end
```

The programmer's natural inclination is to see the pattern and create an abstraction for it:

```ruby
describe Foo do
  def method_must_return_kind_of(meth, instance)
```

```
      _(Foo.new.send(meth)).must_be_kind_of(instance)
   end
```

The programmer would later use that abstraction to attempt to simplify the test code:

```
   it "should have bar return a Bar instance" do
     method_must_return_kind_of(:bar, Bar)
   end

   it "should have baz return a Baz instance" do
     method_must_return_kind_of(:baz, Baz)
   end

   it "should have quux return a Quux instance" do
     method_must_return_kind_of(:quux, Quux)
   end
 end
```

The issue with this approach to abstraction is that it decreases code locality by moving what is being tested away from the inside of the test block. If two of these tests pass, and the third fails inside the method_must_return_kind_of method, debugging the problem is more difficult. This is because the failing line will usually show inside the abstracted method, instead of inside the spec that called it. The other issue here is that someone looking at the specs may not know what method_must_return_kind_of does. The naming doesn't indicate whether it is a class or instance method, for example. By abstracting specs in this way, you are increasing how much context is needed by the programmer trying to fix failing tests.

In general, tests are designed to help avoid and debug problems in library code. The more abstractions you use in your test code, the more likely you are to be debugging your test code instead of your library code. Once you reach a certain level of test abstraction, a failing test gives you no confidence about whether the bug is in the library or the tests themselves, and that is a bad situation to be in.

That does not mean that all abstractions in tests are bad. If you have 10 lines of test code that are called in 100 different specs for a specialized setup, having a method the specs can call for that setup that performs those 10 lines can be hugely helpful. Abstracting setup code in the tests is probably fine, as long as the setup code is identical or at least very similar between all cases. However, attempt to avoid abstracting the parts of the specs that are performing the actual testing, as opposed to setting up for the actual testing.

There is often an alternative to the previous abstraction example, and that is defining multiple test methods using an enumerable, as follows:

```
describe Foo do
  {bar: Bar, baz: Baz, quux: Quux}.each do |meth, klass|
    it "should have #{meth} return a #{klass} instance" do
      _(Foo.new.send(meth)).must_be_kind_of(klass)
    end
  end
end
```

This reduces the duplication of the test methods without the loss of code locality. Assume there is a failure in one of the specs, where the method does not return an object of the expected class. In that case, the test library will report the line inside the spec that failed. That makes it much easier to determine what was actually not working as expected, reducing the amount of time you need to spend debugging.

In this section, you learned about tradeoffs in test complexity and the problems with excessive abstractions in tests. In the next section, you'll learn about the many levels at which you can test code in Ruby.

Understanding the many levels of testing

There are many levels at which you can test code in Ruby. The lowest level of testing is *unit testing*, where you are testing the smallest possible amount of code in your library, such as a single method in a single class, with all dependencies of the method mocked or stubbed. The highest level of testing is some form of *acceptance testing*, which can be automated or manual. In a web application, manual acceptance testing can be just using the development version of the application in a browser and trying different features. Automated acceptance testing of web applications tries to imitate this by running an actual browser and programmatically controlling it by telling it which links to click on and which buttons to press.

There are multiple levels in between. *Model testing* runs at a higher level than unit testing, testing individual methods of objects, but with none of the method's dependencies mocked or stubbed. *Integration testing* involves testing that all parts of the system work together, also without mocking or stubbing anything. Usually, this involves accessing the highest part of the system and get the expected results, which gives reasonable assurance that the lower levels are working correctly. In terms of web applications, integration testing usually involves using the web application's Ruby interface to submit requests.

In general, unit testing Ruby software tends to result in very brittle test code, where changes to the code that will not affect a user's use of the library will break unit tests. This is because unit tests are designed around mocking or stubbing all dependencies of a method. Imagine you have a method such as the following:

```ruby
class Foo
  singleton_class.alias_method(:build, :new)

  def build_foo(arg)
    Foo.build(arg)
  end
end
```

Unit testing the Foo#build_foo method would involve ensuring that it calls Foo.build with the argument, because Foo.build is an external dependency of the method. With the minitest library, this can be handled by combining the use of stubbing the Foo.build method, and returning the result by calling a mock object. Later, you verify the mock object was called with the expected arguments, as follows:

```ruby
describe Foo do
  it "#build_foo should call Foo.build" do
    mock = Minitest::Mock.new
    mock.expect :call, :foo, [1]

    Foo.stub :build, mock do
      _(Foo.new.build_foo(1)).must_equal :foo
    end

    mock.verify
  end
end
```

This issue here is, say you later decide you don't need the `Foo.build` method and change the implementation to use `Foo.new` as follows:

```
class Foo
  def build_foo(arg)
    Foo.new(arg)
  end
end
```

If you do this, you end up breaking the test, even though the functionality is exactly the same. That's because the test is testing what messages the method is sending other objects. In most cases, which messages a method is sending to other objects is an implementation detail of the method, and something not worth testing. This brittleness is a natural, unavoidable consequence of unit testing. You can try to avoid the problem by not stubbing and/or mocking all dependencies of the method, just the ones you think are problematic, but that moves the test from a pure unit test to a hybrid of a unit test and a model test.

The situation is even worse if you keep the `Foo.build` method, but change the behavior to be different. For example, maybe you change it to return a different type of object. In that case, the unit test still passes, even though it should break because the method now returns a different object than it did before. You would have to hope that you have other unit tests of the `Foo.build` method explicitly in order to catch the error.

If unit tests are brittle and miss changes in stubbed and mocked methods by their nature, why do programmers use them? In one word, speed. By stubbing and/or mocking all dependencies, pure unit tests are extremely fast. In cases where you have slow tests that are testing important aspects of the system, having a set of very fast unit tests that execute in a second or a few seconds at most can be valuable. However, unless you are sure you need the extra speed, it's best to stick to model tests. Slow and reliable tests are in general much better than fast tests that break without reason (false positives) and don't catch actual breakage (false negatives).

For web applications, by far the most important tests to have are acceptance tests. You want to be sure as much as possible that high-level usage of your application returns the results you expect. It's also a good idea to have a robust set of model tests, especially for any cases not covered by the acceptance tests. However, if you only have time to implement and maintain a single type of test in your web application, focus on acceptance tests first.

In this section, you learned about the many levels of testing Ruby libraries and applications. In the next section, you'll learn about test coverage and its importance in Ruby.

Realizing that 100% coverage means nothing

Code coverage allows you to check what part of your library or application is actually run. Coverage measurement is generally used as a rough gauge of how thorough your test suites are. There are multiple types of code coverage for Ruby. Using the built-in coverage library, line coverage, branch coverage, and method coverage are all supported.

Line coverage is the simplest type of coverage. It allows you to check whether a line of code was ever executed during the testing process. This is important because any line without coverage during testing means the line was never tested at all. Now, just because the line was covered doesn't mean that the result of the line was actually tested. All it means is that at some point during testing, code somewhere on the line was executed.

Branch coverage takes the same idea as line coverage but takes it a step farther. It ensures that all branches in the code were taken. Suppose if you have the following Foo class with a method named `branch`:

```
class Foo
  attr_accessor :bar

  def branch(v)
    v > 1 ? bar : baz
  end

  def baz; raise; end
end
```

And you add a test for the method as follows:

```
describe Foo do
  it "#branch should return the value of bar" do
    foo = Foo.new
    foo.bar = 3
    (foo.branch(2)).must_equal 3
  end
end
```

This test is OK, but it is incomplete. From a line coverage perspective, this will show 100% line coverage, as all lines are covered. This will even consider the line with the `baz` definition covered, even though `baz` is never called. This is because the line is executed when the `Foo` class definition is evaluated. The line `v > 1 ? bar : baz` will also show as covered, even though the test only executes the `bar` call and not the `baz` call. This is where branch coverage comes in. With branch coverage enabled, the coverage will show that the else branch of code on the line was not covered (the branch taken when `v` is not greater than `1`).

Method coverage is similar to branch coverage, but it only tells you whether the method was executed during the tests. Method coverage with the previous test would be able to tell you that the `baz` method was never called.

Just like line coverage only means the line was executed at one point, branch coverage only tells you the branch was executed at one point. You can write a test that gets full coverage without actually testing anything. Refer to the following code:

```
describe Foo do
  it "#branch should return the value of bar" do
    Foo.new.branch(0) rescue nil
    Foo.new.branch(2) rescue nil
  end
end
```

This code executes all lines, branches, and methods, but provides no useful testing. The tests indicate that either method could raise an exception but doesn't test that either method does, and doesn't test what the return value of either method is.

This brings us to the critical concept in regards to code coverage, which is that 100% coverage means nothing. The corollary to this concept is even more important, and that is that less than 100% coverage means something. Having 100% code coverage does not tell you anything, but having less than 100% code coverage tells you something. At the very least, having less than 100% code coverage means that there are certain parts of your code that you are not testing at all.

Now, maybe you are OK with having untested code in your application. Maybe if you are testing the most important parts of your application, not testing other parts is an appropriate tradeoff. In general, there is limited time for testing, and testing time has to be prioritized, and focusing on code coverage testing may result in a failure to test more important code. However, if you've ever had to add covering tests to a library or application, you will probably quickly see that it finds bugs.

Most of the time adding testing to improve code coverage will feel like boring drudge work. The tests covering the code may not be very valuable. However, what is very valuable is the process of going through the untested code. You'll find that some lines cannot be executed and can be deleted. You'll find that an `if` statement is not necessary, since it is tested in earlier code, and you can eliminate the unnecessary conditional and make your code faster. You'll find cases where error handling was buggy and resulted in an unexpected exception being thrown. You may even find security vulnerabilities. While 100% code coverage itself may not be valuable, the journey to get there often is.

Summary

In this chapter, you've learned why testing in Ruby is more critical than in many other programming languages. You've learned about different approaches to testing, such as manual testing, test after development, test-driven development, and behavior-driven development. You've learned that is important to limit the complexity of your tests by limiting the types of abstractions you use in your tests. You've learned about different levels of testing, and the tradeoffs between them. Finally, you've learned about different types of code coverage, and what 100% coverage means.

Testing your library often alerts you to things you need to change in your library, and in the next chapter, you'll learn about how best to handle change in your libraries.

Questions

1. How do you check the syntax of a Ruby file and report errors and warnings?
2. Is behavior-driven development a good idea if the programmers are going to be writing the specifications?
3. Is it always bad to use abstractions in test code?
4. Why might you prefer model testing to unit testing?
5. What does 100% code coverage mean?

```ruby
  ensure
    checkin_connection(conn) if conn
  end
end
```

Whether it's better to keep both `execute` and `checkout` as extracted methods or to combine them into a single `execute` method depends on whether you have a use for calling `checkout` separately. If there are places in your class where you are checking out a connection but not executing a SQL statement on it, or places where you are checking out a connection and executing multiple SQL statements on it, then it's probably best to keep `checkout` as a separate method. However, if you would never be calling `checkout` separately, it probably does not make sense to keep it as a separate method, and you could make your code faster by having a single `execute` method.

Extracting a class

Extracting a class is less common than extracting a method, but there are still places where it makes sense to do so. As you learned in *Chapter 2, Designing Useful Custom Classes*, classes that deal with only a single responsibility are often easier to maintain, so one reason to extract a class is to take a class that has many responsibilities and break it into separate classes. As you learned, it's not always a good idea to break a large class into smaller classes. You should carefully consider the benefit of using a single class versus the extra cognitive overhead that an extra class entails.

Let's say you are designing a system for tracking clients of a shipping business in the United States named **Shippers Pack Urgently** (**SPU** for short). For each client, you need to keep track of their first and last name, their address, and their phone number. Due to formatting requirements for address label printing, you must keep track of the portions of the address as separate fields. These fields are the street, city, state, and ZIP code. You decide to design a `Client` class to hold client information and initialize instances by assigning all arguments given to instance variables. Refer to the following code:

```ruby
class Client
  def initialize(first_name, last_name, street, city,
                 state, zip, phone)
    @first_name = first_name
    @last_name = last_name
    @street = street
    @city = city
    @state = state
```

```
    @zip = zip
    @phone = phone
  end
```

As you learned in *Chapter 4, Methods and Their Arguments*, this isn't a particularly good approach as the method takes seven positional arguments, but we'll ignore that for now. Clients occasionally need to change either their phone number or their address, so you have the `update_phone` and `update_address` methods to handle updating the phone number and address information:

```
  def update_phone(phone)
    @phone = phone
  end

  def update_address(street, city, state, zip)
    @street = street
    @city = city
    @state = state
    @zip = zip
  end
```

In the normal course of business, the business sends letters to clients, either thanking them for being customers or promoting new services. To handle formatting of address labels for these letters, there is a `format_address_label` method:

```
  def format_address_label
    <<~END
      #{@first_name} #{@last_name}
      #{@street}
      #{@city}, #{@state} #{@zip}
    END
  end
end
```

SPU makes money by packing and shipping high-priority items for clients. They are a little unusual as every package they pack they ship as soon as it is packed, due mainly to the urgency. In other words, each package is a separate shipment, and you decide to use a `Shipment` class for tracking shipments. For each shipment, you need to track the contents of the shipment, the date it was shipped, who the item is being shipped to, and the address information for the shipment. Similar to the `Client` class, you initialize the `Shipment` instances by assigning the arguments to instance variables:

```ruby
class Shipment
  def initialize(contents, ship_date, ship_to,
                 street, city, state, zip)
    @contents = contents
    @ship_date = ship_date
    @ship_to = ship_to
    @street = street
    @city = city
    @state = state
    @zip = zip
  end
```

Unlike the address of a client, the address of a shipment never changes, so there is no method to update the address of a shipment. However, all shipments have a label placed on them, so that SPU employees can look at the package at any point to determine where it is going. Similar to the `Client` class, the `Shipment` class uses `format_address_label` for this:

```ruby
  def format_address_label
    <<~END
      #{@ship_to}
      #{@street}
      #{@city}, #{@state} #{@zip}
    END
  end
end
```

In this example, we are storing address information in both the `Shipment` and `Client` classes. Both `Shipment` and `Client` have a need for address formatting, even if the formatting is slightly different. This is a situation where extracting an `Address` class can be beneficial. The `Address` class will need to store the same street, city, state, and ZIP information that you were storing in `Shipment` and `Client`:

```
class Address
  def initialize(street, city, state, zip)
    @street = street
    @city = city
    @state = state
    @zip = zip
  end
end
```

At this point, you need to decide whether you want to change `Shipment` and `Client` in a backward-compatible manner, or whether you can drop backward compatibility. If this code is in a library used in other applications, and you cannot change all applications using the library at the same time, you probably need to keep backward compatibility. Changing `Client#initialize` while keeping backward compatibility would look like the following:

```
class Client
  def initialize(first_name, last_name, street, city,
                 state, zip, phone)
    @first_name = first_name
    @last_name = last_name
    @address = Address.new(street, city, state, zip)
    @phone = phone
  end
end
```

Similarly, changing `Shipment#initialize` would look like this:

```
class Shipment
  def initialize(contents, ship_date, ship_to,
                 street, city, state, zip)
    @contents = contents
    @ship_date = ship_date
```

```
        @ship_to = ship_to
        @address = Address.new(street, city, state, zip)
      end
  end
```

However, if this is a separate application and it is not too difficult to change all callers of `Client.new` and `Shipment.new`, backward compatibility is not an issue, and it may be a better idea to change the API for `Client` and `Shipment` to accept an `Address` instance:

```
class Client
    def initialize(first_name, last_name, address, phone)
      @first_name = first_name
      @last_name = last_name
      @address = address
      @phone = phone
    end
end
class Shipment
    def initialize(contents, ship_date, ship_to, address)
      @contents = contents
      @ship_date = ship_date
      @ship_to = ship_to
      @address = address
    end
end
```

In this case, dropping backward compatibility makes the code more flexible. For example, if SPU decides to expand to different countries that use different address formats, it is much easier if `Client` and `Shipment` only deal with `Address` objects and not create `Address` objects themselves. This is because the `Address` class may need to change to handle different address formats, and it is easier to make those changes just in the `Address` class, as opposed to making them in the `Address`, `Client`, and `Shipment` classes. It may even be easier to handle foreign addresses using a new `Address` class per country or region that uses a unique addressing format. By accepting an `Address` instance and not the different parts of the address, `Client` and `Shipment` can more easily handle possible future changes in addressing.

A similar issue affects `Client#update_address`. To keep backward compatibility, you could have it continue to accept the four separate arguments, and create an `Address` instance:

```
class Client
  def update_address(street, city, state, zip)
    @address = Address.new(street, city, state, zip)
  end
end
```

Likewise, if backward compatibility is not important, you could change it to accept an `Address` instance:

```
class Client
  def update_address(address)
    @address = address
  end
end
```

Since you'll also need to format labels for addresses, you have a couple of options. One option is just formatting the address part:

```
class Address
  def format_label
    <<~END
    #{@street}
    #{@city}, #{@state} #{@zip}
    END
  end
end
```

With this approach for only formatting the address part and not including the addressee, the `Client` and `Shipment` code to format an address label would look similar to the following:

```
class Client
  def format_address_label
    <<~END
    #{@first_name} #{@last_name}
    #{@address.format_label}
```

```
      END
    end
  end
class Shipment
  def format_address_label
    <<~END
    #{@ship_to}
    #{@address.format_label}
    END
  end
end
```

This isn't terrible, but it may not be the best approach. An alternative approach would be having `Address#format_label` take an argument for the addressee:

```
class Address
  def format_label(addressee)
    <<~END
    #{addressee}
    #{@street}
    #{@city}, #{@state} #{@zip}
    END
  end
end
```

The advantage of this code is that the `Client` and `Shipment` code for formatting the address labels can be simpler:

```
class Client
  def format_address_label
    @address.format_label("#{@first_name} #{@last_name}")
  end
end
class Shipment
  def format_address_label
    @address.format_label(@ship_to)
  end
end
```

Having simpler and less verbose code is definitely good, but the larger conceptual improvement, in this case, is that `Address` is now completely responsible for handling label formatting. If SPU decides to print a barcode or QR code at the top of each label, it can now be accomplished by modifying the code in a single place, `Address#format_label`.

In this section, you learned about the most common Ruby refactoring techniques, extracting a method and extracting a class. In the next section, you'll learn how to approach refactoring when you need to add a new feature that requires refactoring.

Refactoring to add features

One common reason to refactor is to add features that are infeasible to implement with the current design. There are two ways to go about this. We'll call the first way the **cowboy approach**. With the cowboy approach, you just start implementing the new feature and refactor the existing application as needed while you are developing the feature. When you are done implementing the feature, you stop the refactoring.

In the best-case scenario, the cowboy approach saves time. It can also result in the least refactoring changes needed since you only refactor as much as you need to in order to implement the feature you are adding. However, it may result in a partially implemented refactoring, if a full refactoring was not needed to implement the new feature. For the optimistic programmer, the cowboy approach fits better with their natural desire to just get stuff done. It's easy to understand why it is a fairly common approach. Proponents of the cowboy approach mostly have the "*What could go wrong?*" attitude.

Unfortunately, at least two common things can go wrong. First, you could break existing code during the process of refactoring and implementing the new feature. The problem, in this case, is you may not know whether the failure was caused by the refactoring itself or by the implementation of the new feature. Debugging the issue becomes much more difficult because the new feature changes and the refactoring changes are both present and may be hard to separate. You can try backing out only the new feature changes to attempt to isolate the problem, but depending on the complexity of the new feature, that may be difficult by itself. You could also try backing out just the refactoring changes, but then the new feature would break. That may also be difficult to do.

Second, you could run into problems with the new feature. In this case, existing tests pass, but the tests for the new feature do not. In this case, it is probably due to the implementation of the new feature itself, but it's hard to rule out the refactoring changes causing it. Maybe the new feature is exercising parts of the refactored code that the existing code base was not exercising. Even if you are pretty sure the problem is in the new feature implementation, it becomes more difficult to debug simply due to there being more outstanding changes, and it being harder to find the possible bugs in them.

If the cowboy approach isn't the best way to go about implementing a new feature when refactoring is required, what should be done instead? We'll call the alternative approach the **methodical approach**. In the methodical approach, you always refactor first. It doesn't matter how much refactoring is needed or how large the new feature being added is, you always refactor first. Once you've completed the refactoring, you run the tests to make sure the refactoring didn't break anything. At this point, it's a good idea to get updated test coverage information, and add any covering tests needed for the newly refactored code, as you learned about in *Chapter 11, Testing to Ensure Your Code Works*.

After you have fully tested the newly refactored code, you can commit those changes, and then you can begin implementing the feature you need. If during the process you find that additional refactoring is needed, you stash or stage your changes to implement the feature, and then implement and test the refactoring needed. Only after that refactoring has been completed, tested, and committed do you go back to implementing the new feature. After implementing the feature, you can run the tests for the feature and see whether they pass. If one of the existing tests fails at this point, you know something in the new feature is causing the test to fail. You also know that the failure was not caused by the refactoring. Likewise, if one of the new tests fails at this point, you also know it is likely due to the new feature itself and not the refactoring.

Using the methodical approach will probably take a little longer in the best-case scenario. However, it is likely to result in a more complete refactoring, since you complete the refactoring before starting the implementation of the new feature, instead of refactoring just enough to implement the new feature. The greatest advantage of the methodical approach over the cowboy approach is that if something goes wrong, the problem space is significantly reduced, and it is in general much easier to find and fix any bugs found.

In this section, you learned about the methodical and cowboy approaches to adding a feature that requires refactoring. In the next section, you'll learn how to properly remove features from your library.

Removing features properly

Removing features sounds like a bad thing for most new programmers, but it is probably one of the happiest moments for experienced programmers. One important thing to understand is that while most users think of features as assets if you are maintaining a library, features are best thought of as liabilities because every feature has a maintenance cost. When you add a new feature to a library you maintain, you are only increasing your future maintenance burden. By removing a feature in a library that you maintain, you are ridding yourself of a liability. This is one reason removing features is one of the happiest moments for experienced programmers.

Obviously, a library with no features is worthless, so an important quality for a library to have is that the features it contains are useful, and not useless, or worse, actively harmful. However, it is often not possible to foresee when adding a feature whether it will continue to be useful in the years to come. In some cases, a new feature that seems like a great idea when originally implemented turns out to be a major problem in 5 years. The reason that experienced programmers are so happy to get rid of features is the features they generally get rid of are features that are holding the library back or causing the most significant maintenance burden. Simply the knowledge that they will no longer have to deal with the maintenance of the problematic feature is enough to cause significant joy for the remover.

As a responsible library maintainer, you can't just remove features from your library anytime you want, as you are likely to break the code of people relying on your library. In order to ease the burden on your users, for whom feature removal may cause as much pain as removing the feature brings you joy, you need to properly deprecate the feature. How you deprecate the feature depends on what the feature is.

Removing methods

If the feature is a method, the simplest way to deprecate it is to call the `warn` method inside the feature. Make sure to include the name of the method called, which you can get by calling `__callee__`. Also, make sure to use the `:uplevel` keyword argument to `warn`, which will include the caller's filename and line number in the error message. In Ruby 3, it's also a good idea to include the `:category` keyword argument use the `:deprecated` category, as this marks the warning as a deprecation warning. This allows the users of your library to more easily see what method needs to be fixed. Observe the following code:

```ruby
def method_to_be_removed
  warn("#{__callee__} is deprecated",
    uplevel: 1, category: :deprecated)
```

```
  # ...
end
```

Things become more complicated if you still need to call the method internally until it is removed. In this case, it's best to have an internal private alias to the method that doesn't raise a warning, and change all internal callers to use it:

```
def method_to_be_removed
  warn("#{__callee__} is deprecated",
       uplevel: 1, category: :deprecated)
  _method_to_be_removed
end

private def _method_to_be_removed
  # ...
end
```

If the feature being removed is a required positional argument to a method, first you make the required argument optional, and then you only issue the warning if the argument is given. To check whether the argument was given, you can use the technique you learned in *Chapter 7, Designing Your Library*, of setting a local variable inside a default argument value. Say you are planning to remove the argument in this method:

```
def arg_to_be_removed(arg)
  # ...
end
```

You would change this to the following:

```
def arg_to_be_removed(arg=(arg_not_given=true; nil))
  unless arg_not_given
    warn("Passing deprecated argument to #{__callee__}",
         uplevel: 1, category: :deprecated)
  end

  # ...
end
```

Adding a required positional argument is very similar, so we'll give an example here even though it isn't related to removing a feature. If you wanted to add a required argument to the method instead, you use the local variable in the default argument technique, but flip the conditional, as follows:

```
def arg_to_be_added(arg, arg2=(arg2_not_given=true; nil))
  if arg2_not_given
    warn("Should now pass 2 arguments to #{__callee__}",
        uplevel: 1, category: :deprecated)
  end

  # ...
end
```

The technique for removing optional positional arguments or keyword arguments is the same as for removing a required positional argument.

Removing constants

If the feature being removed is a constant and not a method, you can use deprecate_constant:

```
class Foo
  BAR = 1
  deprecate_constant :BAR
end
```

With this approach, any access to the constant will trigger a deprecation warning.

If you still need internal access to the constant until it is removed, you can alias the constant before deprecating it, mark the aliased constant private, and change all internal access to use the private constant:

```
class Foo
  BAR = 1
  BAR_ = BAR
  private_constant :BAR_
  deprecate_constant :BAR
end
```

Notice that the underscore here goes after the constant name and not before because using an underscore first defines a local variable and not a constant.

This doesn't apply just to constants you define in your custom classes; this same approach can be used if you want to deprecate a top-level class, since top-level classes are just constants in `Object`. To deprecate the `Foo` class itself, while keeping `Foo_` for internal reference, use the following:

```
class Object
  Foo_ = Foo
  private_constant :Foo_
  deprecate_constant :Foo
end
```

Note that in Ruby 3, deprecation warnings are not shown by default, even when we have `$VERBOSE = true`. You need to use the `-w` flag when starting Ruby, or set `Warning[:deprecated] = true` if you want deprecation warnings to be displayed.

In general, you should keep the features with the deprecation warnings in your library until you release the next major version of your library. When you release the next major version, you can then feel the joy of removing the deprecated features.

Summary

In this chapter, you've learned how to handle change in your libraries. You've learned reasons to refactor your library, and how to handle the refactoring process. You've learned about implementing the two most common Ruby refactoring techniques, extracting a method and extracting a class. You've learned how important it is to refactor before adding features requiring refactoring. You've also learned about how to properly remove features from your libraries, and the joy of doing so. With all you've learned about refactoring, you are hopefully better able to successfully make appropriate changes to your libraries.

In the next chapter, you'll learn about using common design patterns in your Ruby libraries.

Questions

1. What are three common reasons to refactor in a library?

2. What is the most important prerequisite before starting refactoring?

3. When does it make sense to extract multiple methods instead of a single method?

4. In the best case, what's the fastest approach to implementing a feature that requires refactoring?

5. What keyword arguments should you pass to `Kernel#warn` for deprecation warnings?

13
Using Common Design Patterns

In the last chapter, you learned how best to handle change in your libraries. A couple of common changes are to implement new design patterns or to remove inappropriate design patterns. While design patterns are not as necessary in Ruby as they are in less powerful languages, they are still a useful tool to have in your toolbox. When dealing with design patterns, it is important to understand when it is useful to apply them, and when it is best to abstain from doing so. So in this chapter, you'll also learn when it is appropriate to use specific design patterns.

In this chapter, we will cover the following topics:

- Learning about the many design patterns that are built into Ruby
- Handling cases where there can be only one
- Dealing with nothing
- Visiting objects
- Adapting and strategizing

By the end of this chapter, you'll better understand design patterns that are built into Ruby, and how and why to implement other common design patterns in your libraries and applications.

Technical requirements

In this chapter and all chapters of this book, code given in code blocks is designed to execute on Ruby 3.0. Many of the code examples will work on earlier versions of Ruby, but not all. The code for this chapter is available online at `https://github.com/PacktPublishing/Polished-Ruby-Programming/tree/main/Chapter13`.

Learning about the many design patterns that are built into Ruby

Ruby internally uses many design patterns, supports design patterns in the core classes, and implements design patterns in some standard libraries. In this section, you'll learn about some common design patterns that Ruby uses by default.

The object pool design pattern

With the object pool design pattern, if you need a certain type of object, instead of allocating memory to create a new object, you can reuse an existing object. Ruby's garbage collection system is designed this way. Ruby would be significantly slower and much more prone to memory problems than it already is if it had to manually allocate memory from the operating system each time you created an object. Internally, Ruby uses the object pool pattern to improve object creation speed.

Other than immediate objects such as `true`, `false`, `nil`, symbols, and most integers and floats, all other Ruby objects are stored in an object pool that is referred to as the **Ruby heap**. The Ruby heap is broken up into many sections called **heap pages**, and each of these pages is made up of **slots**. Each object you create in Ruby is stored in one of these slots. When Ruby needs to create an object and there are no free slots left in any heap page, Ruby runs the garbage collector to see if it can free any slots. If it cannot find a free slot after running the garbage collector, then Ruby will need to create a new heap page, and store the object in that new heap page.

By using the object pool design pattern, Ruby reduces the performance and memory fragmentation issues that commonly occur when using `malloc` to allocate and free memory for small objects.

The prototype design pattern

Ruby is often considered to use a class-based object system, but it also supports a prototype-based object system. In a class-based object system, classes and objects (instances of classes) are separate concepts. Classes define the structure, or what types of values are contained in each instance of the class. Objects provide the values for each of those types. In a prototype-based system, there are no classes. Each new object is created by making a copy of an existing object and modifying it.

Most Ruby users use its class-based object system. Ruby nudges you in the direction of using the class-based object by providing special syntax for creating classes:

```
class Foo
end
```

If you ignore this syntax, however, Ruby basically treats the class-based object system and prototype-based object system the same way. You use the class-based object system by creating classes using `Class.new`, and instances of those classes by calling `new` on the resulting class:

```
foo_class = Class.new

foo_class.define_method(:bar) do
  2
end

foo_instance = foo_class.new

foo_instance.bar
# => 2
```

You use the prototype-based object system by taking an empty object and cloning it, then modifying the clone, then creating clones of that object:

```
foo_proto = Object.new

foo_proto.define_singleton_method(:bar) do
  2
end

foo_clone = foo_proto.clone
```

```
foo_clone.bar
# => 2
```

Ruby can support both a class-based object system and a prototype-based object system through the use of singleton classes. It even supports combining both the class-based object system and the prototype-based object systems:

```
foo_class = Class.new

foo_class.define_method(:bar) do
  2
end

foo_class_clone = foo_class.clone

foo_class_clone_instance = foo_class_clone.new

foo_class_clone_clone = foo_class_clone_instance.clone

foo_class_clone_clone.bar
# => 2
```

Being able to support both class-based object systems and prototype-based object systems is a huge advantage of Ruby, and the design of some Ruby libraries, such as Sequel, is only possible by using a mix of the two. In Sequel, each database adapter has its own `Sequel::Dataset` subclass (the class-based object system), and `Sequel::Dataset` instances are frozen and use `clone` to create modified copies of instances, including copies of the dataset's singleton class (the prototype-based object system).

The private class data design pattern

The private class data design pattern reduces the exposure of class-level data so that it cannot be manipulated. Ruby has built-in support for this design pattern using class instance variables:

```
class Foo
  @bar = 1
end
```

Unless encapsulation is deliberately broken through the use of `instance_variable_get`, `instance_variable_set`, or calling a method such as `class_eval`, the `@bar` instance variable is private to this class. It is not available to other objects, to instances of the class, or subclasses of the class.

For methods of the class that should only be accessed by the class itself, you can use `private_class_method`:

```ruby
class Foo
  def self.bar
    2
  end
  private_class_method :bar
end
```

Similarly, unless encapsulation is deliberately broken via `Kernel#send`, this method is not callable by other objects or instances of the class. However, it is available to subclasses of the class. Preventing subclasses of the class from calling the method is possible, but does not happen by default. If you want to prevent a subclass from calling the method, you can do so by checking the value of `self` inside the method:

```ruby
class Foo
  def self.bar
    raise TypeError, "not Foo" unless Foo == self
    2
  end
  private_class_method :bar
end
```

For constants of the class that should be private, you can use `private_constant`:

```ruby
class Foo
  BAR = 3
  private_constant :BAR
end
```

Unless encapsulation is deliberately broken via `Module#const_get`, this constant is not accessible by other objects or instances of the class. However, it is accessible by subclasses of the class, and there isn't a way in Ruby to prevent subclasses from accessing it inside the subclass.

The proxy design pattern

The proxy pattern involves creating wrapper objects for objects and calling methods on those wrapper objects. The wrapper, or proxy, objects, can add useful behavior, such as metrics (the number of calls for each method), caching, or only exposing a subset of the object's methods.

Ruby provides two standard libraries that implement the proxy pattern in a couple of different ways. As you learned in *Chapter 4, Methods and Their Arguments*, the forwardable library can be used to proxy specific methods to other objects:

```ruby
require 'forwardable'

class Proxy
  extend Forwardable

  def initialize(value)
    @value = value
  end

  def_delegator :@value, :to_s
end

Proxy.new(1).to_s
# => "1"
```

forwardable is useful for wrappers that only wrap a subset of the target object's methods. However, if you want to wrap all or almost all of a target object's methods, it is tedious to implement that with forwardable.

For wrapping all or almost all of a target object's methods, Ruby has a separate standard library, delegate. With the delegate library, you can use the SimpleDelegator class to return a proxy object that delegates all methods to the target object, other than those methods defined in the SimpleDelegator class:

```ruby
require 'delegate'

class Proxy2 < SimpleDelegator
  def add_3
    self + 3
  end
```

```
  end

Proxy2.new(1).add_3
# => 4
```

However, `SimpleDelegator` subclasses can wrap any object, not just specific types of objects, so they aren't as useful when you want to deal with proxies for specific types of objects. For more specific proxy types, you can use `Kernel#DelegateClass`, which is also added by the `delegate` library:

```
class HashProxy < DelegateClass(Hash)
  def size_squared
    size ** 2
  end
end

HashProxy.new(a: 1, b: 2, c: 3).size_squared
# => 9
```

In this section, you've learned that Ruby implements the object pool design pattern internally. You've also learned that Ruby offers either core class or standard library support for the prototype, private class data, and proxy design patterns. In the next section, you'll learn how to implement the singleton design pattern in Ruby.

Handling cases where there can be only one

In cases where an application using your library should only have a single instance of the object, you usually would reach for the singleton design pattern. Ruby actually has a standard library for the singleton pattern, appropriately named `singleton`. This library defines the `Singleton` module, which you can include in other classes to turn those classes into singletons. A class that includes `Singleton` no longer has a public `new` method, since you should not be creating multiple instances. Instead, it provides a class method named `instance`, which returns the only instance of the class:

```
require 'singleton'

class OnlyOne
  include Singleton
```

```
  def foo
    :foo
  end
end

only1 = OnlyOne.instance
only2 = OnlyOne.instance

only1.equal?(only2)
# => true
```

The `singleton` library does implement the singleton pattern. So why wasn't it discussed in the previous section, since it is a standard library? This is because, due to the expressive power of Ruby, there is rarely a reason to use it. If you have an existing object where it makes sense to keep the methods, it is better to define the methods as singleton methods on that object or to extend the object with a module that includes the methods. If you need to have a separate object to store the methods, it is usually better in Ruby to instead create an `Object` instance as a constant:

```
OnlyOne = Object.new
```

Then, to define behavior for that object, you would do the same thing you do for every other object in Ruby, which is to define methods directly on this object:

```
def OnlyOne.foo
  :foo
end
```

One of the other aspects of the standard singleton design pattern is called **lazy initialization**, where the singleton instance is not created until access to it is first created by calling the method to access the instance. The implementation of singletons via constants doesn't support this directly, but you can implement this in Ruby using `autoload`. To use `autoload` for lazy initializing, you would put the assigning and setup of the singleton in its own file, and then set Ruby to autoload that file on the first reference to the constant:

```
Object.autoload :OnlyOne, 'only_one'
```

One advantage of the autoload approach for lazy initialization over using the singleton library (without autoload) is that you pay no memory penalty for the singleton definition if the constant is not accessed. However, as you'll learn about in *Chapter 17, Robust Web Application Security*, the use of autoload is problematic in environments that implement filesystem access limiting after application initialization.

Note that you can use autoload even if using the singleton library, as the lazy initialization approach used by autoload is orthogonal to the lazy initialization approach used by the singleton library.

In this section, you learned why it is better to implement the singleton pattern using a standard object as opposed to using the singleton standard library. In the next section, you'll learn about using the null object pattern in Ruby, which has been recommended by some Ruby programmers in recent years.

Dealing with nothing

The null object pattern has gained increased popularity in some parts of the Ruby community in recent years. With the null object pattern, when you deal with another object that may or may not be available, instead of using nil to represent the case where the other object is not available, you use a separate object that implements the same methods.

As an example of this, let's say you are writing an internal application for a company, and you need to represent employees using an Employee class. For each employee, you are tracking the name, position, phone, and supervisor of the employee:

```ruby
class Employee
  attr_reader :name
  attr_reader :position
  attr_reader :phone

  def initialize(name, position, phone, supervisor)
    @name = name
    @position = position
    @phone = phone
    @supervisor = supervisor
  end
```

There is a common need to print information about the employee, such as the employee's name, position, and phone number, and their supervisor's name, position, and phone number:

```ruby
def employee_info
  <<~END
    Name: #{@name}
    Position: #{@position}
    Phone: #{@phone}
    Supervisor Name: #{@supervisor.name}
    Supervisor Position: #{@supervisor.position}
    Supervisor Phone: #{@supervisor.phone}
  END
end
end
```

Then we can check that this works the way we expect, assuming the employee has a supervisor:

```ruby
supervisor = Employee.new("Juan Manuel", "CEO",
                          "246-011-0642", nil)
subordinate = Employee.new("Aziz Karim", "CTO",
                           "707-405-9260", supervisor)

print subordinate.employee_info
# Name: Aziz Karim
# Position: CTO
# Phone: 707-405-9260
# Supervisor Name: Juan Manuel
# Supervisor Position: CEO
# Supervisor Phone: 246-011-0642
```

Unfortunately, this does not work if the employee does not have a supervisor:

```ruby
print supervisor.employee_info
# NoMethodError
```

This is because the `employee_info` method tries to call the `name` method on `@supervisor`, and `@supervisor` is `nil`. Ruby has built-in support for skipping method calls on `nil` values using the lonely operator (`&.`). One way to work around the issue is to use the lonely operator when calling any method on an object that may be `nil`:

```ruby
class Employee
  def employee_info
    <<~END
    Name: #{@name}
    Position: #{@position}
    Phone: #{@phone}
    Supervisor Name: #{@supervisor&.name}
    Supervisor Position: #{@supervisor&.position}
    Supervisor Phone: #{@supervisor&.phone}
    END
  end
end
```

This allows you to call `employee_info` on an `Employee` instance even if the employee doesn't have a supervisor:

```ruby
print supervisor.employee_info
# Name: Juan Manuel
# Position: CEO
# Phone: 246-011-0642
# Supervisor Name:
# Supervisor Position:
# Supervisor Phone:
```

One issue with this approach of using the lonely operator is that you need to remember to add it to every method call on the object that may be `nil`. If you forget one place, you have a `NoMethodError` waiting to be raised. If that sounds problematic, then the null object pattern is right up your alley.

With the null object pattern, instead of using `nil` for the missing object, you use a separate object that supports the same API as the missing object. In this case, to implement the null object pattern, you could add a `NullEmployee` class that uses an empty string for the name, position, and phone, shown as follows:

```
class NullEmployee
  def name
    ""
  end

  def position
    ""
  end

  def phone
    ""
  end
end
```

In order to implement the null object pattern correctly, both of the following conditions must be met:

- The null object needs to implement the same methods as the missing object.
- Calling methods on the null object should return objects of the same type as calling the same methods on the missing object, assuming the same arguments are passed.

The `name`, `position`, and `phone` methods shown previously meet these criteria, because the `Employee` class returns strings for these methods, and so does the `NullEmployee` class.

We can test out this null object by explicitly passing a `NullEmployee` instance as the supervisor when the employee doesn't have a supervisor:

```
supervisor = Employee.new("Juan Manuel", "CEO",
                          "246-011-0642",
                          NullEmployee.new)
```

Then we can test that the `Employee#employee_info` method works correctly with the `NullEmployee` instance, even when using the original `employee_info` method that didn't use the lonely operator:

```
print supervisor.employee_info
# Name: Juan Manuel
# Position: CEO
# Phone: 246-011-0642
# Supervisor Name:
# Supervisor Position:
# Supervisor Phone:
```

We're actually missing something here, and that is that `NullEmployee` doesn't implement the `employee_info` method, in violation of the null object pattern. However, since there is no method you can call to get a `NullEmployee` object, that's not currently a problem. However, as soon as you add a `supervisor` method to `Employee`, you have this issue:

```
Employee.attr_reader :supervisor
```

If we wanted to implement `employee_info` in `NullEmployee`, we could actually define it the same way as we define the `Employee#employee_info` method. However, that just leads to duplication. For this and similar reasons, it's often recommended to make the null object class and the actual object class both be subclasses of the same abstract class. If we want to do that, we can create an `AbstractEmployee` class almost exactly the same way we created the `Employee` class. It defines the same attributes and `employee_info` method:

```
class AbstractEmployee
  attr_reader :name
  attr_reader :position
  attr_reader :phone

  def employee_info
    <<~END
    Name: #{@name}
    Position: #{@position}
    Phone: #{@phone}
    Supervisor Name: #{@supervisor.name}
    Supervisor Position: #{@supervisor.position}
```

```
        Supervisor Phone: #{@supervisor.phone}
    END
  end
end
```

Employee can be a subclass of AbstractEmployee, with an initialize method the same as it was defined previously:

```
class Employee < AbstractEmployee
  attr_reader :supervisor

  def initialize(name, position, phone, supervisor)
    @name = name
    @position = position
    @phone = phone
    @supervisor = supervisor
  end
end
```

Similarly, you can define the NullEmployee class to be a subclass of AbstractEmployee, but instead of defining the methods separately, we can just override initialize to set the null object values. A simple approach would be to do the following:

```
class NullEmployee < AbstractEmployee
  def initialize
    @name = ''
    @position = ''
    @phone = ''
    @supervisor = NullEmployee.new
  end
end
```

This has an advantage over the previous approach that did not subclass from AbstractEmployee, and that is that the name, position, and phone methods return the same object every time you call them on the same object, so the following code works the same way on both Employee and NullEmployee:

```
employee.phone << "x1008"
```

Unfortunately, there's a problem with this approach, and that is it actually causes a `SystemStackError`:

```
NullEmployee.new
# SystemStackError
```

This is because calling `NullEmployee.new` ends up calling `NullEmployee.new` recursively until the stack is exhausted. To prevent this approach, you need to define `supervisor` as a separate method:

```
class NullEmployee
  def initialize
    @name = ''
    @position = ''
    @phone = ''
  end

  def supervisor
    @supervisor ||= NullEmployee.new
  end
end
```

This allows you to create a `NullEmployee` instance without raising an exception:

```
null_employee = NullEmployee.new
```

Unfortunately, you still can't call `employee_info` on the null employee without an exception being raised:

```
null_employee.employee_info
# NoMethodError
```

This is due to the same issue we had before the null object pattern was introduced, and that is because the null employee's supervisor is `nil`. One way to work around this would be to switch the `employee_info` method to call the `supervisor` method instead of accessing the `@supervisor` instance variable. However, that approach will make all calls to `employee_info` slower, even in `Employee`. We could have different implementations of `employee_info` in both `Employee` and `NullEmployee`, but that leads to duplication. A third approach, probably the best way to handle this, would be to override `employee_info` in `NullEmployee`, load the supervisor, then call `super`:

```
class NullEmployee
  def employee_info
    supervisor
    super
  end
end
```

With that change, you can call `employee_info` on the null employee, finally implementing the null object pattern correctly:

```
null_employee.employee_info
# Name:
# Position:
# Phone:
# Supervisor Name:
# Supervisor Position:
# Supervisor Phone:
```

Even though it took a while to set up, you can see the advantage of the null object pattern, in that you don't have to use the lonely operator when calling methods, and everything still works. You can confidently call methods on the employee, and it doesn't matter whether the employee is an `Employee` instance or a `NullEmployee` instance, everything still works.

Knowing the advantages of the null object pattern, does it make sense to use a null object instead of `nil` for all cases where you are dealing with missing data? In general, no, it does not. The null object pattern is only suited to specific cases such as the previous one, where you want to be able to treat the absence of an object the same as the presence of an object.

Let's say you had a smarter version of `employee_info` that only included the supervisor's information if there was a supervisor. First, you can simplify the code by extracting a `specific_employee_info` method that only prints information for a specific employee:

```
class Employee
  def specific_employee_info
    <<~END
    Name: #{@name}
    Position: #{@position}
    Phone: #{@phone}
    END
  end
```

Then you can override `employee_info` to call the `specific_employee_info` method on both the current `employee` and the `supervisor` if the supervisor exists, or just the employee if it does not:

```
  def employee_info
    if @supervisor
      specific_employee_info +
        @supervisor.specific_employee_info
    else
      specific_employee_info
    end
  end
end
```

This results in cleaner output if the employee doesn't have a `supervisor`:

```
supervisor = Employee.new("Juan Manuel", "CEO",
                          "246-011-0642", nil)
supervisor.employee_info
# Name: Juan Manuel
# Position: CEO
# Phone: 246-011-0642
```

In this case, where you actually care whether you have a real employee or a null employee, the null object pattern adds complexity instead of removing complexity. If you were using the null object pattern, you need to use a more complex construction of checking whether the supervisor is actually an object you expect:

```
class Employee
  def employee_info
    if @supervisor.is_a?(Employee)
      specific_employee_info +
        @supervisor.specific_employee_info
    else
      specific_employee_info
    end
  end
end
```

In general, if you have even a small percentage of cases where you are checking for a real object or a null object, you should avoid the null object pattern, and just use the lonely operator to guard calls against the missing object. The null object pattern should only be used if you can always or almost always treat the null object as a real object.

The other issue with using the null object pattern instead of nil is the null object pattern tends to be much slower. nil is an immediate object in Ruby and does not consume any memory, while each null object needs to be allocated before use and garbage collected after use. It's possible to mitigate this issue by using a shared null object, but then the null object needs to be frozen, and that can make it not work the same way as an unfrozen version of a regular object. In general, it is best to avoid the null object pattern in performance-sensitive code, even if it would otherwise be a good fit.

In this section, you learned about applying the null object design pattern to Ruby. In the next section, you'll learn about applying the visitor pattern.

Visiting objects

The visitor pattern is most commonly used when you have many objects of separate classes that you need to handle in some manner. You have a class called a visitor that processes, or visits, each object and does something with the object. Often when using the visitor pattern, you actually have multiple different types of operations that all need to deal with the same objects, so you have multiple visitor classes. However, you do not want to add methods for each visitor class to each of those separate classes. After all, while it is possible to define methods on any class in Ruby, it's generally considered bad practice to define methods on classes that are not part of your library, unless that is the sole purpose of your library.

The visitor pattern is a way around the problem of defining per-visitor methods in each class that is being visited. A classic approach to the visitor pattern results in a ton of complexity and still requires adding a method to the classes being visited. Since you should probably avoid that, you decide to implement a modified visitor pattern. With this modified pattern, the visitor class handles the method dispatch instead of relying on the class being visited.

One approach to implementing the visitor pattern in Ruby is to have a single `visit` method that uses a `case` expression to dispatch each type of supported object to a specific private method. We'll call this example class `ArbitraryVisitor`, since the visiting class just performs some arbitrary actions:

```ruby
class ArbitraryVisitor
  def visit(obj)
    case obj
    when Integer
      visit_integer(obj)
    when String
      visit_string(obj)
    when Array
      visit_array(obj)
    else
      raise ArgumentError, "unsupported object visited"
    end
  end
```

Summary

In this chapter, you've learned about many design patterns and how they apply to Ruby. You've learned that some design patterns are built into Ruby, and others are implemented by core classes and standard libraries. You've also learned how best to implement the singleton, null object, visitor, adapter, and strategy patterns in Ruby. With this knowledge, you are now better able to apply these design patterns correctly in your libraries and make them more maintainable. Additionally, you may be able to recognize and remove inappropriate use of these design patterns from your libraries, also making them more maintainable.

In the next chapter, the last chapter of *Section 2*, you'll learn about optimizing your library.

Questions

1. What design pattern does Ruby's garbage collector use?

2. How do you implement lazy evaluation if using the constant approach to implementing the singleton pattern?

3. When is it not a good idea to implement the null object pattern?

4. Why would you want to use the hash approach to the visitor pattern instead of the case approach?

5. What's the significant difference between the adapter and strategy patterns?

14
Optimizing Your Library

Optimization is often not needed in Ruby, but when it is needed, it should be approached in a principled manner, lest you waste time optimizing the wrong code. Nobody likes slow code, but there is a reason that premature optimization is considered the root of all evil.

In this chapter, you'll learn the importance of profiling in order to decide what to optimize, how the best optimization is deleting code or delaying the execution of code, and what to do when it looks like all parts of your application are slow.

We will cover the following topics in this chapter:

- Understanding that you probably don't need to optimize code
- Profiling first, optimizing second
- Understanding that no code is faster than no code
- Handling code where everything is slow

By the end of this chapter, you'll have a better understanding of when and how to optimize your application.

Technical requirements

In this chapter and all chapters of this book, code given in code blocks is designed to execute on Ruby 3.0. Many of the code examples will work on earlier versions of Ruby, but not all. The code for this chapter is available online at `https://github.com/PacktPublishing/Polished-Ruby-Programming/tree/main/Chapter14`.

Understanding that you probably don't need to optimize code

Programmers in general, and new programmers in particular, often have the idea that all code needs to be fast. Now, there are certainly some environments where super-fast code is a requirement. If you are designing high-frequency trading software, modeling complex astrodynamics or fluid mechanics, or programming in a real-time environment where code must execute in a given number of microseconds, you want to make sure your code is as fast as it can be.

However, if you are using Ruby, that's unlikely to be the case. For one, compared to many other programming languages, Ruby is slow. This isn't a complaint about Ruby. To be fair to Ruby, no language that is as dynamic, easy to use, and programmer-friendly as Ruby is as fast as Ruby. However, Ruby is not known for its performance, at least not in a positive light. If you are using Ruby, it is likely in an environment where the flexibility and ease of use of Ruby outweigh the potential performance issues.

Even in cases where performance is important, such as many business cases, often Ruby's default performance will be fast enough. You should try to avoid implementing a more complex approach that you think will be faster, instead of using a simpler approach that you think will be slower. In many cases, the performance difference will not matter, and either the simpler approach or the more complex approach will perform adequately. In that case, it's usually better to use the simpler approach in order to reduce the maintenance cost.

In many other cases, you are guessing incorrectly that the more complex case will perform better, and it actually performs worse. This can happen even to expert Ruby programmers with many years of experience dealing with the internals of Ruby. Ruby has a lot of internal complexity, and when comparing the performance of a complex case to the performance of a simple case, there is a fair chance that even an expert will be surprised at which is faster.

Often the slow part of the library is not in Ruby itself but in another part of the library. For libraries that access a database, often the slowest part is inside the database, and only by modifying the database queries used can you significantly improve performance. For libraries that make network requests to external servers, the slowest part is usually in the network request, and the time spent executing Ruby code is far less.

A good general principle is to assume that your library will be fast enough, and only if it's proven to be too slow should you attempt to optimize it. Other than bragging rights, having the most optimized library is rarely a significant selling point in Ruby. After all, there is probably a more popular library that is already fast enough. Focus first on making your library easy to use and adding unique and compelling features. Don't worry about performance until you need to.

In this section, you learned that optimization is often not needed in Ruby, since your current implementation is probably fast enough. In the next section, you'll learn what to do in cases where it isn't fast enough.

Profiling first, optimizing second

It's better to never guess where the slow parts of your library are, since you will often be incorrect. There is one way to know where the slow parts of your library are, and that is to profile your library. There are a couple of good options for profiling libraries in Ruby, `ruby-prof` and `stackprof`. There are other profilers for Ruby, such as `rack-mini-profiler` and `rbspy`, but they mostly focus on profiling production applications and not libraries, so we won't discuss them further. However, you may want to remember them if you need to profile a production application.

`ruby-prof` is one of the oldest profiling libraries for Ruby, and still one of the best. It is a tracing profiler, meaning that it keeps track of every single method call Ruby is making, so it generally results in the most accurate profiling. However, because of this, it's the slowest profiler, about two to three times slower than running standard Ruby. This means it's generally not suitable for profiling actual production applications, but it is usually fine for profiling libraries. `ruby-prof` installs as a gem and allows the profiling of specific blocks of code, so it is fairly flexible.

`stackprof` is not as old as `ruby-prof`, but it still has been around for many years. It is a sampling profiler, which means that instead of tracing method calls, it only checks and sees what method Ruby is running every so often, and if you give it a long enough amount of time, statistically it should give a reasonable estimation of what methods are running the majority of the time. Being a sampling profiler, while it may not have the highest accuracy, it has low overhead, so adding profiling to existing code does not slow it down much. `stackprof` also installs as a gem and allows the profiling of specific blocks of code, so it is also fairly flexible.

In the rest of this section, we'll use `ruby-prof` for examples, but the principles of profiling will largely apply to `stackprof` as well.

To learn how to use `ruby-prof`, after installing the gem, you decide to build a simple example class named `MultiplyProf` that can calculate powers of integers, floats, and rationals. Refer to the following code block:

```
class MultiplyProf
  def initialize(vals)
    @i1, @i2 = vals.map(&:to_i)
    @f1, @f2 = vals.map(&:to_f)
    @r1, @r2 = vals.map(&:to_r)
  end
  def integer
    @i1 * @i2
  end
  def float
    @f1 * @f2
  end
  def rational
    @r1 * @r2
  end
end
```

First, before profiling any code, you need to make sure that it works:

```
mp = MultiplyProf.new([2.4r, 4.2r])

mp.integer
# => 8
```

```
mp.float
# => 10.08
```

```
mp.rational
# => (252/25)
```

That looks reasonable. The result for `integer` does not match the result for `float` and `rational` because `integer` doesn't contain the required precision. However, for experimenting with profiling, this example should be fine.

Profiling with `ruby-prof` is easy. After you require the library, surround the block of code you want to test in `RubyProf.profile`, and then print the results. Before running this, see whether you can guess what method will take the most time:

```ruby
require 'ruby-prof'

result = RubyProf.profile do
  1000.times do
    mp = MultiplyProf.new([2.4r, 4.2r])
    mp.integer
    mp.float
    mp.rational
  end
end

# print a graph profile to text
printer = RubyProf::FlatPrinter.new(result)
printer.print(STDOUT, {})
```

Here is an abridged version of the results that will be readable. Hopefully you made a guess before looking at this:

```
# %self    name                     location
# 25.26    Array#map
# 16.84    Integer#times
# 16.69    MultiplyProf#initialize   t.rb:4
#  7.08    Rational#*
#  6.05    Class#new
```

#	5.79	MultiplyProf#rational	t.rb:15
#	5.06	Rational#to_f	
#	4.34	Rational#to_i	
#	4.08	Rational#to_r	
#	3.94	MultiplyProf#integer	t.rb:9
#	3.93	MultiplyProf#float	t.rb:12
#	0.94	[global]#	t.rb:2

So, how accurate was your guess? Did you guess correctly that `Array#map` and `Integer#times` would take up so much time? It probably appeared originally that this was a profile of which of the `integer`, `float`, and `rational` methods of `MultiplyProf` was the fastest. Instead, it actually shows that you need to be careful with what you are profiling.

If your library tends to create a lot of `MultiplyProf` instances and calls `integer`, `float`, or `rational` only once on each, then you want to make `MultiplyProf#initialize` as fast as possible. If your library instead creates a small number of `MultiplyProf` instances and calls `integer`, `float`, or `rational` many times on each, you don't care about `MultiplyProf` initialization speed, but you care to make the `integer`, `float`, and `rational` methods as fast as you can. Make sure what you are profiling matches what your library is typically doing; otherwise, you may optimize for the wrong use case, and make performance worse. If you profile using the previous example but your library only creates a single `MultiplyProf` instance, you may take an approach that makes initialization faster and calling methods on the `MultiplyProf` instance slower, resulting in an overall decrease in the performance of your library.

Let's assume the previous profile is an accurate picture of how your library is typically used. Before you do any optimization, you need a benchmark to produce a baseline of current performance. `ruby-prof` actually does print out the total time taken, but that is with tracing enabled, so there are potential cases where it isn't accurate. You always want a real benchmark both before and after optimization to make sure optimization improved performance.

Ruby has a `benchmark` library built in that could be used for benchmarking. When actually benchmarking, you should probably use many more iterations, ideally enough so the benchmark takes at least 5 seconds. Here's how you could use Ruby's `benchmark` library to benchmark this code:

```ruby
require 'benchmark'

Benchmark.realtime do
  2000000.times do
    mp = MultiplyProf.new([2.4r, 4.2r])
    mp.integer
    mp.float
    mp.rational
  end
end
# => 6.9715518148150295
```

Having to manually adjust the number of iterations is kind of a pain. There's a better approach, and that is using the `benchmark-ips` gem. The API is not as simple, as the gem is designed mostly for the comparative benchmarking of different implementation approaches, but it is still easy to use:

```ruby
require 'benchmark/ips'

Benchmark.ips do |x|
  x.report("MultiplyProf") do
    mp = MultiplyProf.new([2.4r, 4.2r])
    mp.integer
    mp.float
    mp.rational
  end
end
```

The abridged version of the previous code output is as follows:

```
# Warming up ---------------------------------------
#    MultiplyProf      28.531k i/100ms
# Calculating --------------------------------------
#    MultiplyProf      284.095k (± 0.3%) i/s
```

The first number in the `Warming up` section is a short test that `benchmark-ips` runs to warm up the code, which is designed to run enough iterations of the library to generate the fastest possible implementation either via manual caching inside the method or via the Ruby implementation JIT compiler. In most cases, you should ignore the number in the `Warming up` section, and only pay attention to the number in the `Calculating` section. The number in the `Calculating` section basically tells you that it can execute about `284,000` iterations every second. This becomes your baseline, and you'll measure your optimization attempts against it.

So, with the profiling data and the baseline created, now you can start optimizing! How do you do that? You start by looking at the profile. `Array#map` is at the top of the list, so you should start there. All usage is inside `MultiplyProf#initialize`:

```ruby
class MultiplyProf
  def initialize(vals)
    @i1, @i2 = vals.map(&:to_i)
    @f1, @f2 = vals.map(&:to_f)
    @r1, @r2 = vals.map(&:to_r)
  end
end
```

It turns out `Array#map` is completely unnecessary here and can be eliminated completely:

```ruby
class MultiplyProf
  def initialize(vals)
    v1, v2 = vals
    @i1, @i2 = v1.to_i, v2.to_i
    @f1, @f2 = v1.to_f, v2.to_f
    @r1, @r2 = v1.to_r, v2.to_r
  end
end
```

You can skip the `Integer#times` call, as that isn't used inside the `MultiplyProf` library; it comes from the use of `1000.times` inside the profile and benchmark block. For more accurate profiling, it's actually better to skip the use of `Integer#times` and instead use a manual `while` loop:

```
result = RubyProf.profile do
  i = 0
  while i < 1000
    mp = MultiplyProf.new([2.4r, 4.2r])
    mp.integer
    mp.float
    mp.rational
    i += 1
  end
end
```

`MultiplyProf#initialize` is the next highest in terms of time spent inside the method. Unfortunately, after the `Array#map` elimination, it's about as fast as it can get. Let's try reprofiling after the changes to `MultiplyProf#initialize` and by using the `while` loop:

```
# %self      name                     location
# 30.88      MultiplyProf#initialize  t.rb:4
# 24.13      [global]#                t.rb:22
#  7.58      Class#new
#  7.41      MultiplyProf#rational    t.rb:16
#  6.29      Rational#to_f
#  5.23      Rational#to_i
#  5.12      Rational#to_r
#  5.00      MultiplyProf#float       t.rb:13
#  4.99      MultiplyProf#integer     t.rb:10
#  3.37      Rational#*
```

Over half of the time is still spent inside `MultiplyProf.new`, either directly or indirectly. After that, most of the remaining time is spent inside the loop itself. Less than a quarter of the time is spent in the methods doing the multiplication.

At this point, you can check against the baseline by running exactly the same benchmark code as we did previously, using `benchmark-ips`. This time you get the following:

```
# Warming up --------------------------------------
#    MultiplyProf      47.691k i/100ms
# Calculating --------------------------------------
#    MultiplyProf     480.311k (± 0.2%) i/s
```

From the benchmark output, you can see that the simple change to the `MultiplyProf#initialize` method sped up the block of code by around 70%! That's a huge difference for such a small change, and probably not a place you would have considered optimizing if you hadn't reviewed the profile output.

In this section, you learned the importance of profiling before attempting to optimize. In the next section, you'll attempt to further optimize the example in this section, using the principle of *No code is faster than no code.*

Understanding that no code is faster than no code

The phrase *No code is faster than no code* was the motto of the old Ruby web framework named **Merb**, which focused heavily on performance. Another, less poetic way of phrasing the same principle is, *If you can get the same result without executing any code, any approach that requires executing code will be slower.* A simplification of the principle would be, *The fastest code is usually the code that does the least.* In general, if you want the code to be as fast as possible, you need to find a way to get the same results while doing less work.

There are cases where doing less work can require an algorithmic change, such as changing from a linear scan of an array to using a hash table lookup. There are other cases where doing less work can be accomplished by caching results. Sometimes, doing less work can be accomplished by restructuring your code to delay computation until it is needed, or even better, figuring out computation is not needed at all and eliminating it.

With the previous example, there's not a good way to apply this principle, since each instance method of `MultiplyProf` is called exactly once. You were working under that assumption in the previous section, but that's probably not realistic. In most cases, you will be creating a `MultiplyProf` instance many times and only calling one of the methods on it, or you will be creating a `MultiplyProf` instance during application initialization and calling methods on it at runtime, so the `MultiplyProf#initialize` performance isn't important. Let's look at how to optimize both cases.

You decide to first optimize the case where `MultiplyProf` instances are created at runtime but only one of the `MultiplyProf` methods is called. In this case, you want to execute the least code possible in the `MultiplyProf#initialize` method. As shown in the previous section, you should first look at the profiling information for your case, and then the benchmark to create a baseline performance. In the interests of space, we'll skip the profiling output and only show an abridged version of the benchmark output:

```
Benchmark.ips do |x|
  x.report("MultiplyProf") do
    MultiplyProf.new([2.4r, 4.2r]).integer
    MultiplyProf.new([2.4r, 4.2r]).float
    MultiplyProf.new([2.4r, 4.2r]).rational
  end
end
# 189.666k i/s
```

This is a slower baseline than the previous baseline, even with the more optimized code that does not use `Array#map`, because we are creating three `MultiplyProf` instances instead of one. Do not worry if your baseline for a different benchmark is slower than a previous baseline. What matters is the speedup between the baseline performance and the performance after optimization for the same benchmark.

Since you are calling `MultiplyProf#initialize` three times as often in this benchmark, you need to optimize that method as much as possible, and the best way to do that, in this case, is to avoid executing as much code as possible inside the method. What's the absolute simplest `initialize` method you could write? Well, the absolute simplest `initialize` method with the same API is probably the following:

```
class MultiplyProf
  def initialize(vals)
    # do nothing
  end
end
```

However, that throws away the argument and won't allow you to calculate the results. At the very least, you need to store the argument somewhere:

```
class MultiplyProf
  def initialize(vals)
    @vals = vals
  end
```

If the `initialize` method looks like this, then you need to adjust the `integer`, `float`, and `rational` methods to handle the fact that the only instance variable is now `@vals`. Each method needs to access the appropriate argument in `vals` and run the `to_i`, `to_f`, or `to_r` conversion on it:

```
def integer
  @vals[0].to_i * @vals[1].to_i
end
def float
  @vals[0].to_f * @vals[1].to_f
end
def rational
  @vals[0].to_r * @vals[1].to_r
end
end
```

With this new implementation that optimizes the `initialize` performance, we can rerun the benchmark to compare it to the baseline. Running the exact same benchmark with the new implementation, we get the following:

```
# 363.114k i/s
```

With this new approach, there is over a 90% increase in performance! That's a great result, though if you think about it, you did have to rewrite the entire class to achieve it.

Now you decide to try to optimize the second case. This is a case where you create a `MultiplyProf` instance during application initialization, and only call methods on the `MultiplyProf` instance at runtime. You would want to create the baseline, not with the previous implementation with the `@vals` instance variable, but with the implementation that used `v1, v2 = vals` inside `initialize`. A good benchmark for this would look like this:

```
mp = MultiplyProf.new([2.4r, 4.2r])
Benchmark.ips do |x|
  x.report("MultiplyProf") do
    mp.integer
    mp.float
    mp.rational
  end
```

```
end
# 2.130M i/s
```

This baseline result is way faster than the previous baseline, but again, remember that the baseline number means nothing; all that matters is the difference between the baseline result and the result after optimization.

With this benchmark, we can see that we don't need to care about the MultiplyProf#initialize performance; we only need to care about the performance of the integer, float, and rational methods. The important realization here is that the methods are idempotent and the results of the methods will not change at runtime. You can actually precalculate all results upfront and create the integer, float, and rational methods using attr_reader. The Ruby virtual machine executes attr_reader methods faster than methods defined with def, so you should use them when speed is important. This approach appears as in the following code block:

```
class MultiplyProf
  attr_reader :integer
  attr_reader :float
  attr_reader :rational

  def initialize(vals)
    v1, v2 = vals
    @integer = v1.to_i * v2.to_i
    @float = v1.to_f * v2.to_f
    @rational = v1.to_r * v2.to_r
  end
end
```

With this new implementation that optimizes integer, float, and rational performance, we can rerun the benchmark to compare it to the baseline. Running the exact same benchmark with the new implementation, we get the following:

```
# 5.022M i/s
```

That's an increase of over 135%, your best performance improvement yet! With the important realization that the methods are idempotent, you could reoptimize the approach where you were optimizing for performance by caching results:

```
class MultiplyProf
  def initialize(vals)
    @vals = vals
  end
  def integer
    @integer ||= @vals[0].to_i * @vals[1].to_i
  end
  def float
    @float ||= @vals[0].to_f * @vals[1].to_f
  end
  def rational
    @rational ||= @vals[0].to_r * @vals[1].to_r
  end
end
```

You test this approach using the earlier benchmark:

```
Benchmark.ips do |x|
  x.report("MultiplyProf") do
    MultiplyProf.new([2.4r, 4.2r]).integer
    MultiplyProf.new([2.4r, 4.2r]).float
    MultiplyProf.new([2.4r, 4.2r]).rational
  end
end
# 301.952k i/s
```

You can see this is actually slower than the previous optimized approach, which resulted in 363.114k iterations per second. That's because the benchmark doesn't actually use the cached value. You could design a benchmark where it is probably the best performing approach, such as a benchmark where you created a few MultiplyProf instances without calling methods on them, and then created a single MultiplyProf instance and called the integer, float, and rational methods a few times on it.

The most important aspect of a benchmark is how well the benchmark reflects how the library is actually used. When possible, try to create benchmarks that are actual production use cases or similar to production use cases.

In this section, you learned how to optimize by trying to avoid computation in the parts of your code that are called most often. In the next section, you'll learn what to do when all parts of the profile are equally slow, and you don't have a good idea of how to optimize.

Handling code where everything is slow

Sometimes you have a ball of mud, where everything is slow and you cannot figure out why. This is an unfortunate situation to be in. Unfortunately, there is no general advice that will work in all cases. However, there are a few approaches that you can try.

The best place to look first is code that allocates a lot of objects. Allocating too many objects is probably the most common reason that Ruby code is slow. If you can figure out a way to allocate fewer objects, that can improve performance. This is especially true if you can remove allocations of complex objects that themselves allocate a lot of objects. One library that can help you figure out which places to start reducing object allocations is called `memory_profiler`, which can show how much memory and how many objects are allocated and retained by gem, by file, and even by line.

Next, see whether there is a way to move code around so that code that is currently executed in the most common code paths in your library can be moved to less common code paths. In some cases, this is possible, and in other cases, it isn't. However, in cases where it is possible, moving code from commonly used code paths into only the code paths that require the code will generally improve performance. As a specific application of this, look at the `initialize` methods for all of your classes. If you find any code that can be moved from the `initialize` method to a separate method, moving the code to the separate method will improve performance in most cases. There are certainly cases where it will make performance worse, though, so always run a benchmark before optimization to create a baseline, then compare against the baseline after optimization.

If you remember the techniques you learned for using local variables and instance variables for caching back in *Chapter 3, Proper Variable Usage*, now would be a great time to apply them. The proper use of local variables and instance variables for caching can often improve the performance of unoptimized code by three times or more.

For further performance improvements, you can try applying micro-optimizations, such as using the following:

```
array[0]
# and
array[-1]
```

Instead of using the following:

```
array.first
# and
array.last
```

This is because the `[]` method is better optimized internally by Ruby's virtual machine, for array and hash. Additionally, in Ruby 3.0, it's faster to use the following to create a new hash object:

```
Hash[hash]
```

Instead of using the following:

```
hash.dup
```

However, the internal optimizations in the virtual machine can change from version to version. For example, before Ruby 2.5, it was significantly faster to merge hashes using the following:

```
Hash[hash].merge!(hash2)
```

Instead of using the following:

```
hash.merge(hash2)
```

However, since 2.5, the `Hash#merge` approach is faster. If you are going to use these types of micro-optimizations, recheck that they are still faster with each new Ruby release.

One way to find code that you don't need at all is to use the knowledge you gained about branch coverage from *Chapter 11, Testing to Ensure Your Code Works*. By using branch coverage, you can find branches in your code that you must have thought were necessary, but were actually not necessary. By eliminating these branches, you can speed up your code.

There's one cool micro-optimization related to eliminating unnecessary branches. It's kind of a crazy hack, and should only be used in the most performance-sensitive cases, but it's useful to know about. Let's say you have a method with an optional argument where you want different behavior depending on whether the optional argument is given:

```
def foo(bar=(bar_not_given = true))
  return :bar if bar_not_given
  :foo
end
```

Assuming this call to `foo` is very performance-sensitive, there is a way to eliminate the conditional. You can move `return` into the default argument. However, you cannot use the straightforward approach:

```
# Doesn't work:
#def foo(bar=(return :bar))
#   :foo
#end
```

This approach is invalid syntax. You have to fool Ruby's parser to accept it. One way is adding a separate expression after `return`:

```
def foo(bar=(return :bar; nil))
   :foo
end
```

However, this results in a `statement not reached` warning if run in verbose warning mode (`ruby -w`). If you want to avoid verbose warnings, you can use another hack:

```
def foo(bar=nil || (return :bar))
   :foo
end
```

This is valid syntax that doesn't cause the `statement not reached` verbose warning, and Ruby's optimizer optimizes out the conditional. If you have a case where you can use this hack, it is the fastest way to implement the conditional, since the conditional logic is moved out of slower, pure Ruby code and into faster virtual machine handling of default arguments. If you do use `return` from the default argument hack, make sure you have a comment near it explaining what the code does and exactly why performance is so important for this method that the approach is justified.

If all else fails and your code is still slower than you need it to be, one possible route to speed it up is to implement the code as a C extension. This approach is not for the faint of heart. Programming in C is a whole different ballgame than programming in Ruby. However, especially in cases where you are doing a lot of calculations, switching from pure Ruby code to a C extension can speed your code up by a significant amount. Be aware that programming a C extension can result in memory leaks, program crashes (as opposed to Ruby exceptions), and security issues if not done properly. Additionally, programming a C extension takes a lot longer than programming in Ruby, since C is definitely not as programmer-friendly as Ruby. If it is at all possible when programming in C, use Ruby's C API for managing memory, instead of manually attempting to manage memory, as otherwise, it is very easy to introduce a memory leak.

If you are lucky, you won't find yourself in a situation where everything is slow. However, if you get unlucky enough to encounter such a situation, you now have some strategies for handling it.

Summary

In this chapter, you learned all about optimization in Ruby. You learned that you should only optimize if you have identified a bottleneck in your application. You learned that you should profile and benchmark a specific use case before attempting to optimize the use case, so you can test that your optimization actually improved performance. Next, you learned that the best way to improve performance is by running the least amount of code possible. Finally, you learned some techniques and tricks for optimizing when the profile output isn't helpful in alerting you to the cause of the performance issue in your library.

You've now finished *Section 2* of the book, and are ready to move on to the final part of the book, which focuses on principles of Ruby web programming, starting with the most important part, the database. In the next chapter, we will learn why the database is crucial to the design of web applications.

Questions

1. What's the most important thing to do before optimizing your library?

2. After you have identified a bottleneck, what steps should you take before optimizing your library?

3. If you are creating a lot of instances of a specific class, what is the fastest general way to speed that up?

4. If profiling your use case does not help you identify the slow code, where's the best place to look first?

Section 3: Ruby Web Programming Principles

The objective of this section is for you to learn important principles that are specific to web programming, and how to apply them.

This section comprises the following chapters:

15
The Database Is Key

The database is the backbone and most important part of almost all web applications, regardless of the programming language used. This is because the database is where all of an application's data is stored, and in most cases, an application's data is more important than the application itself. In this chapter, you'll learn why proper database design is so important, some important database design principles, and why it is best to use the database's full capabilities. You'll also learn how to choose a model layer for your application, and how to handle database errors when using that model layer.

We will cover the following topics:

- Learning why database design is so important
- Understanding the most important database design principles
- Treating the database as not just dumb storage
- Choosing the model layer
- Handling database and model errors

By the end of this chapter, you'll have a better understanding of database design and usage as it applies to Ruby web applications.

Technical requirements

In this chapter and all chapters of this book, code given in code blocks is designed to execute on Ruby 3.0. Many of the code examples will work on earlier versions of Ruby, but not all. The code for this chapter is available online at `https://github.com/PacktPublishing/Polished-Ruby-Programming/tree/main/Chapter15`.

Learning why database design is so important

In most cases, while your code is important, your data is far more important than your code. Let's say you have an online shop. If you have a bug in your code that prevents you from accepting orders, you are definitely losing money. However, at least the customer that is attempting to order realizes the order didn't go through. They might be annoyed, but they'll probably just shop somewhere else. However, if you suffer data loss or data corruption after accepting an order, that could be way worse. In that case, you have customers that expect to receive orders that they won't be receiving, and they will probably become very irate. It's even worse if the data loss or data corruption happens after the customer was charged, or the data corruption results in orders for customer A being shipped to customer B. Instead of just loss of goodwill, you may have an expensive lawsuit on your hands. For almost all businesses and applications, the data stored is more valuable than the application code itself.

In addition to data being more important than code, data almost always lasts far longer than code. It's not unusual for a business application to be completely rewritten in a new programming language, while the database remains exactly the same. For many large organizations, there is often a wide variety of separate applications that access the same data. The specific applications used may come and go with the ebb and flow of time. However, the data remains stored in the same database and is of primary importance.

Not only is the data more important and longer-lasting than code, but in most cases, the performance of applications is more dependent on how data is stored and structured than on the code itself. In the majority of applications, proper database design and indexing will make a larger performance difference than how code is written in a particular programming language, and often a larger performance difference than which programming language is used. An application written in Ruby using intelligent database design and indexing will often outperform an application written in C with less intelligent database design and improper indexing.

Often, you have a limited amount of time when designing your application, due to external constraints. It's wise to spend the majority of time thinking about the data you will be storing and how best to store it, what your access patterns will be, and how best to design your database indexes to make those access patterns as fast as possible.

Because data is so important, the database you use is probably the most important decision you will make for your application, even more than the choice of programming language. A poorly chosen database almost dooms an application to failure. In general, you should choose the most robust database that meets the needs of your application. Let's see how to decide that in the next section.

Deciding on a database to use

The first decision to make is what type of database to use, such as a relational (SQL) database, a schemaless document database, a key-value database, a graph database, or a more specialized database such as a time-series database. If you value your data at all and your database has any structure at all, a schemaless document database is usually a poor choice that you will end up regretting later when you discover anomalies in your data, far too late to fix them. Most key-value databases are too limited for the use of structured data unless they are treated as document databases, in which case they have the same issues as document databases. Unless you have studied and have had experience with graph databases and are sure they are the best database type for your application, they probably aren't. Similarly, unless you have very specialized needs, a specialized database such as a time series database is probably the wrong choice for your application.

For the vast majority of applications, the best database choice will be a relational database. Because a relational database requires that you explicitly design the schema you will be using, using a relational database requires more upfront thinking about the data you will be storing and how you will be accessing it. It is always worth spending the time thinking upfront about your data. Almost all the time you spend upfront designing a good database structure will be paid back in spades over the life of your application.

Assuming you will be using a relational database, you have to choose which one to use. In terms of open source databases, for the majority of applications, the best choice is PostgreSQL. PostgreSQL is the most robust open source database and has greater support for advanced data types and indexes. It is possible to be successful with MySQL, but you need to be careful to configure MySQL in a way that will not result in silent data loss.

For cases where you must use an embedded database and cannot use a client-server database, SQLite is the natural choice. However, be aware the SQLite does not enforce database types, treating database types as recommendations. If you must use SQLite, make sure to use **CHECK** constraints as much as possible to actually enforce database types. Another thing to be aware of with SQLite is that SQLite's support for altering tables is very limited. Making most changes to a table other than adding a column requires creating a new table with the structure you want, and copying all data from the old table into the new table, then dropping the old table and renaming the new table with the old table's name.

The advantage of designing a mostly client-side application is that it tends to be more responsive once it is fully loaded. Because most of the logic is client-side, it only needs to wait for the server on the occasions where it needs to save data or load additional data. For pages that require a high level of interactivity, a client-side application is usually necessary. For example, if you are designing a game, a photo editing application, a word processor, or a spreadsheet, then a client-side application is the way to go.

The advantage of designing a mostly server-side application is that it tends to load faster and tends to be faster to develop, since almost all the logic lives on the server. Unlike a mostly client-side application, you generally do not have to design two applications. You may only need to implement JavaScript on the few pages that actually need dynamic behavior. Server-side applications are generally easier to debug, especially for errors that only occur in production. This is because you will generally get a full backtrace of where the error occurred so that you can determine the complete environment that the error occurred in, making it easier to reproduce the error.

The downsides of a mostly client-side application are that it tends to take longer to load, it tends to be much more complex, and it tends to be more difficult to debug, especially for errors that occur in production. For errors that occur in production, because they occur in the user's browser, you will not even be aware of them unless you set up a separate service to handle error reports. If the error affects the use of that service, you may never find out about it.

One of the largest downsides to designing a client-side application is that you cannot program it in Ruby; you have to use JavaScript. Now, recent versions of JavaScript are certainly much better than older versions of JavaScript. However, Ruby is, in general, a superior language for application development, in addition to being much more programmer-friendly.

It is possible to write client-side web applications in Ruby and translate the Ruby code into JavaScript using a Ruby implementation named Opal. However, if you do run into any problems, you'll need to be able to handle debugging Ruby, JavaScript, and Opal yourself. Additionally, while the Opal implementation itself is not that large, considering the features it adds, it still has some overhead, so it only makes sense to use Opal if you are planning to build your entire client-side application around it. In other words, using Opal for a small part of the application does not make much sense – you need to be fully invested in Opal for using it to make sense.

With any client-side web application, you must actually design two applications, both the client side and the server side. The server-side part of a mostly client-side application may be smaller than the server-side part of a mostly server-side application, but it is still of reasonable size and complexity. All the database access and anything that's security-sensitive must be implemented on the server side, since the client cannot be trusted. In general, a client-side web application is probably at least twice as difficult to implement as a similar server-side web application.

The main downside of mostly server-side application development is that you are limited in terms of what types of applications you can reasonably build. For most line-of-business, form-based applications, server-side applications work well, but applications that require a high level of dynamism are not a good fit.

In this section, you've learned about what you should take into consideration when you're choosing whether to develop a client-side or server-side web application. In the next section, you'll learn how to decide what web framework to use for your application.

Deciding on a web framework

Once you've decided on whether to build a client-side or server-side application, the next most important decision is which web framework you should use. There are four Ruby web frameworks with significant popularity (that is, over one million downloads) – Ruby on Rails, Sinatra, Grape, and Roda. All web frameworks ship with basic support for handling requests and returning responses. Each has advantages and disadvantages, all of which you'll learn about in the following sections.

Ruby on Rails

Ruby on Rails, or Rails for short, is the most popular Ruby web framework. It is a full-stack framework, which means it comes with many features in addition to being able to handle requests. In *Chapter 15, The Database Is Key*, you learned about **Active Record**, the model layer that comes with Rails.

Rails come with many additional features, including the following:

- **Action Cable**: A framework for real-time communication between the server and client using WebSockets
- **Action Mailbox**: A framework for processing incoming emails
- **Action Mailer**: A framework for sending emails
- **Action Text**: A framework for editing and displaying rich text in web pages

- **Active Job**: A framework for abstracting the handling of background jobs
- **Active Storage**: A framework for processing uploaded files and media

In addition to these features, Rails also supports integration with webpack and sprockets for asset packaging for JavaScript and CSS files.

Rails' largest advantage is due to its popularity. Most Ruby programmers are familiar with Rails and have worked with Rails. Most Ruby libraries that deal with the web in some way work with Rails, and a good portion only work with Rails and not with other frameworks. If you have a problem with Rails and search for it, you'll probably find other people who have had that same problem and found a good fix, or at least a decent workaround.

Another advantage of Rails is that it focuses on convention over configuration. Rails is very much designed around the concept of staying *on the rails*, or doing things the way Rails wants you to do them. If you deviate from that approach, or go *off the rails*, you will have a significantly more difficult time using Rails. Productive use of Rails involves structuring your application to fit Rails, not the other way around.

One disadvantage of Rails is that Rails is very large and complex. It can take a long time to understand. It's also known for being fairly slow. While it does include many features and does a decent job of implementing them, some of these features have superior counterparts outside the framework, such as Shrine for handling uploaded files. While upgrading from one version of Rails to the next has gotten much easier as Rails has matured, it can still be challenging to upgrade, as Rails tends to deprecate features faster than most other frameworks.

Sinatra

Sinatra is the second most popular Ruby web framework. It was the first web framework that showed how simple you could make web applications, such as the two-line `Hello World` application:

```
require 'sinatra'
get('/'){'Hello World'}
```

Sinatra is fairly minimal. It supports a large variety of templating libraries through its use of the `tilt` gem. However, request handling and response generation via templates is basically all Sinatra provides. Everything else, such as email sending or processing, a database or model layer, or processing of uploaded files, must come from external sources.

Sinatra's strength is in how easy it is to get started. By distilling web application development to the most minimal API possible, Sinatra makes it possible to focus on just building your application.

One of the limitations of using Sinatra is that it doesn't give you much to work with. Many people who have used both Rails and Sinatra report that they need to reimplement a lot of what Rails gives them inside their Sinatra applications, which slows down their development compared to having the functionality built-in. Additionally, Sinatra's router uses a linear search of the available routes, which means it doesn't scale well for a large number of routes.

Grape

Grape is significantly less popular than both Sinatra and Rails. Unlike Rails, Sinatra, and Roda, Grape does not focus on generic web application development; instead, it focuses specifically on designing web applications to serve REST-like APIs. For example, Grape was designed to be the backend to a client-side application or to deal with non-web applications that use HTTP to communicate with a server.

As Grape was designed purely for building REST-like APIs, it has built-in support for things such as API versioning, automatically generating API documentation, per-route parameter validation and typecasting, and support for a wide variety of content types, including XML, JSON, and plain text. If you are building a pure REST-like API and need these features, it is a solid choice.

One disadvantage of Grape is that it tends to be even slower than Rails. For performance-critical applications, you will probably want to use a different library.

Roda

Roda is much less popular than the other libraries, barely making it over the one million download threshold. It is significantly faster than Rails, Sinatra, and Grape – often multiple times faster – mostly due to its design, which reduces per-request overhead as much as possible. Roda applications can perform similarly to applications written in faster programming languages.

Roda tries to combine the ease of use of Sinatra with a large number of available but optional features. A basic `Hello World` app in Roda is almost as small as it would be in Sinatra:

```
require 'roda'
Roda.route do |r|
  r.root{'Hello World'}
end
```

Roda is unique among the four frameworks we've discussed as it uses a routing tree, where all the requests that are received by the web application are yielded to the route block, and the routing and request handling are combined, instead of being separated. This allows you to easily share code between different routes in a manner more understandable and less repetitive than in other web frameworks.

Roda uses a plugin system very similar to the plugin system you learned about in *Chapter 8, Designing for Extensibility*. This allows Roda to have a very small, fast, and easy-to-understand core, and use plugins to implement additional features. Roda ships with over 100 plugins, including the following:

- `mail_processor`: A plugin for processing incoming emails
- `mailer`: A plugin for sending emails
- `assets`: A plugin for asset packaging of JavaScript and CSS files

While Roda is not shipped with all of the features that Rails is shipped with, most of the features Roda does not ship with are available in other libraries that integrate with Roda and are superior to the support included in Rails, such as Shrine for handling uploaded files.

One disadvantage of Roda is that due to its lower popularity, fewer Ruby programmers are familiar with it. Additionally, the use of a routing tree to integrate routing and request handling is foreign to many Ruby programmers, and it may take some time for Ruby programmers to adjust to it.

In this section, you learned about the advantages and disadvantages of the four most popular Ruby web frameworks. In the next section, you'll learn about designing URL paths.

Designing URL paths

Once you've selected a web framework, the next important decision to make is how to design the URL path structure for your application. Now, you might be wondering, why does a URL path structure matter for my application, as long as requests are handled as I want them to be handled? Well, how you structure URL paths can affect how your application is designed.

Let's say you have a discussion forum application that deals with forums, topics, and posts. Each forum, such as *Ruby Programming Books*, can have topics such as *Which is the Best Ruby Programming Book?*, and each topic can contain many posts from the members of the forum with their thoughts on that topic. There are many possible ways to design a URL path structure for such a forum application.

You could call one approach the flat approach, where each separate type has its own top-level path. For example, you could have the following three URL paths for the forum application:

- /forums/123, which shows all the topics for the forum with a primary key value of 123.

- /topics/345, which shows all the posts for the topic with a primary key value of 345.

- /posts/567, which shows a specific post with a primary key value of 567.

You could call another approach the nested approach, where the URL path includes the dependency information encoded in it:

- /forums/123, the same as for the flat approach.

- /forums/123/topics/345, which shows all posts for the topic with a primary key of 345 in the forum with a primary key value of 123.

- /forums/123/topics/345/posts/567, which shows the specific post with a primary key value of 567 in the topic with a primary key of 345 in the forum with a primary key value of 123.

In some cases, you may prefer the flat approach, while in other cases, the nested approach may make more sense. For example, if the forum doesn't have any specific authorization code, no user can moderate another user, and any user can post in any forum, then the flat approach may be easier.

However, if the forum application has specific authorization requirements, such as the currently logged-in user can only have access to specific forms or specific topics, the nested approach can have advantages. This is especially true if you are handling the request while the request is being routed, which is possible when using Roda. Let's say the logged-in user tries to navigate to /forums/123/topics/345, but does not have access to the forum with a primary key of 123. If you were using Roda, you could handle this by doing the following:

```ruby
class App < Roda
  route do |r|
    r.on 'forums', Integer do |forum_id|
      forum = Forum[forum_id]
      unless forum.allow_access?(current_user_id)
        response.status = 403
        r.halt
```

```
        end

    #  ...
    end
  end
end
```

With this approach, as soon as Roda has routed the /forums/123 part of the path, it can determine that the current user does not have access to the forum with a primary key of 123. This means it can immediately stop processing the request, regardless of the rest of the path.

With the flat approach, you need to be more involved. You still need to check whether the user has access to the forum if accessing a route such as /forums/123:

```
class App < Roda
  route do |r|
    r.on 'forums', Integer do |forum_id|
      forum = Forum[forum_id]
      unless forum.allow_access?(current_user_id)
        response.status = 403
        r.halt
      end

    #  ...
    end
```

However, to handle the /topics/345 route, you also need to add almost the same code to check whether the user has access to the forum when accessing a topic. Since you don't have the forum's primary key, you need to get the topic first, and from there, get the forum for the topic, before determining whether the user has access to the forum:

```
    r.on 'topics', Integer do |topic_id|
      topic = Topic[topic_id]
      unless topic.forum.allow_access?(current_user_id)
        response.status = 403
        r.halt
      end
```

```
    unless topic.allow_access?(current_user_id)
      response.status = 403
      r.halt
    end

    # ...
    end
  end
end
```

In cases where access checks need to be done at multiple levels, using a nested approach for the URL path structure generally makes more sense than using the flat approach.

In this section, you learned about some principles for designing the URL path structure in your applications. In the next section, you'll learn about how to structure your application as a monolith, as a number of separate microservices, or as an island chain.

Structuring with monoliths, microservices, and island chains

All applications have structures, whether they're intentional or not. In general, it's best to choose an intentional structure based on specific application requirements. In terms of structuring your application processes, there are two common approaches. One approach is using a single monolith, while another is using many separate microservices. There's also a less common approach that can work well in some application types, which we'll refer to as the **island chain approach**.

With the monolith approach, all application code is managed in the same repository, all application data is stored in the same database, and all parts of the application run in the same process. This is the simplest approach in terms of management. It requires little to no coordination to handle changes to other parts of the system since, in a monolithic system, any change to any place in the system can usually occur atomically. However, it may require a high level of coordination with other people working in the system, since they could be modifying a section of the system that you are also modifying, which can result in merge conflicts that are challenging to fix.

With the microservices approach, separate parts of the system are managed in separate repositories, each microservice stores data in its own database, and all of the separate microservices that make up the application run in separate processes. Microservices do not directly access data from the database of a separate microservice; instead, they make an internal request to that microservice to obtain the data if they need it. Making internal changes to a microservice requires very little to no coordination with other developers unless they are also working in the internals of that microservice, since each microservice is independent. However, changes to the external interface of a microservice requires a high level of coordination with all the other microservices that interact with that microservice, to ensure that those microservices do not break.

With the island chain approach, all application code is stored in the same repository and all application data is stored in the same database. However, different parts of the application run in different application processes. Unlike in the microservice approach, where the microservices in the application are separated based on the type of data they deal with, in the island chain approach, the separate processes that make up the application are usually separated based on different security domains.

There are a couple of advantages to the island chain approach compared to the monolith approach, but they depend on specific usage conditions. For the island chain approach to make sense, you must generally have different types of users. For example, in a simple case, you may have admin users and regular users. In this case, admin users may need an entirely different interface than regular users. However, there could be substantial benefits from sharing the same models in both the regular interface and admin interface.

Because separate processes are used for different types of applications in the island chain approach, you can scale the number of processes up and down as needed for each type of process. For example, in most cases, you need far fewer admin processes than regular user processes.

Where the island chain approach shines most is when you can use the separate processes to strictly enforce separate security domains. For example, the process that's exposed to the general public can be locked down, with limited access to the database and filesystem. However, the process running the admin interface, which is only exposed to internal staff, can have more capabilities, since the risk of attack is generally lower. You'll learn more about this defense-in-depth approach to security in *Chapter 17, Robust Web Application Security*.

When using the monolith approach, all the frameworks we discussed previously will work. However, due to the overhead and design of Rails, it is really not conducive to the microservice or island chain approach. You should only use Rails if you want to commit to the monolith approach.

Summary

In this chapter, you learned about the important principles of designing web applications. You learned about what you should consider when deciding between the client-side and server-side approach to application design. You then learned about some of the advantages and disadvantages of using the four most popular Ruby web frameworks. You also learned how URL path structure is important in web application design, especially when routing is integrated with request handling. Finally, you learned about the trade-offs between using a monolith, microservice, or island chain approach to application structure. After reading this chapter, you are hopefully able to make better choices when building and structuring your web applications.

In the next chapter, you'll learn about handling common web application security issues, and using a defense-in-depth approach to integrate database and operating system security features.

Questions

1. Is it better to use a client-side or server-side development approach when designing an application that most involves data input via HTML forms?

2. Of the four most popular Ruby web frameworks, which is the fastest?

3. When should you prefer to use the nested approach for designing URL paths?

4. If your application only has a single user interface, should you consider using the island chain approach to structure the application?

17
Robust Web Application Security

Security is one of the most important considerations when developing a web application. In this chapter, you'll learn about techniques for avoiding common security issues in web applications. Then, you'll learn how to leverage the advanced security techniques provided by the operating system and database to increase the difficulty of attacks, minimize the attack surface, and mitigate damage in the case of a successful attack.

In this chapter, we will cover the following topics:

- Understanding that most security issues in Ruby web applications are high level
- Never trust input
- Performing access control at the highest level possible
- Avoiding injection
- Approaching high-security environments

By the end of this chapter, you'll have a greater understanding of possible security issues in Ruby web applications, as well as how to use both common and advanced techniques to avoid or mitigate them.

Technical requirements

In this chapter and all chapters of this book, the code provided in code blocks was designed to be executed on Ruby 3.0. Many of the code examples will work on earlier versions of Ruby, but not all. The code for this chapter is available online at `https://github.com/PacktPublishing/Polished-Ruby-Programming/tree/main/Chapter17`.

Understanding that most security issues in Ruby web applications are high level

For applications written in C, most security issues tend to be low-level security issues. These security issues are caused by things such as buffer overflows, integer overflows or underflows, and **use-after-free** (**UAF**) vulnerabilities. Ruby itself is mostly written in C, so a bug in Ruby itself could result in one of the previous security issues affecting Ruby. In addition, some Ruby gems include C extensions, either for performance reasons and/or because they need to interface with other libraries written in C. Ruby gems that include C extensions can also experience all these security issues.

Because of how many people use Ruby, low-level vulnerabilities in Ruby itself, while not impossible, are less likely. However, Ruby gems that include C extensions do not generally receive the same level of scrutiny as Ruby itself, so you should be careful when using gems that include C extensions. Really, it helps to be careful when using any gem at all, as any gem that you use could introduce a security issue in your application.

Note that the phrase *low-level vulnerabilities* refers to the type of code it usually affects. Be careful not to think of low-level vulnerabilities as vulnerabilities of low importance, because most of the low-level vulnerabilities mentioned previously are actually critical vulnerabilities that can result in code execution, where your program starts running code that's been submitted by an attacker.

Because Ruby is a high-level language that contains strings that resize as needed, uses an `Integer` type that can handle arbitrary-sized integers, and provides automatic memory management via garbage collection, most Ruby programs are less susceptible to the low-level security issues listed previously. Because of this, most of the security issues that Ruby applications are susceptible to are higher-level issues. However, that doesn't mean these security issues are any less important.

In this section, you learned why most security issues in Ruby are high-level security issues. In the next section, you'll learn why you should never trust input given by a user in a web application.

Never trust input

One of the most common vulnerabilities in Ruby web applications comes from trusting input given by the user. Let's say you have a `Struct` subclass named `Fruit`. This keeps track of individual pieces of fruit, such as the type of fruit, the color of the fruit, and the price of the fruit:

```
Fruit = Struct.new(:type, :color, :price)
```

You store all your `Fruit` instances in a hash named `FRUITS`, keyed by a number assigned to the fruit:

```
FRUITS = {}
FRUITS[1] = Fruit.new('apple', 'red', 0.70)
FRUITS[2] = Fruit.new('pear', 'green', 1.23)
FRUITS[3] = Fruit.new('banana', 'yellow', 1.40)
```

You have a web application where you want to allow the user to ask for either the type, the color, or the price of a specified piece of fruit. You decide to try the Roda web framework to implement this application and find it is very simple to get started with:

```
Roda.route do |r|
  r.get "fruit", Integer, String do |fruit_id, field|
    FRUITS[fruit_id].send(field).to_s
  end
end
```

This seems to work fine. A request for `/fruit/1/type` returns `apple`, a request for `/fruit/2/color` returns `green`, and a request for `/fruit/3/price` returns `1.4`. You deploy this to the web and find that your application has stopped. It doesn't seem to stop right away, but it always stops within a day or so. Confused as to what is going on, you look at the logs and see that the last line in the log shows the final request:

```
# GET /fruit/1/exit
```

Some clever but not-so-nice person on the internet decided to spoil your nice little web application by calling `exit`, which immediately caused the application to shut down. From this, you have learned one valuable lesson, which is that that you should never trust input.

So, how can you avoid this issue? The well-meaning, but deeply silly person uses a blacklist approach to security and decides to prevent this issue by forbidding what is known to cause a problem. They change the web application so that it does the following:

```
Roda.route do |r|
  r.get "fruit", Integer, String do |fruit_id, field|
    next if field == "exit"
    FRUITS[fruit_id].send(field).to_s
  end
end
```

Unfortunately, the application still shuts down after a little while. You check the log again and another clever but also not-so-nice user has changed the request slightly:

```
# GET /fruit/1/exit!
```

This calls the exit! method, which also exits the application (unlike exit, it doesn't run hooks such as at_exit or finalizers). This teaches you the next valuable lesson, which is that you should never try to forbid what is known to be bad (the blacklist approach to security). Instead, you should only allow what you know to be good (the whitelist approach). You change the code one more time to the following:

```
Roda.route do |r|
  r.get "fruit", Integer, String do |fruit_id, field|
    next unless %w[type color price].include?(field)
    FRUITS[fruit_id].send(field).to_s
  end
end
```

Thankfully, after making this change, your application stops exiting.

In more advanced cases, you cannot whitelist all possible valid input. For example, let's say you expand your web application, which allows you to update the type or color of a fruit by submitting a POST request to the same location, which will update the field to the given value and redirect:

```
Roda.route do |r|
  r.is "fruit", Integer, String do |fruit_id, field|
    r.get do
      next unless %w[type color price].include?(field)
```

```
      FRUITS[fruit_id].send(field).to_s
    end

    r.post do
      next unless %w[type color].include?(field)
      FRUITS[fruit_id].send("#{field}=", r.params['value'])
      r.redirect
    end
  end
end
```

This appears to work OK, but you find out that pretty soon, fruit 1 has nil for type and color, while fruit 2 has a hash as the value of type and an array as the value of color. This is because r.params (which comes from the rack gem) performs parameter parsing, which will return a hash, and the values of that hash can be arrays or hashes in addition to plain strings. If you want to ensure the values are strings, you need to convert the values into the expected types. One simple way to do that is by calling to_s on the value of the parameter:

```
r.post do
  next unless %w[type color].include?(field)
  FRUITS[fruit_id].send("#{field}=",
                        r.params['value'].to_s)
  r.redirect
end
```

However, usually, a better approach is to have the web framework perform typecasting for you. Grape supports built-in parameter requirements, while Roda supports typecasting parameters to the expected type via its typecast_params plugin. Unfortunately, neither Rails nor Sinatra support parameter typecasting as part of the framework, though there are external libraries that support parameter typecasting for Rails.

In general, you always want to make sure you convert the parameters that are received in the web application into the expected type. If you don't enforce parameter types, and accidentally pass an array or hash when you're expecting a string, you may end up with security issues, depending on how you programmed your application.

In this section, you learned to never trust user input. In the next section, you'll learn why it is best to perform access control at the highest level possible.

Performing access control at the highest level possible

Many security issues in Ruby web applications are due to missing authentication or authorization checks when processing a request. This is especially common in web frameworks that separate routing from request handling and use some type of conditional `before` hook for performing access control. Let's say you have a Rails controller that uses a `before` hook for access control:

```ruby
class FooController < ApplicationController
  before_action :check_access

  def index
    # ...
  end
  def create
    # ...
  end

  # ...

  private def check_access
    # ...
  end
end
```

This is probably not likely to result in access control vulnerabilities since the access is checked for every action. However, let's say you set the `before_action` hook so that it's conditional, like so:

```ruby
class FooController < ApplicationController
  before_action :check_access, only: [:create]

  # ...
end
```

Here, you really need to be careful when adding any request handling methods to
`FooController`. If they require access control and you don't add them to the `:only`
option, then you have probably introduced a security vulnerability. This is because the
`before_action :only` option uses a fail-open design. It's much better to use the
`before_action :except` option instead:

```
class FooController < ApplicationController
  before_action :check_access, except: [:index, :bars]

  # ...
end
```

It's still bad if you do not update the `:except` option when adding a request handling
method to the controller. However, if you forget, you will end up requiring access control
for a page that does not need it, which is a fail-closed design.

Similarly, let's say you are implementing a global access control hook in
`ApplicationController`:

```
class ApplicationController < ActionController::Base
  before_action :require_login

  # ...
end
```

If you need to have actions in other controllers that do not require a login, you can use the
`skip_before_action` method to skip the login requirement. In these cases, make sure
you use the `:only` option if the `skip_before_action` call needs to be conditional:

```
class BarController < ApplicationController
  skip_before_action :require_login, only: [:index, :bars]

  # ...
end
```

This is because when skipping a before action, `:only` will only skip based on a whitelist,
which uses a fail-closed design, as opposed to `:except`, which will skip based on
a blacklist, which is a fail-open design.

This issue also affects `before` hooks in Sinatra. If you have a conditional access check for a subset of paths in Sinatra, you can do something like the following:

```
before '/foos/(create|bazs)' do
  check_access
end
```

Unfortunately, this is similar to Rails' `:only` option, so it uses a fail-open design. Sinatra doesn't have the direct equivalent of Rails' `:except` option for a fail-closed design, though it is still possible to implement a fail-closed design with some work:

```
before '/foos/:x' do |segment|
  case segment
  when 'index', 'bars'
  else
    check_access
  end
end
```

Roda's routing tree design handles this type of issue more simply. Because routing and request handling are integrated, you can put the access check after the routes that do not need the access check, and before the routes that need the access check. Then, when you're adding your routes, you just need to put them either before or after the access check, depending on whether access control is needed. Refer to the following code:

```
Roda.route do |r|
  r.on "foo" do
    r.get "index" do
      # ...
    end
    # ...

    check_access

    r.get "create" do
      # ...
    end
    # ...
```

```
    end
  end
```

In this section, you learned about performing access control at the highest level possible. In the next section, you'll learn about techniques for avoiding injection.

Avoiding injection

Injection vulnerabilities occur when an attacker can inject code into your application. There are three common types of injection vulnerabilities in Ruby web applications: **script injection**, **SQL injection**, and **code injection** (remote code execution). We'll look at these in more detail in the following subsections.

Script injection

Script injection, otherwise known as **cross-site scripting** or **XSS** for short, is a vulnerability where an attacker can cause their code to be used in your web pages. It's not nearly as bad as SQL injection and code injection, but it can still cause significant problems. For example, let's say you are using Sinatra or Roda for your application, and you have the following code in one of your views:

```
# In your ERB code:
# <p>Added by: <%= params['name'] %></p>
```

Here, an attacker can redirect someone they know who uses your site with a path such as `/path/to/action?name=%3Cscript%3EDo+bad+things%3C%2Fscript%3E`. This will result in the attacker's JavaScript running on your site. Because the attacker's JavaScript is executed in the context of whoever is viewing the page, it can take any action the user could take on the page and possibly the entire website. For example, if you have a banking site that allows users to transfer money from their account to someone else's account, an attacker could potentially use this vulnerability to transfer money from the person viewing the page to the attacker's account.

This doesn't only happen with parameters that are submitted to the current page. Let's say you are reading the name from an `Account` model, which is backed by a database table:

```
# In your ERB code:
# <p>Last update by: <%= Account.last_update_by.name %></p>
```

The same script injection vulnerability still exists. It's actually worse in this case, because if the attacker can get their JavaScript code stored in the database, then every person who views the page could be vulnerable.

Both Roda and Sinatra support the `<%==` tag for automatically escaping output in ERB, thus preventing the script injection:

```
# In your ERB code:
# <p>Added by: <%== params['name'] %></p>
```

Additionally, both Roda and Sinatra support making the default behavior `<%=` to escape the output, and only allow unescaped output via `<%==`. In Sinatra, you can use the following code:

```
require 'erubi'
set :erb, escape_html: true
```

In Roda, you can use the following:

```
Roda.plugin :render, escape: true
```

It is highly recommended that you use this approach to automatically escape output by default if you are using either Roda or Sinatra.

Rails handles escaping differently. Instead of making escaping or not escaping a decision when data is included in the template output, Rails tracks whether the strings in your application are marked as being HTML safe or not. If the strings are marked as HTML safe, they do not get escaped when being output via `<%=` tags. If the strings are not marked as HTML safe, then they get escaped when being output via `<%=` tags. This means that you can use `<%=` for both escaped and unescaped data, but you cannot tell from looking at your templates whether such usage is safe. You must trust that every string you are outputting in your templates has been correctly marked for HTML safety. Verifying that requires tracing the source of every string through the code to make sure it was marked correctly.

One way to mitigate the damage that a script injection attack can do is to set a strict `Content-Security-Policy` header for all the pages that are served by your application. For example, a `Content-Security-Policy` header with `script-src self;` will allow you to load JavaScript files from your site, but will not allow the use of inline JavaScript code. With a strict `Content-Security-Policy` header, the only way for an attacker to get their JavaScript running on your site would be to find a separate vulnerability that allows them to serve the JavaScript as a separate file from your site, which, in general, is much more difficult than exploiting a script injection vulnerability.

SQL injection

A SQL injection vulnerability occurs when an attacker can get their SQL code running in your database. These vulnerabilities are usually very bad because unless you have taken steps to limit the access the database user has, an attacker can generally make any change they want to any table in the database.

This typically happens when you're using Active Record improperly, such as when you're providing an already interpolated string to Active Record, where the string contains input provided by the attacker:

```
Foo.where("bar > #{value}").first
```

This is warned about in the Active Record documentation, and most seasoned Rails programmers know to avoid it, but it still causes vulnerabilities on a regular basis because of how easy it is to introduce. With Active Record, you need to be careful that you always have Active Record do the interpolation safely:

```
Foo.where("bar > ?", value).first
```

Sequel tries to make it more difficult to introduce SQL injections into your application. First, it provides fairly complete support for expressing any SQL expression as a Ruby expression, such as the following:

```
Foo.where(Sequel[:bar] > value).first
```

Second, if you do make a mistake and try to provide an already interpolated string, Sequel will raise an exception:

```
Foo.where("bar > #{value}").first
# raises Sequel::Error, Invalid filter expression
```

Sequel makes you really go out of your way to be vulnerable to SQL injection. It does this by forcing you to wrap any string you would like to use directly as SQL code using Sequel.lit.

Code injection

Code injection, otherwise known as **remote code execution**, occurs when an attacker provides executable code that is run directly by your Ruby application. Let's say you have a metaprogramming method for defining methods, and for performance, you use `class_eval`:

```
class Bar
  def self.column_accessor(name)
    class_eval(<<-END, __FILE__, __LINE__+1)
      def #{name}
        columns.#{name}
      end
    END
  end
end
```

If there is any way for an attacker to call the `Bar.column_accessor` method and provide a value for the `name` argument, then they can run any Ruby code they want in the context of your application. This is worse than the other two vulnerabilities as because once an attacker has this access, they can execute whatever SQL they want on the database and return whatever JavaScript they want to the user.

Thankfully, these vulnerabilities are much less common. Additionally, they are generally much easier to search for. If you search your application for the following:

- `eval`
- `instance_eval`
- `module_eval`
- `class_eval`

You can probably find every place where you are evaluating Ruby code. Make sure there is no case where these methods can be called with user input. Consider switching any metaprogramming that uses the previous methods with metaprogramming that uses `Class.new`, `Module.new`, `define_method`, or `define_singleton_method` instead, unless you really need the extra performance.

In this section, you learned about three types of injection vulnerabilities and how to avoid them in your application. In the next section, you'll learn how to approach Ruby web applications that need to run in high-security environments.

Approaching high-security environments

In a high-security environment, you need to take all the precautions described previously in this chapter. What separates high-security environments from other environments is that you generally need to go further.

In a high-security environment, you should assume that no matter what steps you take, your application will be compromised at some point. Your job is to make this compromise as difficult as possible for the attacker, as well as to take whatever steps you can to mitigate the damage that an attacker can do if they can successfully compromise the application. In this section, you'll learn the basics of the following five techniques which can make compromise more difficult and which can mitigate the damage if compromise is successful:

- Limiting database access
- Internal firewalling
- Randomizing memory layouts
- Limiting filesystem access
- Limiting system call access

Let's go through each of them in the following subsections.

Limiting database access

To limit the damage an attacker can do to the database, the best approach is to limit what the application itself can do to the database. You can do this by running the application using a database user with limited permissions to the database, ideally only allowing the minimal database access necessary for the application to function.

It's fairly easy to set up separate database users, but if your application has not been designed to deal with limited database access, it's tedious to go through the application to find every case where it accesses the database and allow that type of access. Additionally, in monolithic applications, you may find that this approach does not actually add much database security, since the database user needs full access to almost all tables. To fully benefit from limited database access, you may need to break up your monolithic application into separate security domains and use the island chain design approach you learned about in *Chapter 16, Web Application Design Principles*. If you can separate the application into separate security domains and give each security domain only the minimal database access it needs to function, you can significantly mitigate possible damage.

In some cases, you may have a database user that needs partial access to a database table, but you want to limit the type of access they have to the table. For example, you may want to grant them access to summary information for the table, or make a specific type of update to the table, without allowing other updates to the table. For this type of access, it is often best to define a SECURITY DEFINER database function. With a SECURITY DEFINER database function, the database user who creates the function has the necessary access to the table, and programs the function to only perform a specific action on the table, and marks the function as using SECURITY DEFINER. The database user who creates the function then grants access to execute the function to the database user that the application uses. When the application user calls the function, they operate with the permissions of the user who defined the function during function execution, but once the function returns, they lose that access. For specific types of operations, SECURITY DEFINER database functions allow specific necessary access without elevating general access.

Internal firewalling

With internal firewalling, you make sure your application can only access network locations that are specifically allowed. If your application does not need to access external network services, then it may be possible to only allow the application to receive incoming connections and disallow the application from making any outgoing connections. If you do need to make outgoing connections, it's best to limit those connections to specific IP address ranges, domain names, or ports, and only allow the minimum of what is needed.

It is especially important to use internal firewalling if your application runs in an environment that has access to other internal servers that are not accessible to the internet in general, either directly or via a VPN. If your application is compromised, you want to avoid it being used to attack other internal servers.

Randomizing memory layouts

When using a forking web server to serve your application, it can be beneficial to security to use an approach where each forked process that handles requests has a unique memory layout. When forking, the child inherits the memory layout of its parent. However, in cases where all the following are true:

- An attacker can find a low-level vulnerability in your application.
- Successfully exploiting that vulnerability requires knowledge of the memory layout of the application.

- Unsuccessful exploit attempts result in the application crashing.
- The parent process will respawn crashed child processes.

Then, having a child process use the same memory layout as the parent process can result in a vulnerability. An attacker can use an attack technique called **blind return-oriented programming** (**BROP**) to determine the possible memory layouts in the application and construct a successful exploit.

Both Unicorn and Puma are Ruby web servers that fork child processes to handle requests, and both are potentially vulnerable to the BROP attack technique by default. With Unicorn, you can add the following to your Unicorn configuration file to make each Unicorn child process use a separate `exec` system call after forking to generate a new memory layout for the process:

```
worker_exec true
```

However, this approach does not allow the use of application preloading, which can result in it taking much more memory than when application preloading is used. This is because each worker process has a completely separate copy of the application in memory. Even in cases where application preloading was not used, using `worker_exec` requires some additional memory. However, in most high-security environments, the security benefits outweigh the cost of the extra memory.

Limiting filesystem access

To further mitigate potential damage in the case of a compromised application, it can be very helpful to limit what filesystem access is allowed to the application. There are a couple of ways to go about this.

A historical way to implement some filesystem access limiting that works on most Unix-like operating systems is to use `Process.chroot`, which will change the root directory of the process to a given directory, such as the directory that contains the application. This will prevent the application from accessing anything else on the system other than what is under the application directory.

One issue with the `Process.chroot` approach is that you can only use it if you have superuser permissions to the system. Therefore, using `Process.chroot` requires starting your application as root. Then, once your application has been loaded, but before it starts accepting requests, you should use `Process.chroot` to limit filesystem access, and then drop superuser permissions and switch to the user the application runs as.

The other issue with using `Process.chroot` is that if you are loading any libraries that use `autoload` or other forms of runtime requires, they will generally break. Worse, they will only break when the specific path is taken to access the autoloaded constant or trigger the other form of a runtime require. While such a breakage is fail-closed and doesn't introduce a security issue, it's still annoying to figure out which autoload is being attempted, as well as either working around the issue so the autoload doesn't trigger or performing the autoload or other runtime require before calling `Process.chroot`.

Unfortunately, other than using `Process.chroot`, there are no simple ways to implement filesystem access limiting for Ruby web applications on common operating systems. It may be possible to do so on Linux using deep kernel knowledge and `seccomp` with **eBPF**, but at the time of writing, it is far out of reach for Ruby web application programmers. However, one way to do so is to use **OpenBSD**, an operating system known for its security focus. OpenBSD provides a feature known as `unveil`, which implements support for only allowing specific filesystem access, and there is a gem named `pledge` that supports using it.

Let's say you wanted to limit filesystem access after application startup to just reading template files from the `views` directory, and not allowing any other filesystem access. Using the `pledge` gem, you could do the following:

```
require 'unveil'
Pledge.unveil('views' => 'r')
```

This allows access to only read files in the `views` directory. This prevents opening any of the files in the `views` directory for writing, creating any new files under the `views` directory, and opening any other files on the system. With this approach, an attacker who can compromise the application cannot modify any files at all on the filesystem, and they can only gather information from the files inside the `views` directory.

Limiting system call access

The final technique we'll cover for mitigating potential damage is to limit system call access. Most operating system kernels have hundreds of system calls that programs can call, and each system call adds a potential attack surface that an attacker can exploit. If you can limit which system calls the program is allowed to use, you can reduce the possible ways an attacker could attempt to elevate their access.

Unfortunately, similar to filesystem access limiting, there are no simple ways to implement system call limiting for Ruby web applications on common operating systems. Thankfully, similar to `unveil` for filesystem access limiting, OpenBSD provides a feature named `pledge`, which is designed for limiting the allowed system calls. As you would expect, the `pledge` gem supports this feature as well.

While the application is being loaded, it may need a lot of access to the system to read files, open or create log files for writing, or set up filesystem access limiting using `unveil`. However, once the application has been loaded, it may not need much access to the system. It may still need to read files, at least the files in the `views` directory. It may need network access, both to communicate with requests that come into the web server and to communicate with the database. However, it may not need other access.

Let's say you want to limit the system calls that are allowed once your program has been loaded to just those necessary to read files on the filesystem and make network requests. Using the `pledge` gem, you could do the following:

```
require 'pledge'
Pledge.pledge('rpath inet unix')
```

If an attacker compromises the system, one of the first things they may try is writing to a file on the system. With `pledge`, as soon as they try to write to a file, the program immediately exits. Due to the design of `pledge`, any attempt to perform a system call that's not allowed results in the program immediately exiting. `pledge` uses a fail-closed design, and it fails closed hard. Assuming you are monitoring your application processes, you will hopefully immediately be notified that a web server process has crashed due to a `pledge` violation, and you can then determine if it is something that should be allowed, or if it is an early warning that an attacker was able to compromise your system, at which point you can shut the system down before any additional access is gained.

In this section, you learned about five separate techniques that can be implemented in high-security environments to make your Ruby web application more difficult to compromise, as well as to mitigate damage that an attacker can do if they can successfully compromise your application.

You've now finished your journey through this book, and hopefully you've learned a lot of valuable Ruby programming principles, which allow you to write truly polished Ruby code. Best of luck continuing on your journey as a Ruby programmer. May Ruby be with you.

Summary

In this chapter, you learned about many ways to implement security in your web application.

You learned that most of the vulnerabilities in Ruby web applications are high-level vulnerabilities, not low-level vulnerabilities. You learned that you should never trust user input and that you should use a whitelist approach instead of a blacklist approach when handling user input. You also learned how to implement access control at the highest level possible and use a fail-closed design to avoid security issues. Then, you learned techniques for avoiding script injections, SQL injections, and code injections. Finally, you learned about high-security environments and defense-in-depth techniques that make system compromise more difficult and mitigate possible damage in case it occurs.

With the knowledge you've gained in this chapter, you can design secure Ruby web applications.

Questions

1. Why are integer overflow and underflow vulnerabilities less likely in Ruby compared to C?

2. Why should you prefer whitelist security to blacklist security?

3. Why is conditional access control challenging when you're using Sinatra?

4. What response header should you use to mitigate script injection vulnerabilities?

5. For high-security environments where filesystem access limiting and system call limiting are required, what's the best operating system to use when deploying Ruby web applications?

Assessments

Chapter 1

1. `nil` and `false` are the only objects Ruby treats as false in conditional expressions.
2. No. Division is not exact if the division results in a repeating decimal.
3. No. Symbols represent identifiers and strings represent text or data, so they serve different purposes.
4. Hash, but only slightly. `Set` in Ruby 3.0 is implemented internally using a hash.
5. `Class.new` and `Struct.new`.

Chapter 2

1. In most cases, yes.
2. The open-closed principle is almost impossible to implement in Ruby.
3. This depends. If it simplifies the implementation of a class the user uses, then yes.
4. Rarely. In most cases, you should use arrays and hashes, at least until you are dealing with a very large amount of data.

Chapter 3

1. No. However, it is generally a good idea if the scope of the local variable is very long, such as a local variable defined at the top of a long method or class definition containing many blocks.
2. Because if the object is not frozen, the cached value could become invalid, showing the previous value instead. It is possible to handle this by clearing caches when the object is modified.
3. A `Module` or `Class`.

4. Never.

5. Not always, but it is best to only use the built-in global variables and not add your own global variables.

Chapter 4

1. The class's singleton class, or a module that is included in it (for example, via `Object#extend`) or prepended to it.

2. Methods called most frequently should generally have shorter names.

3. An optional keyword argument, because using an optional positional argument will make adding future optional positional arguments awkward.

4. The `deprecate_public` gem.

5. Accept `*args` and pass `*args` to the other method. After method definition, mark the method using `ruby2_keywords` if supported.

Chapter 5

1. Better performance, and it can be simpler if you always remember to check for errors.

2. Unlike using return values, you must handle the error via an exception handler, so you won't silently ignore errors.

3. In general, most errors that are transient will happen again if retried immediately. By waiting and then retrying, you are more likely to be successful.

4. When you need to handle a particular type of error differently than other raised exceptions that currently use the same exception class.

Chapter 6

1. No.

2. `AllCops:DisabledByDefault`.

3. If there was a better approach that was within the arbitrary limit, it would have already been used.

4. `ruby -wc`.

5. When it negatively impacts the understandability of your code.

Chapter 7

1. You should focus on how the user will use your library.

2. In most cases, it does not make sense. You should not increase library size and complexity until you need to.

3. It increases cognitive complexity for the user of the library.

Chapter 8

1. Using `extend` to include the module in the object's singleton class.

2. It allows the user to only load the features they need, so they don't pay a performance or memory cost for features they don't use. Additionally, it generally makes maintenance easier for the library's maintainer.

3. It ensures that no code attempts to modify the core classes while the application is running.

Chapter 9

1. When it makes the code more difficult to understand, instead of easier to understand.

2. When you need to do metaprogramming in a singleton class.

3. Only when you must for performance reasons.

4. Only when the instances of the class need to respond to any method or the number of methods they must respond to is very large.

Chapter 10

1. It simplifies configuration for both the user and the maintainer by centralizing all configuration aspects in a single block.

2. By checking the arity of the block, and if the block accepts an argument, yielding the DSL object. Otherwise, using `instance_exec` to evaluate the block in the context of the DSL object.

3. Implementing a DSL purely to avoid code verbosity is the most likely to cause problems and the least likely to add value.

Chapter 11

1. `ruby -wc filename`.

2. In general, using behavior-driven development is a waste of time if the programmers are writing the specifications, since the programmers could more easily write the executable test code directly, compared to writing the specifications and maintaining the code that converts the specification to executable test code.

3. Not always, it depends on the type of abstraction. Moving setup code to methods and using enumerables to define multiple test methods are both good uses of abstractions in test code.

4. Model testing is in general more reliable and less likely to result in false positives and false negatives compared to unit testing.

5. Nothing. But less than 100% code coverage means some code is not being tested at all.

Chapter 12

1. To simplify the library, to improve performance, and to add extensibility points. There are other good answers, such as being forced to deal with changes forced by external dependencies or to clean up buggy code.

2. A thorough test suite that you can rely on.

3. When the multiple methods being extracted are called in separate places, and one extracted method is not the only place the other extracted method is called.

4. The cowboy approach of refactoring while implementing the feature. However, this approach is also the riskiest.

5. `uplevel: 1` to show the caller's location and `category: :deprecated` to flag the warning as a deprecation warning.

Chapter 13

1. The object pool pattern.

2. Use `autoload` to ensure the constant isn't loaded and evaluated until it is referenced.

3. Whenever you want to treat the null object differently than the real object, or when performance is critical.

4. For a large number of different types, the hash approach will perform better.

5. The adapter pattern wraps another object, while the strategy pattern does not. Both are designed to provide a unified interface to a different implementation.

Chapter 14

1. Make sure you really need to optimize. Only optimize after you have identified a bottleneck.

2. First, create a use case, then profile it to determine why it is slow, then create a benchmark to determine baseline performance.

3. Move as much code as possible out of the class's `initialize` method.

4. The best place to start optimizing if profiling doesn't help is to try to avoid object allocation as much as possible.

Chapter 15

1. Because data is in general far more important than code and lasts longer than code.

2. Only when you absolutely must for performance reasons.

3. There are many good answers to this question, but the most common is to enforce data consistency in related tables.

4. `ActiveRecord`.

5. Sequel.

Chapter 16

1. A server-side development approach.

2. Roda.

3. When you can use information from earlier parts of the path during routing and/or request handling.

4. No.

Chapter 17

1. Ruby has an `Integer` type that supports integers of arbitrary sizes.

2. Blacklist security is a fail-open design that is likely to lead to future security vulnerabilities, while whitelist security is a fail-closed design.

3. Because Sinatra does not offer a simple way to implement a fail-closed design.

4. The `Content-Security-Policy` header, with a strict `script_src` setting that does not allow inline JavaScript.

5. OpenBSD, since the `pledge` gem can be used to enforce both limited filesystem access and limited system call access.

Packt.com

Subscribe to our online digital library for full access to over 7,000 books and videos, as well as industry leading tools to help you plan your personal development and advance your career. For more information, please visit our website.

Why subscribe?

- Spend less time learning and more time coding with practical eBooks and Videos from over 4,000 industry professionals

- Improve your learning with Skill Plans built especially for you

- Get a free eBook or video every month

- Fully searchable for easy access to vital information

- Copy and paste, print, and bookmark content

Did you know that Packt offers eBook versions of every book published, with PDF and ePub files available? You can upgrade to the eBook version at packt.com and as a print book customer, you are entitled to a discount on the eBook copy. Get in touch with us at customercare@packtpub.com for more details.

At www.packt.com, you can also read a collection of free technical articles, sign up for a range of free newsletters, and receive exclusive discounts and offers on Packt books and eBooks.

Other Books You May Enjoy

If you enjoyed this book, you may be interested in these other books by Packt:

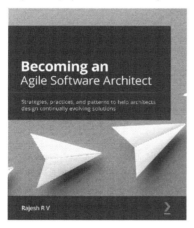

Becoming an Agile Software Architect

Rajesh R V

ISBN: 978-1-80056-384-1

- Acquire clarity on the duties of architects in Agile development
- Understand architectural styles such as domain-driven design and microservices
- Identify the pitfalls of traditional architecture and learn how to develop solutions
- Understand the principles of value and data-driven architecture
- Discover DevOps and continuous delivery from an architect's perspective

- Adopt Lean-Agile documentation and governance

- Develop a set of personal and interpersonal qualities

- Find out how to lead the transformation to achieve organization-wide agility

Supercharge Your Applications with GraalVM

A B Vijay Kumar

ISBN: 978-1-80056-490-9

- Gain a solid understanding of GraalVM and how it works under the hood

- Work with GraalVM's high performance optimizing compiler and see how it can be used in both JIT (just-in-time) and AOT (ahead-of-time) modes

- Get to grips with the various optimizations that GraalVM performs at runtime

- Use advanced tools to analyze and diagnose performance issues in the code

- Compile, embed, run, and interoperate between languages using Truffle on GraalVM

- Build optimum microservices using popular frameworks such as Micronaut and Quarkus to create cloud-native applications

Packt is searching for authors like you

If you're interested in becoming an author for Packt, please visit `authors.packtpub.com` and apply today. We have worked with thousands of developers and tech professionals, just like you, to help them share their insight with the global tech community. You can make a general application, apply for a specific hot topic that we are recruiting an author for, or submit your own idea.

Leave a review - let other readers know what you think

Please share your thoughts on this book with others by leaving a review on the site that you bought it from. If you purchased the book from Amazon, please leave us an honest review on this book's Amazon page. This is vital so that other potential readers can see and use your unbiased opinion to make purchasing decisions, we can understand what our customers think about our products, and our authors can see your feedback on the title that they have worked with Packt to create. It will only take a few minutes of your time, but is valuable to other potential customers, our authors, and Packt. Thank you!

Index

A

abstraction
  cons 232-236
  pros 232-236
acceptance testing 278
Active Record 362
adapter and strategy patterns
  implementing, in Ruby 329-332
application
  structuring, with island chain
    approach 376, 377
  structuring, with microservices
    approach 376, 377
  structuring, with monolith
    approach 376, 377
arbitrary limits
  using, consequences 173-176
arrays
  using 16

B

behavior-driven development
  (BDD) 271, 276
BigDecimal 9, 11, 12

blind return-oriented programming
  (BROP) 393
block-based metaprogramming 241
branch coverage 281, 282

C

circuit breaker 159, 160
circuits
  breaking 159-161
class
  extracting 293-300
  simple, versus complex 42-46
classic exponential backoff algorithm
  implementing 158
class instance variables
  versus constants 79, 80
class methods 94-97
class variables
  replacement, with class instance
    variables using copy to
    subclass approach 88, 89
  replacement, with class instance
    variables using superclass
    lookup approach 86-88

Made in United States
Troutdale, OR
09/06/2023

12687949R00241